Progress Chart

This chart lists all the topics in the book. Once you have completed each page, stick a star in the correct box below.

Page	Topic	Star	Page	Topic	Star	Page	Topic	Star
2	Reading and writing numbers	★	13	Adding two numbers	★	24	Real-life problems	★
3	Multiplying and dividing by 10	★	14	Subtracting three-digit numbers	★	25	Real-life problems	★
4	Ordering sets of large numbers	★	15	Subtracting three-digit numbers	★	26	Areas of rectangles and squares	☆
5	Rounding numbers	★	16	Adding decimals	☆	27	Problems involving time	☆
6	Identifying patterns	★	17	Adding decimals	☆	28	Bar graphs	★
7	Recognizing multiples of 6, 7, and 8	★	18	Subtracting decimals	☆	29	Probability	☆
8	Factors of numbers from 1 to 30	★	19	Subtracting decimals	☆	30	Triangles	☆
9	Recognizing equivalent fractions	★	20	Multiplying by one-digit numbers	★	31	Expanded form	☆
10	Ordering sets of numbers	★	21	Multiplying by one-digit numbers	★	32	Speed trials	★
11	Rounding decimals	★	22	Division with remainders	☆	33	All the 3s	★
12	Adding two numbers	★	23	Division with remainders	☆	34	All the 3s again	★

When you have completed the progress chart in this book, fill in the certificate at the back.

Math
Made Easy

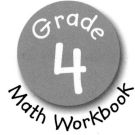

Grade **4** Math Workbook

Author
John Kennedy

Consultant
Sean McArdle

First American Edition, 2003
This edition, 2013
Published in the United States by DK Publishing
345 Hudson Street, New York, New York 10014

Published in Great Britain by Dorling Kindersley Limited.
DK books are available at special discounts when purchased in bulk
for sales promotions, premiums, fund-raising, or educational use.
For details, contact: DK Publishing Special Markets
345 Hudson Street, New York, New York 10014
SpecialSales@dk.com

A cattlog record for this book is available
from the Library of Congress
ISBN: 978-0-7894-5735-6

Printed and bound in China.
All images © Dorling Kindersley.
For futher information see: www.dkimages.com
Discover more at www.dk.com

A WORLD OF IDEAS:
SEE ALL THERE IS TO KNOW

www.dk.com

DK | Penguin Random House

Reading and writing numbers

264,346 in words is Two hundred sixty-four thousand, three hundred forty-six

One million, three hundred twelve thousand, five hundred two is 1,312,502

Write each of these numbers in words.

326,208 ThrEE hundred Twenty six thousand two hundred an Eghit

704,543 SEVEn hundred FOUr thousand FiVE hundred POUNty thrEE

240,701 two hundred Founty thousand SEVEn hundred and one

278,520 two hunDred seventy eight thousand FiVE hundred twenty

---

Write each of these in numbers.

Five hundred seventeen thousand, forty-two 517,042

Six hundred ninety-four thousand, seven hundred eleven 694,711

Eight hundred nine thousand, two hundred three 809,203

Nine hundred thousand, four hundred four 900,404

Write each of these numbers in words.

9,307,012

5,042,390

9,908,434

8,400,642

Write each of these in numbers.

Eight million, two hundred fifty-one

Two million, forty thousand, four hundred four

Seven million, three hundred two thousand, one hundred one

Two million, five hundred forty-one thousand, five

Multiplying and dividing by 10

Write the answer in the box.

26 x 10 = 260

40 ÷ 10 = 4

Write the answer in the box.

76 x 10 = 760   43 x 10 = 430   93 x 10 = 930

66 x 10 = 660   13 x 10 = 130   47 x 10 = 470

147 x 10 = 1,470   936 x 10 = 9,360   284 x 10 = 2,840

364 x 10 = 3,640   821 x 10 = 8,210   473 x 10 = 4,730

Write the answer in the box.

30 ÷ 10 = 3   20 ÷ 10 = 2   70 ÷ 10 = 7

60 ÷ 10 = 6   50 ÷ 10 = 5   580 ÷ 10 = 58

310 ÷ 10 = 31   270 ÷ 10 = 27   100 ÷ 10 = 10

540 ÷ 10 = 54   890 ÷ 10 = 89   710 ÷ 10 = 71

Write the number that has been multiplied by 10.

37 x 10 = 370   64 x 10 = 640   74 x 10 = 740

81 x 10 = 810   10 x 10 = 100   83 x 10 = 830

714 x 10 = 7,140   307 x 10 = 3,070   529 x 10 = 5,290

264 x 10 = 2,640   829 x 10 = 8,290   648 x 10 = 6,480

Write the number that has been divided by 10.

30 ÷ 10 = 3   20 ÷ 10 = 2   90 ÷ 10 = 9

420 ÷ 10 = 42   930 ÷ 10 = 93   740 ÷ 10 = 74

570 ÷ 10 = 57   380 ÷ 10 = 38   860 ÷ 10 = 86

Ordering sets of large numbers

Write these numbers in order, from least to greatest.

2,322	526	404	32	1,240	440
32	404	440	526	1,240	2,322

Write the numbers in each row in order, from least to greatest.

420	190	950	402	905	986
190	402	420	905	950	986
308	640	380	805	364	910
308	380	364	640	805	9 0 0
260	350	26	1,000	620	100
26	100	260	350	620	1,000
20,500	36,820	2,500	45,600	40,560	25,000
2,500	20,500	25,000	36,820	40,560	45,600

Write the numbers in each row in order, from least to greatest.

984,000	8,840,000	8,900	98,240	7,560	75,600
7,500	8,900	75,600	98,240	984,000	8,840,000
301,550	6,405,000	6,450,000	64,500	31,500	3,150
3,150	31,500	64,500	301,550	6,405,000	6,450,000
7,000,100	70,100	7,100,000	710	710,000	7,100
710	7,100	70,100	710,000	7,009,100	7,100,000

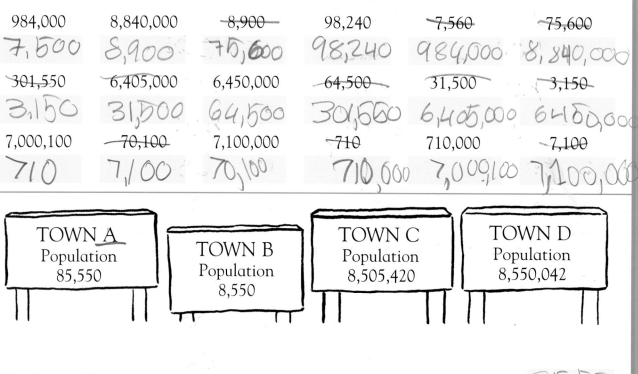

TOWN A
Population
85,550

TOWN B
Population
8,550

TOWN C
Population
8,505,420

TOWN D
Population
8,550,042

Which town has:

The second-smallest population? 85,550

The largest population? 8,550,042   The second-largest population? 8,505,420

Rounding numbers

Round each number.

36 to the nearest ten   40

124 to the nearest hundred   100

4,360 to the nearest thousand   4,000

Remember: If a number is halfway between, round it up.

Round each number to the nearest ten.

24	20	91	90	55	60	73	70
57	60	68	70	49	50	35	40
82	80	37	40	22	20	52	50
46	50	26	30	85	90	99	100
43	40	51	50	78	80	29	30

Round each number to the nearest hundred.

386 =	400	224 =	200	825 =	800	460 =	500
539 =	500	429 =	400	378 =	400	937 =	900
772 =	800	255 =	300	549 =	500	612 =	600
116 =	100	750 =	800	618 =	600	990 =	1,000
940 =	900	843 =	800	172 =	200	868 =	900

Round each number to the nearest thousand.

3,240	3,000	2,500	3,000	9,940	1?	1,051	1,000
8,945	9,000	5,050	5,000	5,530	6,000	4,850	5,000
6,200	6,000	7,250	7,000	8,499	8,000	8,450	8,000
12,501	13,000	8,762	9,000	6,500	7,000	3,292	3,000
1,499	1,000	14,836	15,000	10,650	11,000	11,241	11,000

Identifying patterns

Continue each pattern.

Steps of 9: 5 14 23 32 41 50

Steps of 14: 20 34 48 62 76 90

Continue each pattern.

21	38	55	72	89	106	123	140
13	37	61	85	109	133	157	181
7	25	43	61	79	97	1157	133
32	48	64	80	96	112	128	144
12	31	50	69	88	107	126	145
32	54	76	58	80	102	124	186
24	64	104	144	184	224	264	304
4	34	64	94	124	154	184	214
36	126	216	306	396	486	576	666
12	72	132	192	252	312	372	432
25	45	65	85	105	125	145	165
22	72	122	172	222	272	322	322
25	100	175	250	325	400	475	550
60	165	270	375	480	585	690	795
8	107	206	305	404	503	602	701
10	61	112	163	214	265	316	367
26	127	228	329	430	531	632	733
48	100	152	204	256	308	360	412

Recognizing multiples of 6, 7, and 8

Circle the multiples of 6.

8 (12) 15 (18) 20 (24)

Circle the multiples of 6.

8	22	14	(18)	(36)	40
16	38	44	25	(30)	(60)
(6)	21	19	(54)	56	(24)
(12)	(48)	10	20	35	26
(42)	39	23	28	(36)	32

Circle the multiples of 7.

(7)	17	24	59	(42)	55
15	20	(21)	46	12	70
(14)	27	69	36	47	(49)
65	19	57	(28)	38	63
33	34	(35)	37	60	(56)

Circle the multiples of 8.

(40)	26	15	25	38	(56)
26	(8)	73	41	64	12
75	58	62	(24)	31	(72)
12	(80)	32	46	38	78
(16)	42	66	28	48	68

Circle the number that is a multiple of 6 *and* 7.

18   54   (42)   21   28   63

Circle the numbers that are multiples of 6 *and* 8.

16   (24)   36   (48)   54   42

Circle the number that is a multiple of 7 *and* 8.

(24)   32   40   28   (42)   (56)

Factors of numbers from 1 to 30

The factors of 10 are   1   2   5   10

Circle the factors of 4.   ① ② 3 ④

Write all the factors of each number.

The factors of 26 are   1, 2, 13, 26

The factors of 30 are   1, 3, 10, 30, 2, 15, 6,

The factors of 9 are   1, 3, 9

The factors of 12 are   1, 2, 6, 4, 3, 12

The factors of 15 are   1, 3, 5, 15

The factors of 22 are   1, 22, 11, 2

The factors of 20 are   1, 2, 4, 5, 20

The factors of 21 are   1, 7, 3, 21

The factors of 24 are   1, 6, 4, 8, 24, 3, 12, 2

Circle all the factors of each number.

Which numbers are factors of 14?   ① ② 3 5 ⑦ 9 12 ⑭

Which numbers are factors of 13?   ① 2 3 4 5 6 7 8 9 10 11 ⑬

Which numbers are factors of 7?   ① 2 3 4 5 6 ⑦

Which numbers are factors of 11?   ① 2 3 4 5 6 7 8 9 10 ⑪

Which numbers are factors of 6?   ① ② ③ 4 5 ⑥

Which numbers are factors of 8?   ① ② 3 ④ 5 6 7 ⑧

Which numbers are factors of 17?   ① 2 5 7 12 14 16 ⑰

Which numbers are factors of 18?   ① ② ③ 4 5 ⑥ 8 ⑨ 10 12 ⑱

Some numbers only have factors of 1 and themselves. They are called prime numbers.
Write down all the prime numbers that are less than 30 in the box.

1, 2, 3, 5, 7, 11, 13, 17, 19, 23, 29

Recognizing equivalent fractions

Make each pair of fractions equal by writing a number in the box.

$$\frac{1}{2} = \frac{5}{10} \qquad \frac{3}{4} = \frac{6}{8} \qquad \frac{1}{3} = \frac{3}{9}$$

$$\frac{2}{3} = \frac{8}{12} \qquad \frac{6}{12} = \frac{3}{6} \qquad \frac{4}{8} = \frac{1}{2}$$

$$\frac{1}{5} = \frac{2}{10} \qquad \frac{4}{12} = \frac{2}{6} \qquad \frac{3}{5} = \frac{6}{10}$$

$$\frac{1}{4} = \frac{2}{8} \qquad \frac{6}{18} = \frac{1}{3} \qquad \frac{3}{12} = \frac{1}{4}$$

$$\frac{3}{9} = \frac{1}{3} \qquad \frac{4}{10} = \frac{2}{5} \qquad \frac{3}{4} = \frac{9}{12}$$

$$\frac{4}{16} = \frac{1}{4} \qquad \frac{15}{20} = \frac{3}{4} \qquad \frac{6}{12} = \frac{1}{2}$$

$$\frac{3}{5} = \frac{6}{10} \qquad \frac{3}{6} = \frac{1}{2} \qquad \frac{9}{12} = \frac{3}{4}$$

Make each row of fractions equal by writing a number in each box.

$$\frac{1}{2} = \frac{2}{4} = \frac{3}{6} = \frac{4}{8} = \frac{5}{10} = \frac{6}{12}$$

$$\frac{1}{4} = \frac{2}{8} = \frac{3}{12} = \frac{4}{16} = \frac{5}{20} = \frac{6}{24}$$

$$\frac{3}{4} = \frac{6}{8} = \frac{9}{12} = \frac{12}{16} = \frac{15}{20} = \frac{18}{24}$$

$$\frac{1}{3} = \frac{2}{6} = \frac{3}{9} = \frac{4}{12} = \frac{5}{15} = \frac{12}{36}$$

$$\frac{1}{5} = \frac{2}{10} = \frac{3}{15} = \frac{4}{20} = \frac{5}{25} = \frac{6}{30}$$

$$\frac{2}{3} = \frac{4}{6} = \frac{6}{9} = \frac{8}{12} = \frac{10}{15} = \frac{14}{21}$$

Ordering sets of numbers

Write the numbers in order, from least to greatest.

$$2 \qquad 1\frac{1}{2} \qquad \frac{1}{2} \qquad \frac{1}{4} \qquad 1\frac{3}{4}$$

$$\frac{1}{4} \qquad \frac{1}{2} \qquad 1\frac{1}{2} \qquad 1\frac{3}{4} \qquad 2$$

Write each row of numbers in order, from least to greatest.

$$4 \qquad 2\frac{1}{2} \qquad 1\frac{3}{4} \qquad 1\frac{1}{4} \qquad 3\frac{1}{2}$$
(student answers) $1\frac{1}{4} \quad 1\frac{3}{4} \quad 2\frac{1}{2} \quad 3\frac{1}{2} \quad 4$

$$2 \qquad 1\frac{1}{2} \qquad 1 \qquad 2\frac{1}{4} \qquad 3$$
(student answers) $1\frac{1}{2} \quad 2\frac{1}{2} \quad 2 \quad 2\frac{1}{4} \quad 3$

$$2 \qquad 1\frac{1}{4} \qquad 3\frac{1}{2} \qquad 1\frac{1}{2} \qquad 2\frac{1}{2}$$
(student answers) $1\frac{1}{4} \quad 1\frac{1}{2} \quad 2 \quad 2\frac{1}{2} \quad 3\frac{1}{2}$

$$7\frac{1}{2} \qquad 3\frac{1}{4} \qquad 1\frac{1}{2} \qquad 1\frac{1}{4} \qquad 2\frac{3}{4}$$
(student answers) $1\frac{1}{4} \quad 1\frac{1}{2} \quad 2\frac{3}{4} \quad 3\frac{1}{4} \quad 7\frac{1}{2}$

$$4\frac{1}{4} \qquad 3\frac{1}{2} \qquad 2\frac{3}{4} \qquad 2\frac{1}{2} \qquad 3\frac{1}{4}$$
(student answers) $2\frac{1}{2} \quad 2\frac{3}{4} \quad 3\frac{1}{4} \quad 3\frac{1}{2} \quad 4\frac{1}{4}$

$$3\frac{3}{4} \qquad 3\frac{1}{3} \qquad 4\frac{1}{4} \qquad 3\frac{2}{3} \qquad 3\frac{1}{2}$$
(student answers) $3\frac{1}{3} \quad 3\frac{1}{2} \quad 3\frac{2}{3} \quad 3\frac{3}{4} \quad 4\frac{1}{4}$

STOP Roc tomorrow

$$4\frac{2}{3} \qquad 4\frac{1}{2} \qquad 4\frac{3}{4} \qquad 4\frac{1}{3} \qquad 5\frac{1}{4}$$
(student answers) $4\frac{1}{3} \quad 4\frac{1}{2} \quad 4\frac{2}{3} \quad 4\frac{3}{4} \quad 5\frac{1}{4}$

$$7\frac{1}{2} \qquad 6\frac{2}{3} \qquad 7\frac{3}{4} \qquad 7\frac{1}{4} \qquad 6\frac{1}{2}$$
(student answers) $6\frac{1}{2} \quad 6\frac{2}{3} \quad 7\frac{1}{4} \quad 7\frac{1}{2} \quad 7\frac{3}{4}$

$$14\frac{1}{2} \qquad 15\frac{3}{4} \qquad 15\frac{1}{2} \qquad 14\frac{3}{4} \qquad 13\frac{3}{4}$$
(student answers) $13\frac{3}{4} \quad 14\frac{1}{2} \quad 14\frac{3}{4} \quad 15\frac{1}{2} \quad 15\frac{3}{4}$

$$7\frac{1}{3} \qquad 8\frac{1}{2} \qquad 7\frac{3}{4} \qquad 8\frac{1}{5} \qquad 7\frac{2}{3}$$
(student answers) $7\frac{1}{3} \quad 7\frac{2}{3} \quad 7\frac{3}{4} \quad 8\frac{1}{2} \quad 8\frac{1}{5}$

$$10\frac{1}{5} \qquad 9\frac{3}{4} \qquad 10\frac{1}{2} \qquad 9\frac{1}{5} \qquad 9\frac{1}{2}$$
(student answers) $9\frac{1}{5} \quad 9\frac{1}{2} \quad 9\frac{3}{4} \quad 10\frac{1}{2} \quad 10\frac{1}{5}$

Rounding decimals

Round each decimal to the nearest whole number.

3.4   3

5.7   6

4.5   5

If the whole number has 5 after it, round it to the whole number above.

Round each decimal to the nearest whole number.

6.2	6.0	2.5	3.0	1.5	2.0	3.8	4.0
5.5	6.0	2.8	3.0	3.2	3.0	8.5	9.0
5.4	5.0	7.9	8.0	3.7	4.0	2.3	2.0
1.1	1.0	8.6	9.0	8.3	8.0	9.2	9.0
4.7	5.0	6.3	6.0	7.3	7.0	8.7	9.0

Round each decimal to the nearest whole number.

14.4	10.0	42.3	40.0	74.1	60.0	59.7	6
29.9	30.0	32.6	40.0	63.5	70.0	96.4	9
18.2	10.0	37.5	40.0	39.6	40.0	76.3	7
40.1	40.0	28.7	30.0	26.9	30.0	12.5	2
29.5	30.0	38.5	40.0	87.2	8	41.6	5

Round each decimal to the nearest whole number.

137.6	200.0	423.5	5	426.2	4	111.8	2
641.6	7	333.5	4	805.2	8	246.8	3
119.5	2	799.6	8	562.3	5	410.2	4
682.4	6	759.6	8	531.5	6	829.9	9
743.4	7	831.1	8	276.7	3	649.3	6

Adding two numbers

Find each sum.

```
  271        483
+ 524      + 571
  795      1,054
```

Remember to regroup if you need to.

Find each sum.

```
  334        352        723        843
+ 265      + 127      + 345      + 291
  599        479       1,068      1,134
```

```
  385        363        535        392
+ 606      + 147      + 187      + 488
  991        510        722        880
```

Write the answer in the box.

213 + 137 = 350

535 + 167 = 602

Write the missing number in the box.

```
  3 6 2      2   6      7   1      7 3 9
+ 4 1 9    + 5 8 1    + 2 6 4    + 2 4 0
  7 8 1      8 3 7      9 8        9 7 9
```

Find each sum.

```
  204
+ 148
  352
```

One jar contains 204 candies, and another contains 148 candies. How many candies are there altogether?

352

```
  159
+ 136
  295
```

A boy has 136 baseball cards, and his sister has 159. How many cards do they have altogether?

295

Adding two·numbers

(handwritten working top-right)
3,642
+2,013
5,655

Find each sum.

4,321	3,794
+ 2,465	+ 5,325
6,786	9,119

Remember to carry if you need to.

Find each sum.

2,642	4,325	2,471
+ 3,241	+ 2,653	+ 4,238
5,883	6,978	6,709

3,749	5,764	8,482
+ 2,471	+ 3,915	+ 1,349
6,220	9,679	9,831

Write the answer in the box.

$1{,}342 + 1{,}264 = $ **2606** $2{,}531 + 4{,}236 = $ **6,767**

$2{,}013 + 3{,}642 = $ **5,655** $1{,}738 + 4{,}261 = $ **5,999**

Write the missing number in the box.

3,7 4 1	1,6 5 2	3, 6 4 2
+ 2, 9 4 **3**	+ 3, 2 **6** 4	+ **4** 8 3 **1**
6, 6 8 4	4, 9 2 6	8, 4 7 3

Find each sum.

(handwritten working)
362
+419
1

5,621 people saw the local soccer team play on Saturday, and 3,246 people watched the midweek match. How many people saw the soccer team play that week?

8,867

5,621
+ 3,246
8,867

6,214 people went to the rock concert on Saturday night, and 3,471 people went on Sunday night. How many people saw the rock concert that weekend?

6,214
3,471
9,685

9685

13

Subtracting three-digit numbers

$$\begin{array}{r} 3\cancel{6}5 \\ -\,1\cancel{6}3 \\ \hline 242 \end{array}$$

Write the difference between the lines.

$$\begin{array}{r} 364 \\ -\,223 \\ \hline 141 \end{array} \qquad \begin{array}{r} \overset{6\,11}{4\cancel{7}\cancel{1}}\text{ cm} \\ -\,252\text{ cm} \\ \hline 219\text{ cm} \end{array}$$

Write the difference between the lines.

$$\begin{array}{r} 263 \\ -\,151 \\ \hline 112 \end{array} \qquad \begin{array}{r} 478 \\ -\,234 \\ \hline 244 \end{array} \qquad \begin{array}{r} 845 \\ -\,624 \\ \hline 221 \end{array} \qquad \begin{array}{r} 793 \\ -\,581 \\ \hline 212 \end{array}$$

$$\begin{array}{r} 580\text{ ft} \\ -\,230\text{ ft} \\ \hline 350\text{ ft} \end{array} \qquad \begin{array}{r} 659\text{ m} \\ -\,318\text{ m} \\ \hline 341\text{ m} \end{array} \qquad \begin{array}{r} 850\text{ yd} \\ -\,740\text{ yd} \\ \hline 110\text{ yd} \end{array} \qquad \begin{array}{r} 372\text{ m} \\ -\,262\text{ m} \\ \hline 110\text{ m} \end{array}$$

Write the difference in the box.

$365 - 123 = 242$ $799 - 354 = 945$

$\$876 - \$515 = 861$ $\$940 - \$730 = 210$

$\$684 - \$574 = 110$ $\$220 - \$120 = 100$

Write the difference between the lines.

$$\begin{array}{r} \overset{5}{3}\overset{\,1}{6}3 \\ -\,145 \\ \hline 218 \end{array} \qquad \begin{array}{r} 484 \\ -\,237 \\ \hline 247 \end{array} \qquad \begin{array}{r} \overset{5}{5}61 \\ -\,342 \\ \hline 219 \end{array} \qquad \begin{array}{r} 394 \\ -\,185 \\ \hline 209 \end{array}$$

$$\begin{array}{r} 9\overset{2}{3}7 \\ -\,719 \\ \hline 218 \end{array} \qquad \begin{array}{r} 5\overset{5}{6}8 \\ -\,209 \\ \hline 359 \end{array} \qquad \begin{array}{r} 225 \\ -\,116 \\ \hline 109 \end{array} \qquad \begin{array}{r} 752 \\ -\,329 \\ \hline 423 \end{array}$$

Find the answer to each problem.

A grocer has 234 apples. He sells 127. How many apples does he have left?

107 apples

A store has 860 videos to rent. 420 are rented. How many are left in the store?

440 videos

There are 572 children in a school. 335 are girls. How many are boys?

247 children

Subtracting three-digit numbers

Write the difference between the lines.

```
  311              10
                 6Ø11
 4̷15             71̷1 m
-152            -392 m
─────           ──────
 263             319 m
```

Write the difference between the lines.

```
 524 m          319 m          647 ft          915 yd
- 263 m        - 137 m        - 456 ft        - 193 yd
──────         ──────         ───────         ───────
 261 m          182 m          191 ft          722 yd
```

```
 714            926            421            815
- 407          - 827          - 355          - 786
─────          ─────          ─────          ─────
 307            99             66             29
```

Write the difference in the box.

512 – 304 = 208   648 – 239 = 409

831 – 642 = 189   377 – 198 = 179

Write the difference between the lines.

```
 423            615            312            924
- 136          - 418          - 113          - 528
─────          ─────          ─────          ─────
 287            197            199            396
```

Write the missing number in the box.

```
 7 2 3          5 6 2          8 3 4          5 3 2
-1 2 8         -3 1 7         -2 5 7         -1 8 5
──────         ──────         ──────         ──────
 5 9 5          2 4 5          5 7 7          3 4 7
```

Find the answer to each problem.

A theater holds 645 people. 257 people buy tickets. How many seats are empty?

388 seats

```
 645
-257
─────
 388
```

There are 564 people in a park. 276 are boating on the lake. How many are taking part in other activities?

288 people

Adding decimals

Write the answer between the lines.

$5.25
+ $2.40
$7.65

2.25 m
+ 3.50 m
5.75 m

Write the answer between the lines.

$2.25
+ $4.50
_____

$7.50
+ $2.25
_____

$3.35
+ $1.50
_____

$6.45
+ $2.35
_____

$3.15
+ $4.75
_____

$1.50
+ $3.95
_____

5.50 m
+ 2.35 m
_____

3.60 m
+ 4.15 m
_____

7.30 m
+ 1.65 m
_____

6.15 m
+ 2.20 m
_____

3.30 m
+ 6.55 m
_____

5.20 m
+ 1.75 m
_____

Write the answer in the box.

$5.25 + $3.30 =

6.15 m + 1.50 m =

$6.35 + $2.30 =

$5.20 + $2.55 =

2.45 m + 5.10 m =

$7.45 + $1.50 =

Find the answer to each problem.

Lorna has $2.50. Her brother has $2.75. How much do they have together?

Max has 9.50 m of track for a model train. His friend has 7.75 m of track. If they joined their tracks, how long would the new track be?

16

Adding decimals

Write the answer between the lines.

    $3.35   3.45 m
+ $5.55   + 1.25 m
─────   ────────
   $8.90   4.70 m

Write the answer between the lines.

$3.60	$1.25	$7.45
+ $2.25	+ $4.55	+ $2.35

$3.60	$7.35	$5.25
+ $3.25	+ $1.45	+ $2.65

3.45 m	8.55 m	1.75 m
+ 4.35 m	+ 1.35 m	+ 5.20 m

2.40 m	7.15 m	3.85 m
+ 1.45 m	+ 1.35 m	+ 4.10 m

Write the answer in the box.

$2.75 + $4.15 =   3.75 m + 2.75 m = $3.65 + $1.50 =

$6.25 + $1.50 =   8.65 m + 2.55 m = $3.45 + $1.55 =

Work out the answer to each sum.

George buys two magazines that cost $2.55 and $1.75. How much does he spend?

Jennifer buys two rolls of tape. One is 7.75 m long, and the other is 6.75 m. How much tape does she have altogether?

Subtracting decimals

Write the difference between the lines.

$\begin{array}{r} \$\,6.55 \\ -\ \$\,3.20 \\ \hline \$3.35 \end{array}$ $\begin{array}{r} 4.70\ \text{m} \\ -\ 2.50\ \text{m} \\ \hline 2.20\ \text{m} \end{array}$

Write the difference between the lines.

$\begin{array}{r} \$7.45 \\ -\ \$3.30 \\ \hline \end{array}$ $\begin{array}{r} \$9.60 \\ -\ \$7.20 \\ \hline \end{array}$ $\begin{array}{r} \$5.55 \\ -\ \$2.40 \\ \hline \end{array}$

$\begin{array}{r} \$8.35 \\ -\ \$3.25 \\ \hline \end{array}$ $\begin{array}{r} \$3.95 \\ -\ \$1.75 \\ \hline \end{array}$ $\begin{array}{r} \$6.55 \\ -\ \$2.40 \\ \hline \end{array}$

Write the difference between the lines.

$\begin{array}{r} 3.90\ \text{m} \\ -\ 1.40\ \text{m} \\ \hline \end{array}$ $\begin{array}{r} 4.75\ \text{m} \\ -\ 3.35\ \text{m} \\ \hline \end{array}$ $\begin{array}{r} 9.20\ \text{m} \\ -\ 2.20\ \text{m} \\ \hline \end{array}$

$\begin{array}{r} 7.55\ \text{m} \\ -\ 1.15\ \text{m} \\ \hline \end{array}$ $\begin{array}{r} 2.15\ \text{m} \\ -\ 1.00\ \text{m} \\ \hline \end{array}$ $\begin{array}{r} 3.35\ \text{m} \\ -\ 2.20\ \text{m} \\ \hline \end{array}$

Write the difference in the box.

$\$4.15\ -\ \$1.10\ =$ $\$3.55\ -\ \$2.50\ =$

$\$9.75\ -\ \$4.30\ =$ $\$8.85\ -\ \$6.05\ =$

$7.55\ \text{m} - 2.30\ \text{m}\ =$ $6.15\ \text{m} - 4.05\ \text{m}\ =$

Find the answer to each problem.

Mei-ling has $4.65 to spend. She buys a book for $3.45. How much money does she have left?

Shawn is given $9.50 for his birthday. If he spends $3.20 at the mall, how much money will he have left?

Subtracting decimals

Write the difference between the lines.

4 13	6 13
$5.35	7.35 m
− $2.40	− 1.65 m
$2.95	5.70 m

Write the difference between the lines.

$6.55	$7.45	$8.65
− $2.75	− $3.65	− $4.75

$3.15	$5.70	$4.15
− $1.25	− $2.90	− $1.75

Write the difference between the lines.

5.35 m	7.25 m	4.15 m
− 2.55 m	− 2.55 m	− 2.25 m

5.45 m	8.15 m	7.30 m
− 2.55 m	− 2.20 m	− 3.50 m

Write the difference in the box.

$6.25 − $2.50 = $4.35 − $2.55 =

$5.20 − $3.30 = $7.40 − $3.80 =

6.45 m − 2.55 m =   7.35 m − 3.55 m =

Find the answer to each problem.

Keisha has a piece of wood 4.55 m long. She cuts off a piece 1.65 m long. How long a piece of wood is left?

Eli's long-jump result is 2.35 m. Steven's is 1.40 m. How much longer is Eli's jump than Steven's?

Multiplying by one-digit numbers

Find each product.

	₁	₁
32	26	34
x 2	x 3	x 4
64	78	136

Find each product.

¹
27
x   2
54

32
x   3
96

²
16
x   4
64

¹
19
x   2
38

22
x   3
66

²
25
x   4
100

⁶
18
x   6
108

¹
33
x   5
165

¹
39
x   2
78

¹
26
x   2
52

41
x   2
82

²
38
x   3
114

²
29
x   3
87

¹
45
x   2
90

²
28
x   3
84

³
16
x   6
96

10
x   5
50

40
x   2
80

20
x   4
80

50
x   3
150

Find the answer to each problem.

Laura has 36 marbles, and
Sarah has twice as many.
How many marbles does
Sarah have?

A ruler is 30 cm long.
How long will 4 rulers be?

30
x 4
120

120

Multiplying by one-digit numbers

Find each product.

$$\begin{array}{r} 53 \\ \times\ 3 \\ \hline 159 \end{array} \qquad \begin{array}{r} \overset{3}{76} \\ \times\ 6 \\ \hline 456 \end{array} \qquad \begin{array}{r} \overset{3}{25} \\ \times\ 7 \\ \hline 175 \end{array}$$

Find each product.

$$\begin{array}{r} \overset{4}{56} \\ \times\ 8 \\ \hline 448 \end{array} \qquad \begin{array}{r} \overset{4}{48} \\ \times\ 5 \\ \hline 240 \end{array} \qquad \begin{array}{r} \overset{4}{46} \\ \times\ 7 \\ \hline 322 \end{array} \qquad \begin{array}{r} \overset{1}{32} \\ \times\ 6 \\ \hline 192 \end{array} \qquad \begin{array}{r} 36 \\ \times\ 9 \\ \hline 324 \end{array}$$

$$\begin{array}{r} \overset{2}{45} \\ \times\ 4 \\ \hline 180 \end{array} \qquad \begin{array}{r} \overset{1}{33} \\ \times\ 6 \\ \hline 198 \end{array} \qquad \begin{array}{r} \overset{1}{73} \\ \times\ 5 \\ \hline 365 \end{array} \qquad \begin{array}{r} 96 \\ \times\ 3 \\ \hline 288 \end{array} \qquad \begin{array}{r} \overset{5}{58} \\ \times\ 7 \\ \hline 406 \end{array}$$

$$\begin{array}{r} 81 \\ \times\ 3 \\ \hline 243 \end{array} \qquad \begin{array}{r} 24 \\ \times\ 9 \\ \hline 216 \end{array} \qquad \begin{array}{r} 19 \\ \times\ 8 \\ \hline 152 \end{array} \qquad \begin{array}{r} 64 \\ \times\ 4 \\ \hline 256 \end{array} \qquad \begin{array}{r} 52 \\ \times\ 6 \\ \hline 312 \end{array}$$

$$\begin{array}{r} 37 \\ \times\ 7 \\ \hline 259 \end{array} \qquad \begin{array}{r} 40 \\ \times\ 8 \\ \hline 320 \end{array} \qquad \begin{array}{r} 50 \\ \times\ 3 \\ \hline 150 \end{array} \qquad \begin{array}{r} 30 \\ \times\ 7 \\ \hline 210 \end{array} \qquad \begin{array}{r} 20 \\ \times\ 9 \\ \hline 180 \end{array}$$

Find the answer to each problem.

A school bus holds 36 children. How many children can travel in 6 busloads?

216

Each of 28 children brings 7 drawings to school. How many drawings do they have altogether?

196

Division with remainders

Find each quotient.

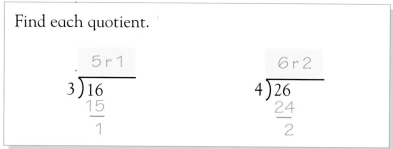

$$5 r 1$$
$$3 \overline{)16}$$
$$\underline{15}$$
$$1$$

$$6 r 2$$
$$4 \overline{)26}$$
$$\underline{24}$$
$$2$$

Find each quotient.

17 R1
2)35
-2
15
-14
1

11 R2
4)46
-4
06
-4
2

07
3)22
-0
22
21
1

0a R4
5)49
-0
4a
45
4

14 R2
4)58
-4
18
18
2

12 R3
5)63
-5
13
-10
3

09 R2
5)37
-0
37
35
2

12 R2
4)50
-4
10
8
2

25 R1
3)76
-6
16
15
1

14 R5
4)59
-4
19
14
5

17 R9
5)94
-5
34
35
9

16 R3
5)83
-5
33
30
3

49 R1
2)99
-8
19
-18
1

18 R3
4)75

15 R2
5)77
-3
27
-25
2

18 R1
2)37
-2
17
16
1

Write the answer in the box.

What is 27 divided by 4?   Divide 78 by 5.

What is 46 divided by 3?   Divide 63 by 2.

Division with remainders

Find each quotient.

$$6\overline{)34}$$ 5 r 4
$$30$$
$$4$$

$$7\overline{)50}$$ 7 r 1
$$49$$
$$1$$

Find each quotient.

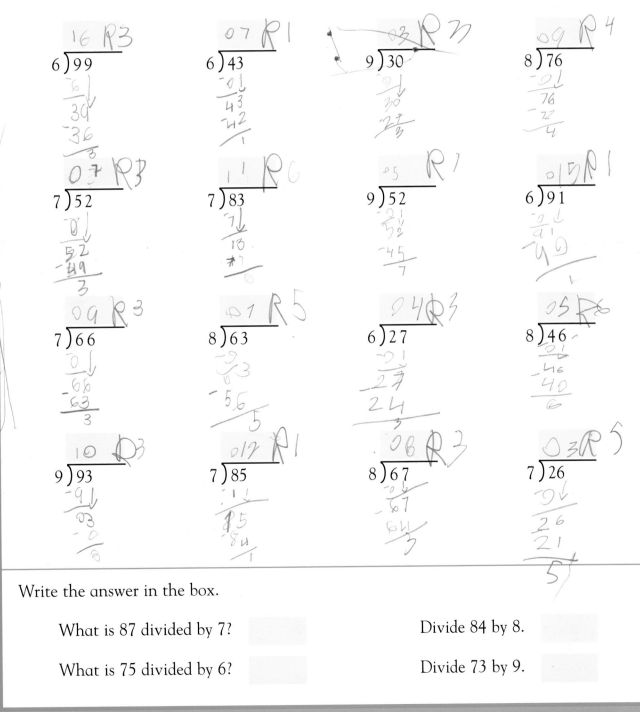

$$6\overline{)99}$$

$$6\overline{)43}$$

$$9\overline{)30}$$

$$8\overline{)76}$$

$$7\overline{)52}$$

$$7\overline{)83}$$

$$9\overline{)52}$$

$$6\overline{)91}$$

$$7\overline{)66}$$

$$8\overline{)63}$$

$$6\overline{)27}$$

$$8\overline{)46}$$

$$9\overline{)93}$$

$$7\overline{)85}$$

$$8\overline{)67}$$

$$7\overline{)26}$$

Write the answer in the box.

What is 87 divided by 7?

What is 75 divided by 6?

Divide 84 by 8.

Divide 73 by 9.

Real-life problems

Write the answer in the box.

Yasmin has $4.60 and she is given another $1.20.
How much money does she have?

$5.80

```
   $4.60
 +$1.20
   $5.80
```

David has 120 marbles.
He divides them equally among his 5 friends.
How many marbles
does each get?　　24

```
      24
   5)120
     10
     20
     20
      0
```

Write the answer in the box.

Michael buys a ball for $5.50 and a flashlight for $3.65.
How much does he spend?

```
 $5.50
+$3.65
 $9.1.5
```

$9.15

How much does he have left from $10?

$0.85

The 32 children of a class bring in $5 each for a school trip.
What is the total of the amount brought in?

$160

A set of 5 shelves can be made from a piece of wood 4 yards long.
What fraction of a yard will each shelf be?

$\frac{4}{5}$ y

Each of 5 children has $16.
How much do they have altogether?

$80

If the above total were shared among 8 children, how much would
each child have?

$10

Real-life problems

Find the answer to each problem.

A box is 16 in. wide. How wide will 6 boxes side by side be?

96 in.

$$\begin{array}{r} 3 \\ 16 \text{ in.} \\ \times 6 \\ \hline 96 \text{ in.} \end{array}$$

Josh is 1.20 m tall. His sister is 1.55 m tall. How much taller than Josh is his sister?

0.35 m

$$\begin{array}{r} 1.55 \text{ m} \\ - 1.20 \text{ m} \\ \hline 0.35 \text{ m} \end{array}$$

Find the answer to each problem.

A can contains 56 g of lemonade mix. If 12 g are used, how much is left?

44g

$$\begin{array}{r} 56g \\ -12g \\ \hline 44g \end{array}$$

A large jar of coffee weighs 280 g. A smaller jar weighs 130 g. How much heavier is the larger jar than the smaller jar?

150 g

$$\begin{array}{r} 280g \\ -130g \\ \hline 150g \end{array}$$

There are 7 shelves of books. 5 shelves are 1.2 m long. 2 shelves are 1.5 m long. What is the total length of the 7 shelves?

A rock star can sign 36 photographs in a minute. How many can he sign in 30 seconds?

18 photographs

$$\begin{array}{r} 18 \\ 2\overline{)36} \\ -20 \\ \hline 16 \\ 16 \\ \hline 0 \end{array}$$

Shana has read 5 pages of a 20-page comic book. If it has taken her 9 minutes, how long is it likely to take her to read the whole comic book?

Areas of rectangles and squares

Find the area of this rectangle.

5 ft

15 ft²

3 ft

To find the area of a rectangle or square, multiply length (*l*) by width (*w*).
Area → *l* x *w* → 5 ft x 3 ft = 15 ft²

Find the area of each rectangle and square.

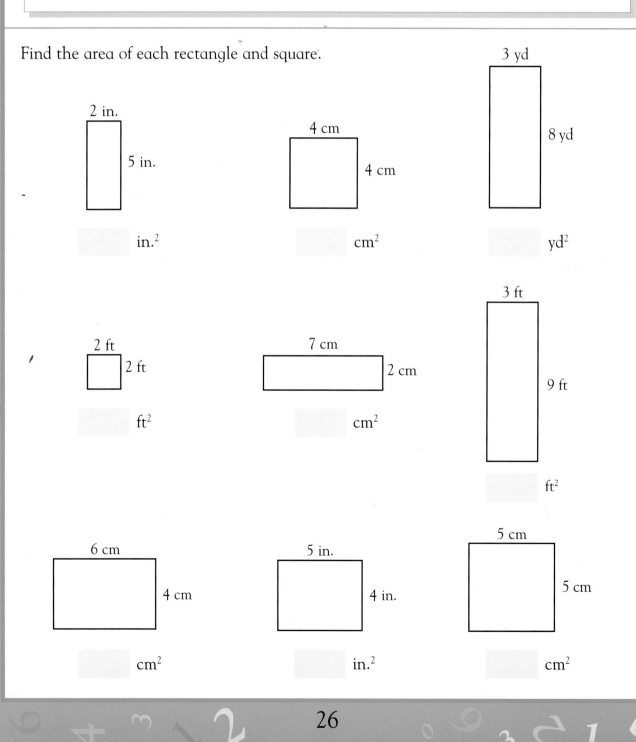

2 in.

5 in.

in.²

4 cm

4 cm

cm²

3 yd

8 yd

yd²

2 ft

2 ft

ft²

7 cm

2 cm

cm²

3 ft

9 ft

ft²

6 cm

4 cm

cm²

5 in.

4 in.

in.²

5 cm

5 cm

cm²

Problems involving time

Find the answer to this problem.

A train leaves the station at 7:30 A.M. and arrives at the end of the line at 10:45 A.M. How long did the journey take?

3 hours 15 minutes

7:30 → 10:30 = 3 h
10:30 → 10:45 = 15 min
Total = 3 h 15 min

Find the answer to each problem.

A film starts at 7:00 P.M. and finishes at 8:45 P.M. How long is the film?

A cake takes 2 hours 25 minutes to bake. If it begins baking at 1:35 P.M., at what time will the cake be done?

Sanjay needs to clean his bedroom and wash the car. It takes him 1 hour 10 minutes to clean his room and 45 minutes to clean the car. If he starts at 10:00 A.M., at what time will he finish?

A car is taken in for repair at 7:00 A.M. It is finished at 1:50 P.M. How long did the repairs take?

Claire has to be at school by 8:50 A.M. If she takes 1 hour 30 minutes to get ready, and the trip takes 35 minutes, at what time does she need to get up?

A bus leaves the bus station at 8:45 A.M. and arrives back at 10:15 A.M. How long has its trip taken?

27

Bar graphs

Use this bar graph to answer each question.

Caps sold

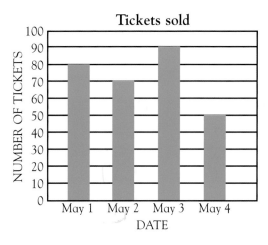

What color cap was sold the most? `red`

How many more green
caps were sold than blue caps? `10`

Use this bar graph to answer each question.

Tickets sold

How many tickets
were sold on May 1?

How many more
tickets were sold on
May 2 than on May 4?

On which date were 90 tickets sold?

Use this bar graph to answer each question.

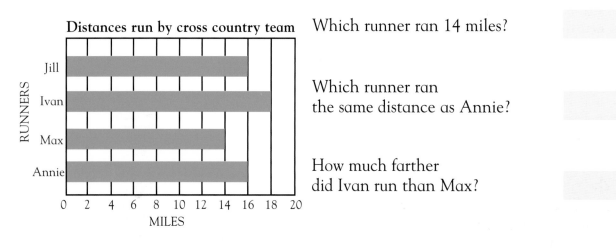

Distances run by cross country team

Which runner ran 14 miles?

Which runner ran
the same distance as Annie?

How much farther
did Ivan run than Max?

Probability

Mark each event on the probability line.

```
        c                    b                    a
        ↓                    ↓                    ↓
   |_____|_____|_____|_____|
impossible   poor     even     good   certain
            chance   chance   chance
```

a) It will get dark tonight.
b) When I toss a coin, it will land showing heads.
c) Abraham Lincoln will come for lunch.

Mark each event on the probability line.

```
   |_____|_____|_____|_____|
impossible   poor     even     good   certain
            chance   chance   chance
```

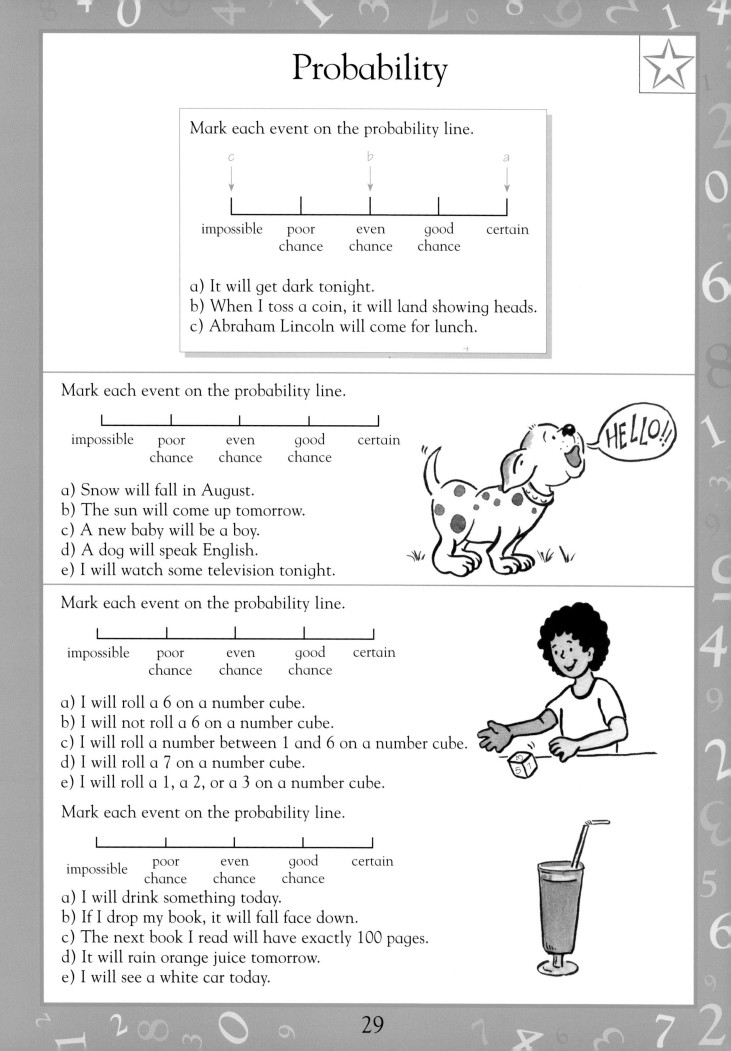

a) Snow will fall in August.
b) The sun will come up tomorrow.
c) A new baby will be a boy.
d) A dog will speak English.
e) I will watch some television tonight.

Mark each event on the probability line.

```
   |_____|_____|_____|_____|
impossible   poor     even     good   certain
            chance   chance   chance
```

a) I will roll a 6 on a number cube.
b) I will not roll a 6 on a number cube.
c) I will roll a number between 1 and 6 on a number cube.
d) I will roll a 7 on a number cube.
e) I will roll a 1, a 2, or a 3 on a number cube.

Mark each event on the probability line.

```
   |_____|_____|_____|_____|
impossible   poor     even     good   certain
            chance   chance   chance
```

a) I will drink something today.
b) If I drop my book, it will fall face down.
c) The next book I read will have exactly 100 pages.
d) It will rain orange juice tomorrow.
e) I will see a white car today.

Triangles

Look at these different triangles.

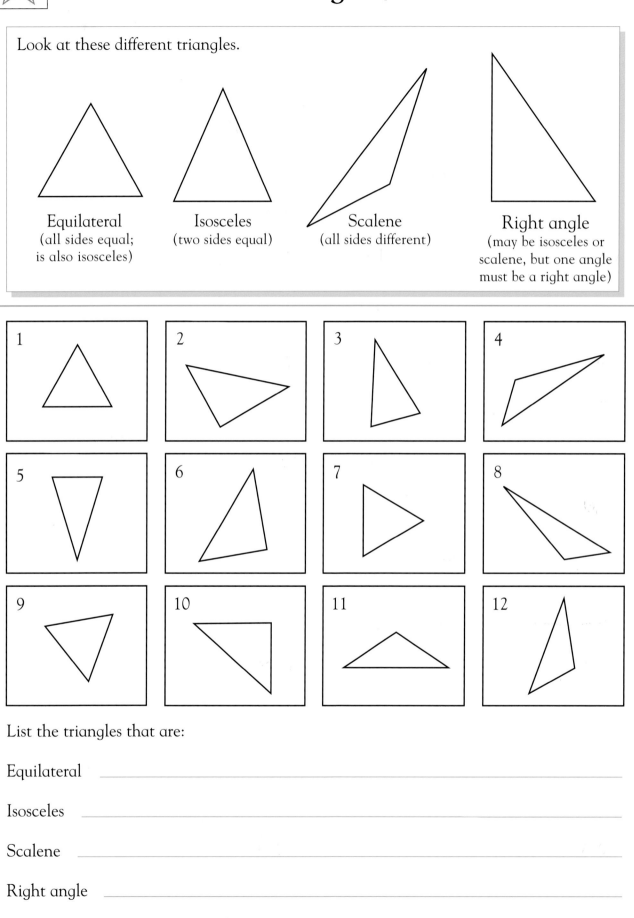

Equilateral
(all sides equal;
is also isosceles)

Isosceles
(two sides equal)

Scalene
(all sides different)

Right angle
(may be isosceles or
scalene, but one angle
must be a right angle)

1

2

3

4

5

6

7

8

9

10

11

12

List the triangles that are:

Equilateral _____

Isosceles _____

Scalene _____

Right angle _____

Expanded form

What is the value of 3 in 2,308?   300

Write 3,417 in expanded form.

(3 x 1,000) + (4 x 100) + (1 x 10) + (7 x 1)

3,000 + 400 + 10 + 7

What is the value of 5 in each of these numbers?

25   5,904   52   2,512   805

What is the value of 8 in each of these numbers?

8,300   982   1,805   768   19,873

Circle each number in which 7 has the value of 70.

7,682   927   870   372   707

171   767   875   7,057   70,000

Write each number in expanded form.

3,897   24,098

50,810   8,945

6,098   14,003

Speed trials

yasmin

Write the answers as fast as you can, but get them right!

$4 \times 10 = $ 40 $8 \times 2 = $ 16 $6 \times 5 = $ 30

Write the answers as fast as you can, but get them right!

$3 \times 2 = 6$	$0 \times 5 = 6$	$3 \times 10 = 30$	$0 \times 3 = 6$
$5 \times 2 = 10$	$10 \times 5 = 50$	$5 \times 10 = 50$	$10 \times 3 = 30$
$1 \times 2 = 2$	$8 \times 5 = 40$	$1 \times 10 = 10$	$8 \times 3 = 24$
$4 \times 2 = 8$	$6 \times 5 = 30$	$4 \times 10 = 40$	$6 \times 3 = 18$
$7 \times 2 = 14$	$2 \times 5 = 10$	$7 \times 10 = 70$	$2 \times 3 = 6$
$2 \times 2 = 4$	$7 \times 5 = 35$	$2 \times 10 = 20$	$7 \times 3 = 21$
$6 \times 2 = 12$	$4 \times 5 = 20$	$6 \times 10 = 60$	$4 \times 3 = 12$
$8 \times 2 = 16$	$1 \times 5 = 5$	$8 \times 10 = 80$	$1 \times 3 = 3$
$10 \times 2 = 20$	$5 \times 5 = 25$	$10 \times 10 = 100$	$5 \times 3 = 15$
$0 \times 2 = 0$	$3 \times 5 = 15$	$0 \times 10 = 0$	$3 \times 3 = 9$
$9 \times 2 = 18$	$5 \times 3 = 15$	$9 \times 10 = 90$	$6 \times 4 = 24$
$2 \times 7 = 14$	$5 \times 8 = 40$	$10 \times 7 = 70$	$3 \times 4 = 12$
$2 \times 1 = 2$	$5 \times 6 = 30$	$10 \times 1 = 10$	$7 \times 4 = 28$
$2 \times 4 = 8$	$5 \times 9 = 45$	$10 \times 4 = 40$	$4 \times 4 = 16$
$3 \times 7 = 21$	$5 \times 7 = 35$	$10 \times 7 = 70$	$10 \times 4 = 40$
$2 \times 5 = 10$	$5 \times 4 = 20$	$10 \times 5 = 50$	$8 \times 4 = 32$
$2 \times 9 = 18$	$5 \times 1 = 5$	$10 \times 9 = 90$	$0 \times 4 = 0$
$2 \times 6 = 12$	$4 \times 7 = 28$	$10 \times 6 = 60$	$9 \times 4 = 36$
$2 \times 8 = 16$	$5 \times 10 = 50$	$10 \times 8 = 80$	$5 \times 4 = 20$
$2 \times 3 = 6$	$5 \times 2 = 10$	$10 \times 3 = 30$	$2 \times 4 = 8$

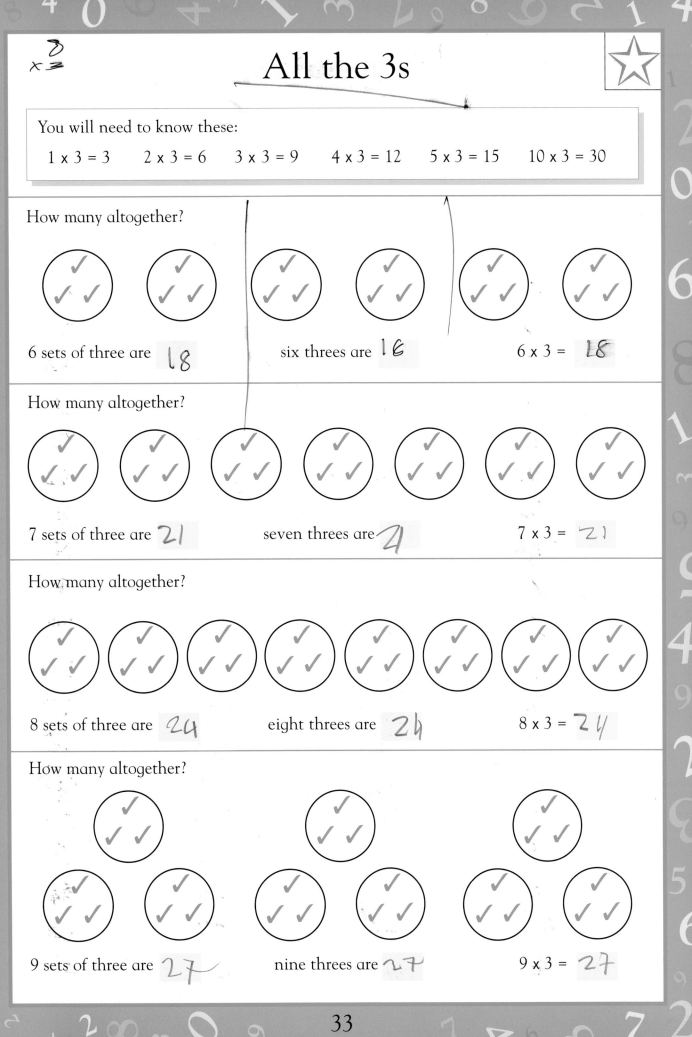

All the 3s

x 8
x 3

You will need to know these:

1 x 3 = 3   2 x 3 = 6   3 x 3 = 9   4 x 3 = 12   5 x 3 = 15   10 x 3 = 30

How many altogether?

6 sets of three are _18_   six threes are _16_   6 x 3 = _18_

How many altogether?

7 sets of three are _21_   seven threes are _21_   7 x 3 = _21_

How many altogether?

8 sets of three are _24_   eight threes are _24_   8 x 3 = _24_

How many altogether?

9 sets of three are _27_   nine threes are _27_   9 x 3 = _27_

33

All the 3s again

You should know all of the three times table by now.

1 x 3 = 3	2 x 3 = 6	3 x 3 = 9	4 x 3 = 12	5 x 3 = 15
6 x 3 = 18	7 x 3 = 21	8 x 3 = 24	9 x 3 = 27	10 x 3 = 30

Say these to yourself a few times.

Cover the three times table with a sheet of paper so you can't see the numbers.
Write the answers. Be as fast as you can, but get them right!

1 x 3 = 3	5 x 3 = 15	6 x 3 = 18
2 x 3 = 6	7 x 3 = 21	9 x 3 = 27
3 x 3 = 9	9 x 3 = 27	4 x 3 = 12
4 x 3 = 12	4 x 3 = 12	5 x 3 = 15
5 x 3 = 15	6 x 3 = 18	3 x 7 = 21
6 x 3 = 18	8 x 3 = 24	3 x 4 = 12
7 x 3 = 21	10 x 3 = 30	2 x 3 = 6
8 x 3 = 24	1 x 3 = 3	10 x 3 = 30
9 x 3 = 27	3 x 3 = 9	3 x 9 = 27
10 x 3 = 30	2 x 3 = 6	3 x 6 = 18
3 x 1 = 3	3 x 5 = 15	3 x 5 = 15
3 x 2 = 6	3 x 7 = 21	3 x 8 = 24
3 x 3 = 9	3 x 9 = 27	7 x 3 = 21
3 x 4 = 12	3 x 4 = 12	3 x 2 = 6
3 x 5 = 15	3 x 6 = 18	3 x 10 = 30
3 x 6 = 18	3 x 8 = 24	8 x 3 = 24
3 x 7 = 21	3 x 10 = 30	3 x 0 = 0
3 x 8 = 24	3 x 1 = 3	1 x 3 = 3
3 x 9 = 27	3 x 0 = 0	3 x 3 = 3
3 x 10 = 30	3 x 2 = 6	3 x 9 = 27

All the 4s

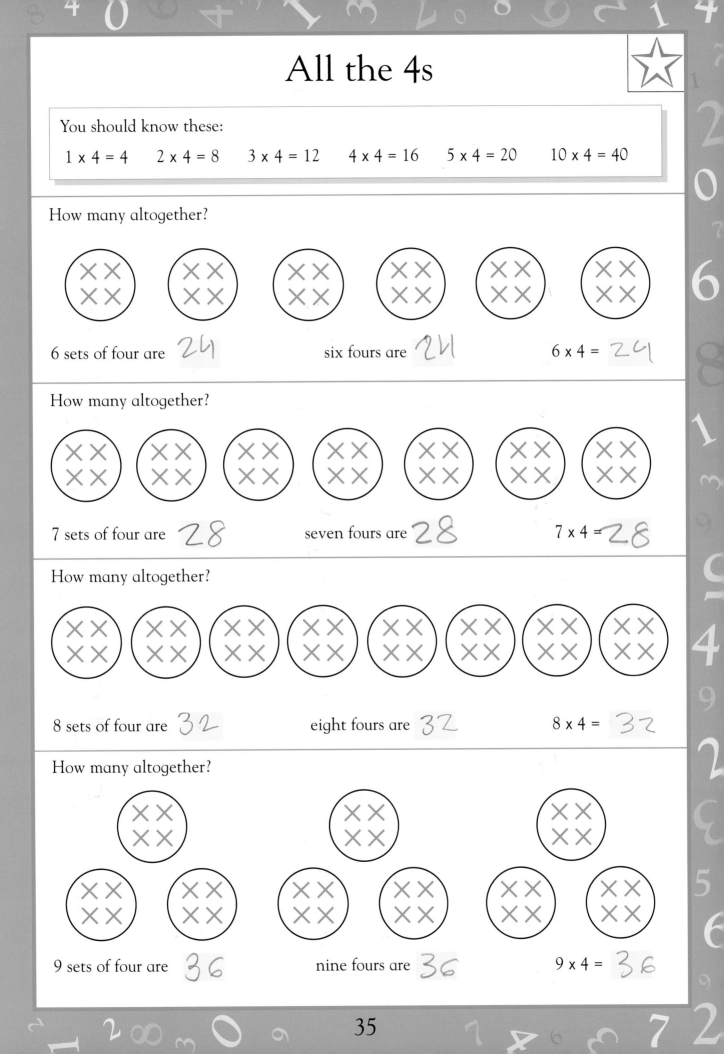

How many altogether?

6 sets of four are *24*   six fours are *24*   6 x 4 = *24*

How many altogether?

7 sets of four are *28*   seven fours are *28*   7 x 4 = *28*

How many altogether?

8 sets of four are *32*   eight fours are *32*   8 x 4 = *32*

How many altogether?

9 sets of four are *36*   nine fours are *36*   9 x 4 = *36*

All the 4s again

Cover the four times table with a sheet of paper so you can't see the numbers.
Write the answers. Be as fast as you can, but get them right!

$1 \times 4 = 4$	$5 \times 4 = 40$	$6 \times 4 = 24$
$2 \times 4 = 8$	$7 \times 4 = 28$	$9 \times 4 = 36$
$3 \times 4 = 12$	$9 \times 4 = 36$	$4 \times 1 = 4$
$4 \times 4 = 16$	$3 \times 4 = 12$	$5 \times 4 = 20$
$5 \times 4 = 20$	$6 \times 4 = 24$	$4 \times 7 = 28$
$6 \times 4 = 24$	$8 \times 4 = 32$	$3 \times 4 = 12$
$7 \times 4 = 28$	$10 \times 4 = 40$	$2 \times 4 = 8$
$8 \times 4 = 32$	$1 \times 4 = 4$	$10 \times 4 = 40$
$9 \times 4 = 36$	$4 \times 4 = 16$	$4 \times 3 = 12$
$10 \times 4 = 40$	$2 \times 4 = 8$	$4 \times 6 = 24$
$4 \times 1 = 4$	$4 \times 5 = 26$	$4 \times 5 = 20$
$4 \times 2 = 8$	$4 \times 7 = 28$	$4 \times 8 = 32$
$4 \times 3 = 12$	$4 \times 9 = 36$	$7 \times 4 = 28$
$4 \times 4 = 16$	$4 \times 4 = 16$	$4 \times 2 = 8$
$4 \times 5 = 20$	$4 \times 6 = 24$	$4 \times 10 = 40$
$4 \times 6 = 24$	$4 \times 8 = 32$	$8 \times 4 = 32$
$4 \times 7 = 28$	$4 \times 10 = 40$	$4 \times 0 = 0$
$4 \times 8 = 32$	$4 \times 1 = 4$	$1 \times 4 = 4$
$4 \times 9 = 36$	$4 \times 0 = 0$	$4 \times 4 = 16$
$4 \times 10 = 40$	$4 \times 2 = 8$	$4 \times 9 = 36$

Speed trials

You should know all of the 1, 2, 3, 4, 5, and 10 times tables by now, but how quickly can you do them?
Ask someone to time you as you do this page.
Remember, you must be fast but also correct.

4 x 2 = 08
8 x 3 = 24
7 x 4 = 28
6 x 5 = 30
8 x 10 = 80
8 x 2 = 16
5 x 3 = 15
9 x 4 = 36
5 x 5 = 25
7 x 10 = 70
0 x 2 = 0
4 x 3 = 12
6 x 4 = 24
3 x 5 = 15
4 x 10 = 40
7 x 2 = 14
3 x 3 = 9
2 x 4 = 8
7 x 5 = 35
9 x 10 = 90

6 x 3 = 18
3 x 4 = 12
7 x 5 = 35
3 x 10 = 30
1 x 2 = 2
7 x 3 = 21
4 x 4 = 16
6 x 5 = 30
4 x 10 = 40
6 x 2 = 12
5 x 3 = 15
8 x 4 = 32
0 x 5 = 0
2 x 10 = 20
7 x 2 = 14
8 x 3 = 24
9 x 4 = 36
5 x 5 = 25
7 x 10 = 70
5 x 2 = 10

9 x 5 = 45
8 x 10 = 80
7 x 2 = 14
6 x 3 = 18
5 x 4 = 20
4 x 5 = 25
3 x 10 = 30
2 x 2 = 4
1 x 3 = 3
0 x 4 = 0
10 x 5 = 50
9 x 2 = 18
8 x 3 = 24
7 x 4 = 28
6 x 5 = 30
5 x 10 = 50
4 x 0 = 0
3 x 2 = 6
2 x 8 = 16
1 x 9 = 9

Some of the 6s

You should already know parts of the 6 times table because they are parts of the 1, 2, 3, 4, 5, and 10 times tables.

1 x 6 = 6	2 x 6 = 12	3 x 6 = 18
4 x 6 = 24	5 x 6 = 30	10 x 6 = 60

Find out if you can remember them quickly and correctly.

Cover the six times table with paper so you can't see the numbers.
Write the answers as quickly as you can.

What is three sixes? $3 \times 6 = 18$

What is ten sixes? $10 \times 6 = 60$

What is two sixes? $2 \times 6 = 12$

What is four sixes? $4 \times 6 = 24$

What is one six? $1 \times 6 = 6$

What is five sixes? $5 \times 6 = 30$

Write the answers as quickly as you can.

How many sixes make 12? 2

How many sixes make 6? 1

How many sixes make 30? 5

How many sixes make 18? 3

How many sixes make 24? 4

How many sixes make 60? 10

Write the answers as quickly as you can.

Multiply six by three. 18

Multiply six by ten. 60

Multiply six by two. 12

Multiply six by five. 30

Multiply six by one. 6

Multiply six by four. 24

Write the answers as quickly as you can.

4 x 6 = 24   2 x 6 = 12   10 x 6 = 60

5 x 6 = 30   1 x 6 = 6   3 x 6 = 18

Write the answers as quickly as you can.

A box contains six eggs. A man buys five boxes. How many eggs does he have? 30

$6 \times 5 =$

A pack contains six sticks of gum.
How many sticks will there be in 10 packs? 60

The rest of the 6s

You need to learn these:
6 x 6 = 36   7 x 6 = 42   8 x 6 = 48   9 x 6 = 54

This work will help you remember the 6 times table.

Complete these sequences.

6   12   18   24   30   *36*   *42*   *48*   *54*   *60*

5 x 6 = 30   so   6 x ~6~ *5* = 30 plus another 6 = *36*

18   24   30   *36*   *42*   *48*   *54*   *60*

6 x 6 = 36   so   7 x 6 = ~36~ *42* plus another 6 = *48*

6   12   18   *24*   *30*   *36*   *42*   48   *54*   60

7 x 6 = 42   so   8 x 6 = ~42~ *48* plus another 6 = *54*

6   *12*   18   24   30   *36*   *42*   *48*   *54*   *60*

8 x 6 = 48   so   9 x 6 = ~48~ *54* plus another 6 = *60*

8   *12*   *18*   24   *30*   *36*   42   *48*   *54*   60

Test yourself on the rest of the 6 times table.
Cover the above part of the page with a sheet of paper.

What is six sixes?   *36*   What is seven sixes?   *42*

What is eight sixes?   *48*   What is nine sixes?   *54*

8 x 6 = *48*   7 x 6 = *42*   6 x 6 = *36*   9 x 6 = *54*

Practice the 6s

You should know all of the 6 times table now, but how quickly can you remember it?
Ask someone to time you as you do this page.
Remember, you must be fast but also correct.

1 x 6 = 6	2 x 6 = 12	7 x 6 = 42
2 x 6 = 12	4 x 6 = 24	3 x 6 = 18
3 x 6 = 18	6 x 6 = 36	9 x 6 = 54
4 x 6 = 24	8 x 6 = 48	6 x 4 = 24
5 x 6 = 30	10 x 6 = 60	1 x 6 = 6
6 x 6 = 36	1 x 6 = 6	6 x 2 = 12
7 x 6 = 42	3 x 6 = 18	6 x 8 = 48
8 x 6 = 48	5 x 6 = 30	0 x 6 = 0
9 x 6 = 54	7 x 6 = 42	6 x 3 = 18
10 x 6 = 60	9 x 6 = 54	5 x 6 = 30
6 x 1 = 6	6 x 3 = 18	6 x 7 = 42
6 x 2 = 12	6 x 5 = 30	2 x 6 = 12
6 x 3 = 18	6 x 7 = 42	6 x 9 = 54
6 x 4 = 24	6 x 9 = 54	4 x 6 = 24
6 x 5 = 30	6 x 2 = 12	8 x 6 = 48
6 x 6 = 36	6 x 4 = 24	10 x 6 = 60
6 x 7 = 42	6 x 6 = 36	6 x 5 = 30
6 x 8 = 48	6 x 8 = 48	6 x 0 = 0
6 x 9 = 54	6 x 10 = 60	6 x 1 = 6
6 x 10 = 60	6 x 0 = 0	6 x 6 = 36

Speed trials

8, 16, 24

4 x 6 = 24	6 x 3 = 18	9 x 6 = 54
5 x 3 = 15	8 x 6 = 48	8 x 6 = 48
7 x 3 = 21	6 x 6 = 36	7 x 3 = 21
6 x 5 = 30	3 x 10 = 30	6 x 6 = 36
6 x 10 = 60	6 x 2 = 12	5 x 4 = 20
8 x 2 = 16	7 x 3 = 21	4 x 6 = 24
5 x 3 = 15	4 x 6 = 24	3 x 6 = 18
9 x 6 = 54	6 x 5 = 30	2 x 6 = 12
5 x 5 = 25	6 x 10 = 60	6 x 3 = 18
7 x 6 = 42	6 x 2 = 12	0 x 6 = 0
0 x 2 = 0	5 x 3 = 15	10 x 5 = 50
6 x 3 = 18	8 x 4 = 32	6 x 2 = 12
6 x 6 = 36	0 x 6 = 0	8 x 3 = 24
3 x 5 = 15	5 x 10 = 50	7 x 6 = 42
4 x 10 = 40	7 x 6 = 42	6 x 5 = 30
7 x 10 = 70	8 x 3 = 24	5 x 10 = 50
3 x 6 = 18	9 x 6 = 54	6 x 0 = 0
2 x 4 = 8	5 x 5 = 25	3 x 10 = 30
6 x 9 = 54	7 x 10 = 70	2 x 8 = 16
9 x 10 = 90	5 x 6 = 30	1 x 8 = 8

Some of the 7s

You should already know parts of the 7 times table because they are parts of the 1, 2, 3, 4, 5, 6 and 10 times tables.

$1 \times 7 = 7$ $2 \times 7 = 14$ $3 \times 7 = 21$ $4 \times 7 = 28$

$5 \times 7 = 35$ $6 \times 7 = 42$ $10 \times 7 = 70$

Find out if you can remember them quickly and correctly.

Cover the seven times table with paper and write the answers to these questions as quickly as you can.

What is three sevens?   21   What is ten sevens?   70

What is two sevens?   14   What is four sevens?   28

What is six sevens?   42   What is five sevens?   35

Write the answers as quickly as you can.

How many sevens make 14?   2   How many sevens make 42?   6

How many sevens make 35?   5   How many sevens make 21?   3

How many sevens make 28?   4   How many sevens make 70?   10

Write the answers as quickly as you can.

Multiply seven by three.   21   Multiply seven by ten.   70

Multiply seven by two.   14   Multiply seven by five.   35

Multiply seven by six.   42   Multiply seven by four.   28

Write the answers as quickly as you can.

$4 \times 7 =$ 28 $2 \times 7 =$ 14 $10 \times 7 =$ 70

$5 \times 7 =$ 35 $1 \times 7 =$ 7 $3 \times 7 =$ 21

Write the answers as quickly as you can.

A bag has seven candies. Ann buys five bags. How many candies does she have?   35
   7   5   7 x 5 =

How many days are there in six weeks?   42

The rest of the 7s

You should now know all of the 1, 2, 3, 4, 5, 6, and 10 times tables.

You need to learn only these parts of the seven times table.

7 x 7 = 49   8 x 7 = 56   9 x 7 = 63

This work will help you remember the 7 times table.

7 x 7 = 49
8 x 7 = 49 + 7 = 56

Complete these sequences.

| 7 | 14 | 21 | 28 | 35 | 42 | 49 | 56 | 63 | 70 |

6 x 7 = 42   so   7 x 7 = 42 plus another 7 = **49**

| 21 | 28 | 35 | 42 | 49 | 56 | 63 | 70 |

7 x 7 = 49   so   8 x 7 = 49 plus another 7 = **56**

| 7 | 14 | 21 | 28 | 35 | 42 | 49 | 56 | 63 | 70 |

8 x 7 = 56   so   9 x 7 = 56 plus another 7 = **63**

| 7 | 14 | 21 | 28 | 35 | 42 | 49 | 56 | 63 | 70 |

Test yourself on the rest of the 7 times table.
Cover the section above with a sheet of paper.

What is seven sevens?   **49**   What is eight sevens?   **56**

What is nine sevens?   **63**   What is ten sevens?   **70**

8 x 7 = **56**   7 x 7 = **49**   9 x 7 = **63**   10 x 7 = **70**

How many days are there in eight weeks?   **56**

A package contains seven pens.
How many pens will there be in nine packets?   **6 3**

How many sevens make 56?   **8**

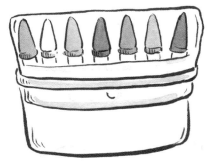

Practice the 7s

You should know all of the 7 times table now, but how quickly can you remember it?
Ask someone to time you as you do this page.
Remember, you must be fast but also correct.

1 x 7 = 7	2 x 7 = 14	7 x 6 = 42
2 x 7 = 14	4 x 7 = 28	3 x 7 = 21
3 x 7 = 21	6 x 7 = 42	9 x 7 = 63
4 x 7 = 28	8 x 7 = 56	7 x 4 = 28
5 x 7 = 35	10 x 7 = 70	1 x 7 = 7
6 x 7 = 42	1 x 7 = 7	7 x 2 = 14
7 x 7 = 49	3 x 7 = 21	7 x 8 = 56
8 x 7 = 56	5 x 7 = 35	0 x 7 = 0
9 x 7 = 63	7 x 7 = 49	7 x 3 = 21
10 x 7 = 70	9 x 7 = 63	5 x 7 = 35
7 x 1 = 7	7 x 3 = 21	7 x 7 = 49
7 x 2 = 14	7 x 5 = 35	2 x 7 = 14
7 x 3 = 21	7 x 7 = 49	7 x 9 = 63
7 x 4 = 28	7 x 9 = 63	4 x 7 = 28
7 x 5 = 35	7 x 2 = 14	8 x 7 = 56
7 x 6 = 42	7 x 4 = 28	10 x 7 = 70
7 x 7 = 49	7 x 6 = 42	7 x 5 = 35
7 x 8 = 56	7 x 8 = 56	7 x 0 = 0
7 x 9 = 63	7 x 10 = 70	7 x 1 = 7
7 x 10 = 70	7 x 0 = 0	6 x 7 = 42

Speed trials

1 2 3 4 1
4, 8, 12, 16,
5
20, 24, 28,
6 7
32

You should know all of the 1, 2, 3, 4, 5, 6, 7, and 10 times tables by now, but how quickly can you remember them?
Ask someone to time you as you do this page.
Remember, you must be fast but also correct.

4 x 7 = 28	7 x 3 = 21	9 x 7 = 63
5 x 10 = 50	8 x 7 = 56	7 x 6 = 42
7 x 5 = 35	6 x 6 = 36	8 x 3 = 24
6 x 5 = 30	5 x 10 = 50	6 x 6 = 36
6 x 10 = 60	6 x 3 = 18	7 x 4 = 28
8 x 7 = 56	7 x 5 = 35	4 x 6 = 24
5 x 8 = 40	4 x 6 = 24	3 x 7 = 21
9 x 6 = 54	6 x 5 = 30	2 x 8 = 16
5 x 7 = 35	7 x 10 = 70	7 x 3 = 21
7 x 6 = 42	6 x 7 = 42	0 x 6 = 0
0 x 5 = 0	5 x 7 = 35	10 x 7 = 70
6 x 3 = 18	8 x 4 = 32	6 x 2 = 12
6 x 7 = 42	0 x 7 = 0	8 x 7 = 56
3 x 5 = 15	5 x 8 = 40	7 x 7 = 49
4 x 7 = 28	7 x 6 = 42	6 x 5 = 30
7 x 10 = 70	8 x 3 = 24	5 x 10 = 50
7 x 8 = 56	9 x 6 = 54	7 x 0 = 0
2 x 7 = 14	7 x 7 = 49	3 x 10 = 30
4 x 9 = 36	9 x 10 = 90	2 x 7 = 14
9 x 10 = 90	5 x 6 = 30	7 x 8 = 56

Some of the 8s

You should already know some of the 8 times table because it is part of the 1, 2, 3, 4, 5, 6, 7, and 10 times tables.

$1 \times 8 = 8$ $2 \times 8 = 16$ $3 \times 8 = 24$ $4 \times 8 = 32$

$5 \times 8 = 40$ $6 \times 8 = 48$ $7 \times 8 = 56$ $10 \times 8 = 80$

Find out if you can remember them quickly and correctly.

Cover the 8 times table with paper so you can't see the numbers.
Write the answers as quickly as you can.

What is three eights? **24**   What is ten eights? **80**

What is two eights? **16**   What is four eights? **32**

What is six eights? **48**   What is five eights? **40**

Write the answers as quickly as you can.

How many eights equal 16? **2**   How many eights equal 40? **10**

How many eights equal 32? **4**   How many eights equal 24? **3**

How many eights equal 56? **7**   How many eights equal 48? **5**

Write the answers as quickly as you can.

Multiply eight by three. **24**   Multiply eight by ten. **80**

Multiply eight by two. **16**   Multiply eight by five. **40**

Multiply eight by six. **48**   Multiply eight by four. **32**

Write the answers as quickly as you can.

$6 \times 8 =$ **48** $2 \times 8 =$ **16** $10 \times 8 =$ **80**

$5 \times 8 =$ **40** $7 \times 8 =$ **56** $3 \times 8 =$ **24**

Write the answers as quickly as you can.

A pizza has eight slices. John buys six pizzas.

How many slices does he have? **48**

Which number multiplied by 8 gives the answer 56? **7 x 8 =**

The rest of the 8s

You need to learn only these parts of the eight times table.
8 x 8 = 64   9 x 8 = 72

This work will help you remember the 8 times table.

Complete these sequences.

| 8 | 16 | 24 | 32 | 40 | 48 | 56 | 64 | 72 | 80 |

7 x 8 = 56   so   8 x 8 = 56 plus another 8 = 64

| 24 | 32 | 40 | 48 | 56 | 64 | 72 | 80 |

8 x 8 = 64   so   9 x 8 = 64 plus another 8 = 80

| 8 | 16 | 24 | 32 | 40 | 48 | 56 | 64 | 72 | 80 |

| 8 | 16 | 24 | 32 | 40 | 48 | 56 | 64 | 72 | 80 |

Test yourself on the rest of the 8 times table.
Cover the section above with a sheet of paper.

What is seven eights? 56   What is eight eights? 64

What is nine eights? 72   What is eight nines? 72

8 x 8 = 64   9 x 8 = 72   8 x 9 = 72   10 x 8 = 80

What number multiplied by 8 gives the answer 72? 9

A number multiplied by 8 gives the answer 80. What is the number? 10

David puts out building bricks in piles of 8.
How many bricks will there be in 10 piles? 80

What number multiplied by 5 gives the answer 40? 8

How many 8s make 72? 9

Practice the 8s

1 x 8 = 8		2 x 8 = 16		8 x 6 = 48
2 x 8 = 16		4 x 8 = 32		3 x 8 = 24
3 x 8 = 24		6 x 8 = 48		9 x 8 = 72
4 x 8 = 32		8 x 8 = 64		8 x 4 = 32
5 x 8 = 40		10 x 8 = 80		1 x 8 = 8
6 x 8 = 48		1 x 8 = 8		8 x 2 = 16
7 x 8 = 56		3 x 8 = 24		7 x 8 = 56
8 x 8 = 64		5 x 8 = 40		0 x 8 = 0
9 x 8 = 72		7 x 8 = 56		8 x 3 = 24
10 x 8 = 80		9 x 8 = 72		5 x 8 = 40
8 x 1 = 8		8 x 3 = 24		8 x 8 = 64
8 x 2 = 16		8 x 5 = 40		2 x 8 = 16
8 x 3 = 24		8 x 8 = 64		8 x 9 = 72
8 x 4 = 32		8 x 9 = 72		4 x 8 = 32
8 x 5 = 40		8 x 2 = 16		8 x 6 = 48
8 x 6 = 48		8 x 4 = 32		10 x 8 = 80
8 x 7 = 56		8 x 6 = 48		8 x 5 = 40
8 x 8 = 64		8 x 8 = 64		8 x 0 = 0
8 x 9 = 72		8 x 10 = 80		8 x 1 = 8
8 x 10 = 80		8 x 0 = 0		6 x 8 = 48

Speed trials

You should know all of the 1, 2, 3, 4, 5, 6, 7, 8, and 10 times tables now,
but how quickly can you remember them?
Ask someone to time you as you do this page.
Be fast but also correct.

4 x 8 = 32

5 x 10 = 50

7 x 8 = 56

8 x 5 = 40

6 x 10 = 80

8 x 7 = 56

5 x 8 = 40

9 x 8 = 72

8 x 8 = 64

7 x 6 = 42

7 x 5 = 35

6 x 8 = 48

6 x 7 = 42

5 x 7 = 35

8 x 4 = 32

7 x 10 = 70

2 x 8 = 16

4 x 7 = 28

6 x 9 = 54

9 x 10 = 90

7 x 8 = 56

8 x 7 = 56

6 x 8 = 48

8 x 10 = 80

6 x 3 = 18

7 x 7 = 49

5 x 6 = 30

6 x 7 = 42

7 x 10 = 70

6 x 9 = 54

5 x 8 = 40

8 x 4 = 32

0 x 8 = 0

5 x 9 = 45

7 x 6 = 42

8 x 3 = 24

9 x 6 = 54

8 x 6 = 48

9 x 10 = 90

6 x 6 = 36

9 x 8 = 72

7 x 6 = 42

8 x 3 = 24

8 x 8 = 64

7 x 4 = 28

4 x 8 = 32

3 x 7 = 21

2 x 8 = 16

7 x 3 = 21

0 x 8 = 0

10 x 8 = 80

6 x 2 = 12

8 x 6 = 48

7 x 8 = 56

6 x 5 = 30

8 x 10 = 80

8 x 7 = 56

5 x 10 = 50

8 x 2 = 16

8 x 9 = 72

Some of the 9s

You should already know nearly all of the 9 times table because it is part of the 1, 2, 3, 4, 5, 6, 7, 8, and 10 times tables.

1 x 9 = 9	2 x 9 = 18	3 x 9 = 27	4 x 9 = 36	5 x 9 = 45
6 x 9 = 54	7 x 9 = 63	8 x 9 = 72	10 x 9 = 90	

Find out if you can remember them quickly and correctly.

Cover the nine times table so you can't see the numbers.
Write the answers as quickly as you can.

What is three nines? 27

What is ten nines? 90

What is two nines? 18

What is four nines? 36

What is six nines? 54

What is five nines? 45

What is seven nines? 63

What is eight nines? 72

Write the answers as quickly as you can.

How many nines equal 18? 2

How many nines equal 54? 6

How many nines equal 90? 10

How many nines equal 27? 3

How many nines equal 72? 8

How many nines equal 36? 4

How many nines equal 45? 5

How many nines equal 63? 7

Write the answers as quickly as you can.

Multiply nine by seven. 63

Multiply nine by ten. 90

Multiply nine by two. 18

Multiply nine by five. 45

Multiply nine by six. 54

Multiply nine by four. 36

Multiply nine by three. 27

Multiply nine by eight. 72

Write the answers as quickly as you can.

6 x 9 = 54   2 x 9 = 18   10 x 9 = 90

5 x 9 = 45   3 x 9 = 27   8 x 9 = 72

0 x 9 = 0   7 x 9 = 63   4 x 9 = 36

The rest of the 9s

You need to learn only this part of the nine times table.

9 x 9 = 81

This work will help you remember the 9 times table.

Complete these sequences.

9   18   27   36   45   54   *63*   *72*   *81*   *90*

8 x 9 = 72   so   9 x 9 = 72 plus another 9 = *81*

27   36   45   *54*   *63*   *72*   *81*   *90*

9   18   27   *36*   *45*   *54*   *63*   72   *81*   90

9   *18*   27   *36*   45   *54*   *63*   *72*   *81*   *90*

Look for a pattern in the nine times table.

1	x	9	=	09
2	x	9	=	18
3	x	9	=	27
4	x	9	=	36
5	x	9	=	45
6	x	9	=	54
7	x	9	=	63
8	x	9	=	72
9	x	9	=	81
10	x	9	=	90

Write down any patterns you can see. (There is more than one.)

_____

_____

_____

_____

_____

_____

_____

Practice the 9s

You should know all of the 9 times table now, but how quickly can you remember it?
Ask someone to time you as you do this page.
Be fast and correct.

1 x 9 = 09	2 x 9 = 18	9 x 6 = 54
2 x 9 = 18	4 x 9 = 36	3 x 9 = 27
3 x 9 = 27	6 x 9 = 54	9 x 9 = 81
4 x 9 = 36	9 x 7 = 63	9 x 4 = 36
5 x 9 = 45	10 x 9 = 90	1 x 9 = 9
6 x 9 = 54	1 x 9 = 9	9 x 2 = 18
7 x 9 = 63	3 x 9 = 27	7 x 9 = 63
8 x 9 = 72	5 x 9 = 45	0 x 9 = 0
9 x 9 = 81	7 x 9 = 63	9 x 3 = 27
10 x 9 = 90	9 x 9 = 81	5 x 9 = 45
9 x 1 = 09	9 x 3 = 27	9 x 9 = 81
9 x 2 = 18	9 x 5 = 45	2 x 9 = 18
9 x 3 = 27	0 x 9 = 0	8 x 9 = 72
9 x 4 = 36	9 x 1 = 9	4 x 9 = 36
9 x 5 = 45	9 x 2 = 18	9 x 7 = 63
9 x 6 = 54	9 x 4 = 36	10 x 9 = 90
9 x 7 = 63	9 x 6 = 54	9 x 5 = 45
9 x 8 = 72	9 x 8 = 72	9 x 0 = 0
9 x 9 = 81	9 x 10 = 90	9 x 1 = 9
9 x 10 = 90	9 x 0 = 0	6 x 9 = 54

Speed trials

You should know all of the times tables by now, but how quickly can you remember them?
Ask someone to time you as you do this page.
Be fast and correct.

6 x 8 = 48			4 x 8 = 32			8 x 10 = 80		
9 x 10 = 90			9 x 8 = 72			7 x 9 = 63		
5 x 8 = 40			6 x 6 = 36			8 x 5 = 40		
7 x 5 = 35			8 x 9 = 72			8 x 7 = 56		
6 x 4 = 24			6 x 4 = 24			7 x 4 = 28		
8 x 8 = 64			7 x 3 = 21			4 x 9 = 36		
5 x 10 = 50			5 x 9 = 40			6 x 7 = 42		
9 x 8 = 72			6 x 8 = 48			4 x 6 = 24		
8 x 3 = 24			7 x 7 = 49			7 x 8 = 56		
7 x 7 = 49			6 x 9 = 54			6 x 9 = 54		
9 x 5 = 45			7 x 8 = 56			10 x 8 = 80		
4 x 8 = 32			8 x 4 = 32			6 x 5 = 30		
6 x 7 = 42			0 x 9 = 0			8 x 8 = 64		
2 x 9 = 18			10 x 10 = 100			7 x 6 = 42		
8 x 4 = 32			7 x 6 = 42			6 x 8 = 48		
7 x 10 = 70			8 x 7 = 56			9 x 10 = 90		
2 x 8 = 16			9 x 6 = 54			8 x 4 = 32		
4 x 7 = 28			8 x 6 = 48			7 x 10 = 70		
6 x 9 = 54			9 x 9 = 81			5 x 8 = 40		
9 x 9 = 81			6 x 7 = 42			8 x 9 = 72		

53

Times tables for division

Knowing the times tables can also help with division problems. Look at these examples.

3 x 6 = 18 which means that 18 ÷ 3 = 6 and that 18 ÷ 6 = 3
4 x 5 = 20 which means that 20 ÷ 4 = 5 and that 20 ÷ 5 = 4
9 x 3 = 27 which means that 27 ÷ 3 = 9 and that 27 ÷ 9 = 3

Use your knowledge of the times tables to work these division problems.

3 x 8 = 24 which means that 24 ÷ 3 = 8 and that 24 ÷ 8 = 3

4 x 7 = 28 which means that 28 ÷ 4 = 7 and that 28 ÷ 7 = 4

3 x 5 = 15 which means that 15 ÷ 3 = 5 and that 15 ÷ 5 = 3

4 x 3 = 12 which means that 12 ÷ 3 = 4 and that 12 ÷ 4 = 3

3 x 10 = 30 which means that 30 ÷ 3 = 10 and that 30 ÷ 10 = 3

4 x 8 = 32 which means that 32 ÷ 4 = 8 and that 32 ÷ 8 = 4

3 x 9 = 27 which means that 27 ÷ 3 = 9 and that 27 ÷ 9 = 3

4 x 10 = 40 which means that 40 ÷ 4 = 10 and that 40 ÷ 10 = 4

These division problems help practice the 3 and 4 times tables.

20 ÷ 4 = 5	15 ÷ 3 = 5	16 ÷ 4 = 4
24 ÷ 4 = 6	27 ÷ 3 = 9	30 ÷ 3 = 10
12 ÷ 3 = 4	18 ÷ 3 = 6	28 ÷ 4 = 7
24 ÷ 3 = 8	32 ÷ 4 = 8	21 ÷ 3 =

How many fours in 36? 9	Divide 27 by three. 9
Divide 28 by 4. 7	How many threes in 21? 7
How many fives in 35? 7	Divide 40 by 5. 8
Divide 15 by 3. 5	How many eights in 48? 6

Times tables for division

This page will help you remember times tables by dividing by 2, 3, 4, 5, and 10.

$20 \div 5 =$ 4 $18 \div 3 =$ 6 $60 \div 10 =$ 6

Complete the problems.

$40 \div 10 = 4$ $14 \div 2 = 7$ $32 \div 4 = 8$

$25 \div 5 = 5$ $21 \div 3 = 7$ $16 \div 4 = 4$

$24 \div 4 = 6$ $28 \div 4 = 7$ $12 \div 2 = 6$

$45 \div 5 = 9$ $35 \div 5 = 7$ $12 \div 3 = 4$

$10 \div 2 = 5$ $40 \div 10 = 4$ $12 \div 4 = 3$

$20 \div 10 = 2$ $20 \div 2 = 10$ $20 \div 2 = 6$

$6 \div 2 = 3$ $18 \div 3 = 6$ $20 \div 4 = 5$

$24 \div 3 = 8$ $32 \div 4 = 8$ $20 \div 5 = 4$

$30 \div 5 = 6$ $40 \div 5 = 9$ $20 \div 10 = 2$

$30 \div 10 = 3$ $80 \div 10 = 8$ $18 \div 2 = 9$

$40 \div 5 = 8$ $6 \div 2 = 3$ $18 \div 3 = 6$

$21 \div 3 = 7$ $15 \div 3 = 5$ $15 \div 3 = 5$

$14 \div 2 = 7$ $24 \div 4 = 6$ $15 \div 5 = 3$

$27 \div 3 = 9$ $15 \div 5 = 3$ $24 \div 3 = 8$

$90 \div 10 = 9$ $10 \div 10 = 1$ $24 \div 4 = 6$

$15 \div 5 = 3$ $4 \div 2 = 2$ $50 \div 5 = 10$

$15 \div 3 = 5$ $9 \div 3 = 3$ $50 \div 10 = 5$

$20 \div 5 = 4$ $4 \div 4 = 1$ $30 \div 3 = 10$

$20 \div 4 = 5$ $10 \div 5 = 2$ $30 \div 5 = 6$

$16 \div 2 = 8$ $100 \div 10 = 10$ $30 \div 10 = 3$

Times tables for division

This page will help you remember times tables by dividing by 2, 3, 4, 5, 6, and 10.

$30 \div 6 =$ 5 $12 \div 6 =$ 2 $60 \div 10 =$ 6

Complete the problems.

$18 \div 6 =$ 3 $27 \div 3 =$ 9 $48 \div 6 =$

$30 \div 10 =$ 3 $18 \div 6 =$ 3 $35 \div 5 =$

$14 \div 2 =$ 7 $20 \div 2 =$ 10 $36 \div 4 =$

$18 \div 3 =$ 6 $24 \div 6 =$ $24 \div 3 =$

$20 \div 4 =$ 5 $24 \div 3 =$ $20 \div 2 =$

$15 \div 5 =$ 3 $24 \div 4 =$ $30 \div 6 =$

$36 \div 6 =$ 6 $30 \div 10 =$ $25 \div 5 =$

$50 \div 10 =$ 5 $18 \div 2 =$ $32 \div 4 =$

$8 \div 2 =$ 4 $18 \div 3 =$ $27 \div 3 =$

$15 \div 3 =$ 5 $36 \div 4 =$ $16 \div 2 =$

$16 \div 4 =$ 4 $36 \div 6 =$ $42 \div 6 =$

$25 \div 5 =$ 5 $40 \div 5 =$ $5 \div 5 =$

$6 \div 6 =$ 3 $100 \div 10 =$ $4 \div 4 =$

$10 \div 10 =$ 10 = 1 $16 \div 4 =$ $28 \div 4 =$

$42 \div 6 =$ 7 $42 \div 6 =$ $14 \div 2 =$

$24 \div 4 =$ 6 $48 \div 6 =$ $24 \div 6 =$

$54 \div 6 =$ 9 $54 \div 6 =$ $18 \div 6 =$

$90 \div 10 =$ 9 $60 \div 6 =$ $54 \div 6 =$

$30 \div 6 =$ 5 $60 \div 10 =$ $60 \div 6 =$

$30 \div 5 =$ 6 $30 \div 6 =$ $40 \div 5 =$

Times tables for division

Complete the problems.

$21 \div 7 =$	$18 \div 6 =$	$49 \div 7 =$
$35 \div 5 =$	$28 \div 7 =$	$35 \div 5 =$
$14 \div 2 =$	$24 \div 6 =$	$35 \div 7 =$
$18 \div 6 =$	$24 \div 4 =$	$24 \div 6 =$
$20 \div 5 =$	$24 \div 2 =$	$21 \div 3 =$
$15 \div 3 =$	$21 \div 7 =$	$70 \div 7 =$
$36 \div 4 =$	$42 \div 7 =$	$42 \div 7 =$
$56 \div 7 =$	$18 \div 3 =$	$32 \div 4 =$
$18 \div 2 =$	$49 \div 7 =$	$27 \div 3 =$
$15 \div 5 =$	$36 \div 4 =$	$16 \div 4 =$
$49 \div 7 =$	$36 \div 6 =$	$42 \div 6 =$
$25 \div 5 =$	$40 \div 5 =$	$45 \div 5 =$
$7 \div 7 =$	$70 \div 7 =$	$40 \div 4 =$
$63 \div 7 =$	$24 \div 3 =$	$24 \div 3 =$
$42 \div 7 =$	$42 \div 6 =$	$14 \div 7 =$
$24 \div 6 =$	$48 \div 6 =$	$24 \div 4 =$
$54 \div 6 =$	$54 \div 6 =$	$18 \div 3 =$
$28 \div 7 =$	$60 \div 6 =$	$56 \div 7 =$
$30 \div 6 =$	$63 \div 7 =$	$63 \div 7 =$
$35 \div 7 =$	$25 \div 5 =$	$48 \div 6 =$

Times tables for division

This page will help you remember times tables by dividing by 2, 3, 4, 5, 6, 7, 8, and 9.

$16 \div 8 =$ 2 $35 \div 7 =$ 5 $27 \div 9 =$ 3

Complete the problems.

$42 \div 6 =$	$81 \div 9 =$	$56 \div 7 =$
$32 \div 8 =$	$56 \div 7 =$	$45 \div 5 =$
$14 \div 7 =$	$72 \div 9 =$	$35 \div 7 =$
$18 \div 9 =$	$24 \div 8 =$	$18 \div 9 =$
$63 \div 7 =$	$27 \div 9 =$	$21 \div 3 =$
$72 \div 9 =$	$72 \div 9 =$	$28 \div 7 =$
$72 \div 8 =$	$42 \div 6 =$	$64 \div 8 =$
$56 \div 7 =$	$27 \div 3 =$	$32 \div 8 =$
$18 \div 6 =$	$14 \div 7 =$	$27 \div 9 =$
$81 \div 9 =$	$36 \div 4 =$	$16 \div 8 =$
$63 \div 9 =$	$36 \div 6 =$	$42 \div 6 =$
$45 \div 5 =$	$48 \div 8 =$	$45 \div 9 =$
$54 \div 9 =$	$21 \div 7 =$	$40 \div 4 =$
$70 \div 7 =$	$24 \div 3 =$	$24 \div 8 =$
$42 \div 7 =$	$40 \div 8 =$	$63 \div 7 =$
$30 \div 5 =$	$45 \div 9 =$	$24 \div 6 =$
$54 \div 6 =$	$54 \div 6 =$	$18 \div 6 =$
$56 \div 8 =$	$42 \div 7 =$	$56 \div 8 =$
$30 \div 5 =$	$63 \div 9 =$	$63 \div 9 =$
$35 \div 7 =$	$50 \div 5 =$	$48 \div 8 =$

Times tables practice grids

This is a times tables grid.

X	3	4	5
7	21	28	35
8	24	32	40

Complete each times tables grid.

X	1	3	5	7	9
2					
3					

X	4	6
6		
7		
8		

X	6	7	8	9	10
3					
4					
5					

X	10	7	8	4
3				
5				
7				

X	6	2	4	7
5				
10				

X	8	7	9	6
9				
7				

Times tables practice grids

Here are more times tables grids.

X	2	4	6
5			
7			

X	8	3	9	2
5				
6				
7				

X	2	3	4	5
8				
9				

X	10	9	8	7
6				
5				
4				

X	3	8
2		
3		
4		
5		
6		
7		

X	2	4	6	8
1				
3				
5				
7				
9				
0				

Times tables practice grids

Here are some other times tables grids.

X	8	9
7		
8		

X	9	8	7	6	5	4
9						
8						
7						

X	2	5	9
4			
7			
8			

X	2	3	4	5	7
4					
6					
8					

X	3	5	7
2			
8			
6			
0			
4			
7			

X	8	7	9	6
7				
9				
0				
10				
8				
6				

Speed trials

Try this final test.

27 ÷ 3 =	4 x 9 =	14 ÷ 2 =
7 x 9 =	18 ÷ 2 =	9 x 9 =
64 ÷ 8 =	6 x 8 =	15 ÷ 3 =
90 ÷ 10 =	21 ÷ 3 =	8 x 8 =
6 x 8 =	9 x 7 =	24 ÷ 4 =
45 ÷ 9 =	36 ÷ 4 =	7 x 8 =
3 x 7 =	4 x 6 =	30 ÷ 5 =
9 x 5 =	45 ÷ 5 =	6 x 6 =
48 ÷ 6 =	8 x 5 =	42 ÷ 6 =
7 x 7 =	42 ÷ 6 =	9 x 5 =
3 x 9 =	7 x 4 =	49 ÷ 7 =
56 ÷ 8 =	35 ÷ 7 =	8 x 6 =
36 ÷ 4 =	9 x 3 =	72 ÷ 8 =
24 ÷ 3 =	24 ÷ 8 =	9 x 7 =
36 ÷ 9 =	8 x 2 =	54 ÷ 9 =
6 x 7 =	36 ÷ 9 =	7 x 6 =
4 x 4 =	6 x 10 =	10 ÷ 10 =
32 ÷ 8 =	80 ÷ 10 =	7 x 7 =
49 ÷ 7 =	6 x 9 =	16 ÷ 8 =
25 ÷ 5 =	16 ÷ 2 =	7 x 9 =
56 ÷ 7 =	54 ÷ 9 =	63 ÷ 7 =

Addition, multiplication, and division ☆

Write the missing number in the box.

$7 + ? = 7$ $3 \times ? = 3$

$7 + \boxed{0} = 7$ $3 \times \boxed{1} = 3$

Write the missing number in the box.

$4 + \boxed{} = 4$ $12 \times \boxed{} = 12$ $\boxed{} \times 9 = 9$ $6 + \boxed{} = 6$

$3 + \boxed{} = 15$ $17 + \boxed{} = 25$ $\boxed{} + 8 = 19$ $\boxed{} + 17 = 26$

$4 + \boxed{} = 9$ $12 + \boxed{} = 17$ $35 \div \boxed{} = 5$ $25 + \boxed{} = 40$

$\boxed{} + 60 = 75$ $14 + \boxed{} = 20$ $\boxed{} + 32 = 53$ $\boxed{} + 9 = 58$

$5 \times \boxed{} = 30$ $12 \div \boxed{} = 3$ $50 \div \boxed{} = 5$ $8 \times \boxed{} = 48$

$\boxed{} \times 6 = 54$ $100 \div \boxed{} = 5$ $63 \times \boxed{} = 630$ $\boxed{} \div 9 = 4$

Rewrite each equation, and fill in the missing number.

$3 \times (6 \times 4) = (3 \times ?) \times 4$

$(7 \times 9) \times 3 = 7 \times (? \times 3)$

$(2 \times 5) \times 9 = ? \times (5 \times 9)$

$8 \times (8 \times 7) = (8 \times 8) \times ?$

$5 \times (10 + 3) = (5 \times 10) + (? \times 3)$

$(8 + 6) \times 7 = (8 \times 7) + (6 \times ?)$

$(3 + 7) \times 2 = (? \times 2) + (7 \times 2)$

$9 \times (5 + 12) = (? \times 5) + (? \times 12)$

Place value to 10,000,000

| How many hundreds are there in 7,000? | 70 | hundreds (70 x 100 = 7,000) |
| What is the value of the 9 in 694? | 90 | (because the 9 is in the tens column) |

Write how many tens there are in:

400	tens	600	tens	900	tens
200	tens	1,300	tens	4,700	tens
4,800	tens	1,240	tens	1,320	tens
2,630	tens	5,920	tens	4,350	tens

What is the value of the 7 in these numbers?

| 76 | | 720 | | 137 | |
| 7,122 | | 74,301 | | 724 | |

What is the value of the 3 in these numbers?

| 324,126 | | 3,927,141 | | 214,623 | |
| 8,254,320 | | 3,711,999 | | 124,372 | |

Write how many hundreds there are in:

6,400	hundreds	8,500	hundreds
19,900	hundreds	36,200	hundreds
524,600	hundreds	712,400	hundreds

What is the value of the 8 in these numbers?

| 8,214,631 | | 2,398,147 | | 463,846 | |
| 287,034 | | 8,110,927 | | 105,428 | |

Multiplying and dividing by 10

Write the answer in the box.

37 x 10 = <u>370</u>   58 ÷ 10 = <u>5.8</u>

Write the product in the box.

94 x 10 =   13 x 10 =   37 x 10 =

36 x 10 =   47 x 10 =   54 x 10 =

236 x 10 =   419 x 10 =   262 x 10 =

531 x 10 =   674 x 10 =   801 x 10 =

Write the quotient in the box.

92 ÷ 10 =   48 ÷ 10 =   37 ÷ 10 =

18 ÷ 10 =   29 ÷ 10 =   54 ÷ 10 =

345 ÷ 10 =   354 ÷ 10 =   723 ÷ 10 =

531 ÷ 10 =   262 ÷ 10 =   419 ÷ 10 =

Find the missing factor.

＿＿ x 10 = 230   ＿＿ x 10 = 750   ＿＿ x 10 = 990

＿＿ x 10 = 480   ＿＿ x 10 = 130   ＿＿ x 10 = 250

＿＿ x 10 = 520   ＿＿ x 10 = 390   ＿＿ x 10 = 270

＿＿ x 10 = 620   ＿＿ x 10 = 860   ＿＿ x 10 = 170

Find the dividend.

＿＿ ÷ 10 = 4.7   ＿＿ ÷ 10 = 6.8   ＿＿ ÷ 10 = 12.4

＿＿ ÷ 10 = 25.7   ＿＿ ÷ 10 = 36.2   ＿＿ ÷ 10 = 31.4

＿＿ ÷ 10 = 40.8   ＿＿ ÷ 10 = 67.2   ＿＿ ÷ 10 = 80.9

＿＿ ÷ 10 = 92.4   ＿＿ ÷ 10 = 32.7   ＿＿ ÷ 10 = 56.3

Ordering sets of measures

Write these measures in order, from least to greatest.

3,100 km	24 km	1,821 km	247 km	4 km	960 km
4 km	24 km	247 km	960 km	1,821 km	3,100 km

Write these measures in order, from least to greatest.

$526	$15,940	$1,504	$826	$37,532

720 mi	7,200 mi	27,410 mi	15 mi	247 mi

70,000 gal	650 gal	26,000 gal	6,500 gal	7,000 gal

656 lb	9,565 lb	22,942 lb	752,247 lb	1,327 lb

9,520 yrs	320 yrs	4,681 yrs	8,940 yrs	20,316 yrs

217,846 kg	75,126 kg	8,940 kg	14,632 kg	175 kg

9,420 km	764 km	25,811 km	114,243 km	7,240 km

$37,227	$1,365,240	$143,820	$950	$4,212

24,091 ft	59,473 ft	1,237 ft	426 ft	837,201 ft

47,632 oz	847 oz	9,625 oz	103,427 oz	2,330 oz

7,340 m	249 m	12,746 m	32 m	17,407,321 m

Appropriate units of measure

Choose the best units to measure the length of each item.

inches	feet	yards

notebook	car	swimming pool
inches	feet	yards

Choose the best units to measure the length of each item.

inches	feet	yards

bed   bicycle   toothbrush   football field

shoe   driveway   canoe   fence

The height of a door is about 7 _____ .

The length of a pencil is about 7 _____ .

The height of a flagpole is about 7 _____ .

Choose the best units to measure the weight of each item.

ounces	pounds	tons

train   kitten   watermelon   tennis ball

shoe   bag of potatoes   elephant   washing machine

The weight of a hamburger is about 6 _____ .

The weight of a bag of apples is about 5 _____ .

The weight of a truck is about 4 _____ .

Identifying patterns

Continue each pattern.

| Intervals of 6: | 1 | 7 | 13 | 19 | 25 | 31 | 37 |
| Intervals of 3: | 27 | 24 | 21 | 18 | 15 | 12 | 9 |

Continue each pattern.

0	10	20				
15	20	25				
5	7	9				
2	9	16				
4	7	10			19	
2	10	18		34		

Continue each pattern.

44	38	32				
33	29	25				
27	23	19				
56	48	40			16	
49	42	35				
28	25	22				10

Continue each pattern.

36	30	24		12		
5	14	23				
3	8	13				
47	40	33			12	
1	4	7				

Recognizing multiples

Circle the multiples of 10.

14   (20)   25   (30)   47   (60)

Circle the multiples of 6.

| 20 | 48 | 56 | 72 | 25 | 35 |
| 1 | 3 | 6 | 16 | 26 | 36 |

Circle the multiples of 7.

| 14 | 24 | 35 | 27 | 47 | 49 |
| 63 | 42 | 52 | 37 | 64 | 71 |

Circle the multiples of 8.

| 25 | 31 | 48 | 84 | 32 | 8 |
| 18 | 54 | 64 | 35 | 72 | 28 |

Circle the multiples of 9.

17	81	27	35	92	106
45	53	108	90	33	95
64	9	28	18	36	98

Circle the multiples of 10.

| 15 | 35 | 20 | 46 | 90 | 100 |
| 44 | 37 | 30 | 29 | 50 | 45 |

Circle the multiples of 11.

24	110	123	54	66	90
45	33	87	98	99	121
43	44	65	55	21	22

Circle the multiples of 12.

136	134	144	109	108	132
24	34	58	68	48	60
35	29	72	74	84	94

Factors of numbers from 31 to 65

The factors of 40 are   1   2   4   5   8   10   20   40

Circle the factors of 56.

(1)   (2)   3   (4)   5   6   (7)   (8)   (14)   (28)   32   (56)

Find all the factors of each number.

The factors of 31 are

The factors of 47 are

The factors of 60 are

The factors of 50 are

The factors of 42 are

The factors of 32 are

The factors of 48 are

The factors of 35 are

The factors of 52 are

Circle all the factors of each number.

Which numbers are factors of 39?

1   2   3   4   5   8   9   10   13   14   15   20   25   39

Which numbers are factors of 45?

1   3   4   5   8   9   12   15   16   21   24   36   40   44   45

Which numbers are factors of 61?

1   3   4   5   6   10   15   16   18   20   26   31   40   61

Which numbers are factors of 65?

1   2   4   5   6   8   9   10   12   13   14   15   30   60   65

Some numbers have only factors of 1 and themselves. They are called prime numbers.
Write all the prime numbers between 31 and 65 in the box.

70

Writing equivalent fractions

Make these fractions equal by writing the missing number.

$$\frac{20}{100} = \frac{2}{10} = \frac{1}{5}$$

$$\frac{5}{15} = \frac{1}{3}$$

Make these fractions equal by writing a number in the box.

$$\frac{10}{100} = \frac{\square}{10} \qquad \frac{8}{100} = \frac{\square}{25} \qquad \frac{4}{100} = \frac{\square}{25}$$

$$\frac{2}{20} = \frac{\square}{10} \qquad \frac{5}{100} = \frac{\square}{20} \qquad \frac{6}{20} = \frac{\square}{10}$$

$$\frac{3}{5} = \frac{\square}{20} \qquad \frac{5}{6} = \frac{\square}{12} \qquad \frac{2}{8} = \frac{\square}{24}$$

$$\frac{2}{3} = \frac{\square}{24} \qquad \frac{2}{18} = \frac{\square}{9} \qquad \frac{4}{50} = \frac{\square}{25}$$

$$\frac{11}{12} = \frac{\square}{36} \qquad \frac{12}{15} = \frac{\square}{5} \qquad \frac{8}{20} = \frac{\square}{5}$$

$$\frac{2}{12} = \frac{1}{\square} \qquad \frac{5}{20} = \frac{1}{\square} \qquad \frac{5}{8} = \frac{10}{\square}$$

$$\frac{7}{8} = \frac{21}{\square} \qquad \frac{15}{100} = \frac{3}{\square} \qquad \frac{6}{24} = \frac{1}{\square}$$

$$\frac{5}{25} = \frac{1}{\square} \qquad \frac{8}{20} = \frac{2}{\square} \qquad \frac{15}{20} = \frac{3}{\square}$$

$$\frac{5}{30} = \frac{1}{\square} \qquad \frac{12}{14} = \frac{6}{\square} \qquad \frac{1}{5} = \frac{4}{\square}$$

$$\frac{9}{18} = \frac{1}{\square} \qquad \frac{24}{30} = \frac{4}{\square} \qquad \frac{25}{30} = \frac{5}{\square}$$

$$\frac{1}{8} = \frac{\square}{16} = \frac{3}{\square} = \frac{\square}{32} = \frac{\square}{40} = \frac{6}{\square}$$

$$\frac{20}{100} = \frac{\square}{25} = \frac{2}{\square} = \frac{1}{\square} = \frac{\square}{50} = \frac{\square}{200}$$

$$\frac{2}{5} = \frac{6}{\square} = \frac{\square}{20} = \frac{10}{\square} = \frac{\square}{50} = \frac{40}{\square}$$

$$\frac{1}{6} = \frac{\square}{12} = \frac{3}{\square} = \frac{4}{\square} = \frac{5}{\square} = \frac{6}{\square}$$

$$\frac{2}{3} = \frac{\square}{24} = \frac{\square}{36} = \frac{\square}{21} = \frac{\square}{\square} = \frac{\square}{300}$$

Fraction models

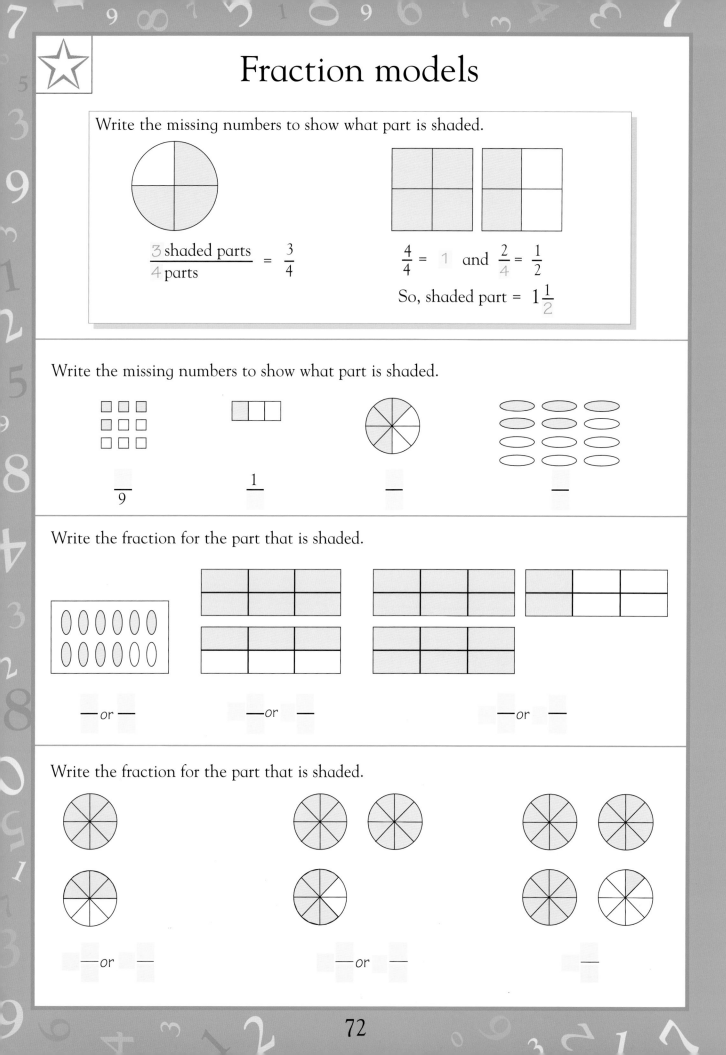

Write the missing numbers to show what part is shaded.

$\dfrac{3 \text{ shaded parts}}{4 \text{ parts}} = \dfrac{3}{4}$

$\dfrac{4}{4} = 1$ and $\dfrac{2}{4} = \dfrac{1}{2}$

So, shaded part = $1\dfrac{1}{2}$

Write the missing numbers to show what part is shaded.

$\dfrac{}{9}$ $\dfrac{1}{}$ $\dfrac{}{}$ $\dfrac{}{}$

Write the fraction for the part that is shaded.

$\dfrac{}{}$ or $\dfrac{}{}$ $\dfrac{}{}$ or $\dfrac{}{}$ $\dfrac{}{}$ or $\dfrac{}{}$

Write the fraction for the part that is shaded.

$\dfrac{}{}$ or $\dfrac{}{}$ $\dfrac{}{}$ or $\dfrac{}{}$ $\dfrac{}{}$

Converting fractions and decimals

Write these fractions as decimals.

$\dfrac{7}{10}$ = *0.7*

$\dfrac{3}{100}$ = *0.03*

Write these fractions as decimals.

0.2 = *$\dfrac{2}{10}$* = *$\dfrac{1}{5}$*

0.47 = *$\dfrac{47}{100}$*

Write these fractions as decimals.

$\dfrac{3}{10}$ =
$\dfrac{2}{10}$ =
$\dfrac{1}{2}$ = =

$\dfrac{7}{10}$ =
$\dfrac{1}{10}$ =
$\dfrac{8}{10}$ =

$\dfrac{9}{10}$ =
$\dfrac{6}{10}$ =
$\dfrac{4}{10}$ =

Write these decimals as fractions.

0.1 = $\dfrac{1}{}$

0.4 = $\dfrac{4}{}$ = $\dfrac{2}{}$

0.7 = $\dfrac{7}{}$

0.2 = $\dfrac{2}{}$ = $\dfrac{1}{}$

0.5 = $\dfrac{5}{}$ = $\dfrac{1}{}$

0.8 = $\dfrac{8}{}$ = $\dfrac{4}{}$

0.3 = $\dfrac{3}{}$

0.6 = $\dfrac{6}{}$ = $\dfrac{3}{}$

0.9 = $\dfrac{9}{}$

Change these fractions to decimals.

$\dfrac{1}{100}$ =
$\dfrac{15}{100}$ =
$\dfrac{24}{100}$ =

$\dfrac{3}{100}$ =
$\dfrac{25}{100}$ =
$\dfrac{56}{100}$ =

$\dfrac{7}{100}$ =
$\dfrac{49}{100}$ =
$\dfrac{72}{100}$ =

Change these decimals to fractions.

0.39 =
0.83 =
0.51 =

0.47 =
0.91 =
0.43 =

0.21 =
0.73 =
0.17 =

Using information in tables

Use the table to answer the questions.

Student's favorite sports

Sport	Number of votes
Basketball	4
Soccer	10
Softball	5
Swimming	6

How many students voted for softball?   5

What is the most popular sport?   *soccer*

Use the table to answer the questions.

Pieces made by pottery club

Name	Cups	Bowls	Plates
Carl	5	9	11
Marta	7	2	9
Assam	3	1	12
Colin	8	8	10
Renee	6	9	2

How many plates did Colin make?

Who made 7 cups?

Who made the same
number of bowls as Renee?

Complete the table, and answer the questions.

Olympic medals 1998

Country	Gold	Silver	Bronze	Total
Austria	3	5	9	17
Canada	6	5	4	
Germany	12	9	8	
Norway	10	10	5	
Russia	9	6	3	
United States	6	3	4	

How many more gold medals
did Russia win than bronze medals?

Which country won
the most silver medals?

Which country won
three times as many
bronze medals as gold medals?

Coordinate graphs

Write the coordinates for each point.
Remember to write the coordinate
for the x-axis first.

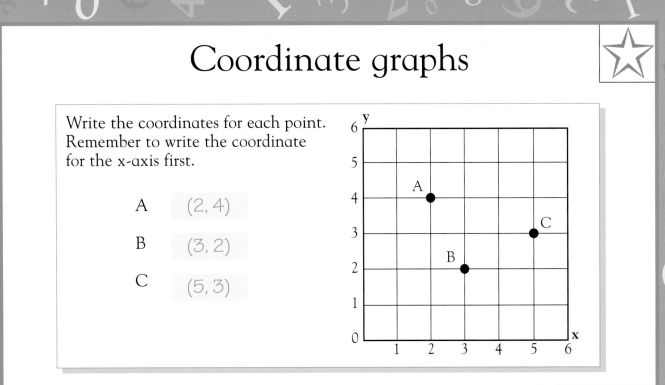

A   (2, 4)

B   (3, 2)

C   (5, 3)

Write the coordinates for each symbol.

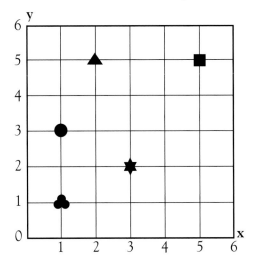

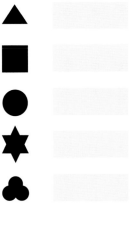

Place each of the points on the graph.

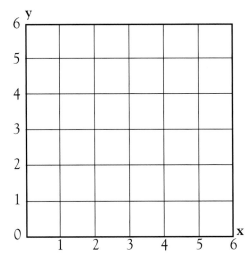

A   (2, 3)

B   (5, 4)

C   (2, 4)

D   (5, 3)

E   (4, 4)

Properties of polygons

Circle the polygon that has two pairs of parallel sides.

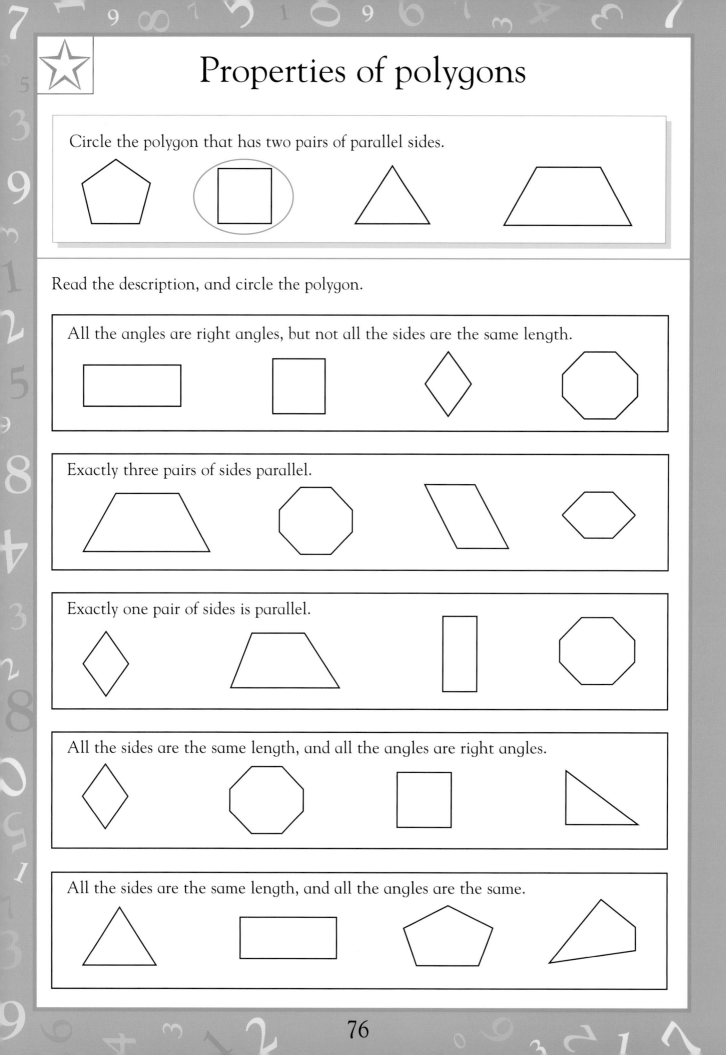

Read the description, and circle the polygon.

All the angles are right angles, but not all the sides are the same length.

Exactly three pairs of sides parallel.

Exactly one pair of sides is parallel.

All the sides are the same length, and all the angles are right angles.

All the sides are the same length, and all the angles are the same.

Naming polygons

Polygons are named for the number of sides they have.

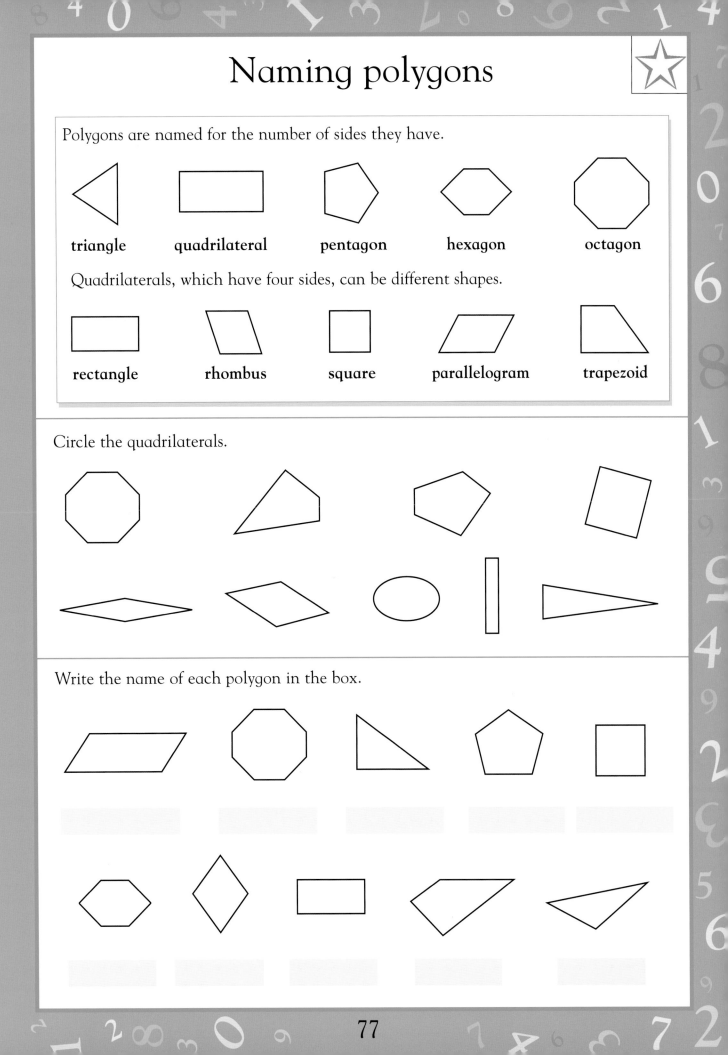

triangle   quadrilateral   pentagon   hexagon   octagon

Quadrilaterals, which have four sides, can be different shapes.

rectangle   rhombus   square   parallelogram   trapezoid

Circle the quadrilaterals.

Write the name of each polygon in the box.

Adding decimals

Find each sum. Remember to regroup.

$$\begin{array}{r} \overset{1}{}\$7.49 \\ +\ \ \$1.36 \\ \hline \$8.85 \end{array}$$

$$\begin{array}{r} \overset{1}{}4.18 \\ +\ \ 5.59 \\ \hline 9.77 \end{array}$$

Find each sum.

$$\begin{array}{r} \$5.22 \\ +\ \ \$3.49 \\ \hline \end{array}$$
$$\begin{array}{r} 4.34 \\ +\ \ 2.56 \\ \hline \end{array}$$
$$\begin{array}{r} \$8.21 \\ +\ \ \$4.49 \\ \hline \end{array}$$
$$\begin{array}{r} 3.28 \\ +\ \ 9.22 \\ \hline \end{array}$$

Find each sum.

$$\begin{array}{r} 2.77\text{ m} \\ +\ 4.59\text{ m} \\ \hline \end{array}$$
$$\begin{array}{r} 6.58\text{ km} \\ +\ 3.54\text{ km} \\ \hline \end{array}$$
$$\begin{array}{r} 7.37\text{ cm} \\ +\ 2.76\text{ cm} \\ \hline \end{array}$$
$$\begin{array}{r} 8.09\text{ m} \\ +\ 4.96\text{ m} \\ \hline \end{array}$$

Write each sum in the box.

$\$3.39\ +\ \$5.52\ =\ $

$\$6.37\ +\ \$5.09\ =\ $

$\$7.46\ +\ \$9.53\ =\ $

$\$8.22\ +\ \$1.19\ =\ $

$3.77\text{ km} + 1.99\text{ km}\ =\ $

$5.24\text{ m} + 8.37\text{ m}\ =\ $

Solve each problem.

Sandra has saved $3.99. Her mom gives her $1.62. How much does she now have?

Mrs. Jones's car is 4.53 m long. Mr. Jones's car is 5.24 m long. How long must their driveway be in order to fit both cars end to end?

Adding decimals

Find each sum. Remember to regroup.

```
   1
  $4.96
+ $2.83
───────
  $7.79
```

```
  1 1
  7.92 km
+ 1.68 km
─────────
  9.60 km
```

Find each sum.

```
  8.94
+ 5.88
──────
```

```
  $9.57
+ $9.99
───────
```

```
  $7.96
+ $4.78
───────
```

```
  5.73
+ 9.97
──────
```

```
  6.43 m
+ 8.57 m
────────
```

```
  7.34 cm
+ 9.99 cm
─────────
```

```
  8.62 km
+ 8.08 km
─────────
```

```
  3.04
+ 5.76
──────
```

Write each sum in the box.

$5.03 + $6.49 =

2.74 + 9.61 =

$8.32 + $9.58 =

1.29 + 4.83 =

5.26 km + 9.19 km =

2.04 m + 9.97 m =

Solve each problem.

Anna buys a can of soda for 45¢ and a sandwich for $1.39. How much does she pay?

Mr. Bailey buys two wardrobes. One is 1.29 m wide and the other is 96 cm wide. How much space will they take up if he puts them side by side?

Subtracting decimals

Find each difference. Remember to regroup.

$$\begin{array}{r} {\scriptstyle 7\ 11\ 13} \\ 8.2\overset{11}{\cancel{3}} \\ -\ 4.78 \\ \hline 3.45 \end{array} \qquad \begin{array}{r} {\scriptstyle 1\ 15\ 14} \\ 2.6\overset{}{\cancel{4}} \\ -\ 1.77 \\ \hline 0.87 \end{array}$$

Find each difference.

$$\begin{array}{r} 8.24 \\ -\ 5.36 \\ \hline \end{array} \qquad \begin{array}{r} \$6.27 \\ -\ \$3.48 \\ \hline \end{array} \qquad \begin{array}{r} 3.12 \\ -\ 1.23 \\ \hline \end{array} \qquad \begin{array}{r} \$9.47 \\ -\ \$4.79 \\ \hline \end{array}$$

Find each difference.

$$\begin{array}{r} 5.21 \\ -\ 2.99 \\ \hline \end{array} \qquad \begin{array}{r} 3.64\ m \\ -\ 1.99\ m \\ \hline \end{array} \qquad \begin{array}{r} 9.12\ km \\ -\ 3.99\ km \\ \hline \end{array} \qquad \begin{array}{r} 6.63\ cm \\ -\ 2.94\ cm \\ \hline \end{array}$$

Write each difference in the box.

$2.22 \quad - \quad \$1.63 \quad = \qquad\qquad 8.14 \quad - \quad 3.25 \quad =$

$9.76 \quad - \quad \$3.87 \quad = \qquad\qquad 5.71 \quad - \quad 1.92 \quad =$

$7.71 \quad - \quad 1.99 \quad = \qquad\qquad 3.55 \quad - \quad 1.89 \quad =$

Solve each problem.

Kofi's mother gave him $5.75 to spend at the store.
He came back with $1.87.
How much did he spend?

The end of Mrs. Brophy's hose was damaged.
The hose was 4 m 32 cm long, and she cut off 1 m 49 cm.
How much did she have left?

Subtracting decimals

Find each difference. Remember to regroup.

$$\begin{array}{r} \$8.31 \\ - \ \$2.94 \\ \hline \$5.37 \end{array}$$

$$\begin{array}{r} 6.23 \text{ m} \\ - \ 2.84 \text{ m} \\ \hline 3.39 \text{ m} \end{array}$$

Find each difference.

$\$5.31$	8.24	7.23	$\$6.23$	$\$4.11$
$- \ \$1.89$	$- \ 2.87$	$- \ 3.44$	$- \ \$1.24$	$- \ \$1.12$

Find each difference.

8.14 m	6.33 km	9.11 cm	6.23	7.48 m
$- \ 2.97$ m	$- \ 2.94$ km	$- \ 1.32$ cm	$- \quad 2.24$	$- \ 3.49$ m

Write each difference in the box.

$7.14 \quad - \quad 3.17 \quad =$

$\$3.39 \quad - \quad \$1.47 \quad =$

$8.51 \quad - \quad 6.59 \quad =$

$\$6.23 \quad - \quad \$5.34 \quad =$

$8.14 \quad - \quad 3.46 \quad =$

7.42 m $- \quad 4.57$ m $=$

Solve each problem.

Suzanne goes to the park with $\$5.13$ to spend. She buys a hot dog for $\$2.49$. How much does she have left?

Gita's garden is 7.43 m long. Josh's garden is 9.21 m long. How much longer is Josh's garden than Gita's?

⭐ Multiplying by one-digit numbers

Find each product. Remember to regroup.

```
  11              3              34
 465            391            278
x   3          x   4          x   5
─────          ─────          ─────
1,395          1,564          1,390
```

Find each product.

```
 563            910            437            812
x   3          x   2          x   3          x   2
─────          ─────          ─────          ─────
```

```
 572            831            406            394
x   4          x   3          x   5          x   6
─────          ─────          ─────          ─────
```

Find each product.

```
 318            223            542            217
x   3          x   4          x   4          x   3
─────          ─────          ─────          ─────
```

```
 127            275            798            365
x   4          x   5          x   6          x   6
─────          ─────          ─────          ─────
```

```
 100            372            881            953
x   5          x   4          x   4          x   3
─────          ─────          ─────          ─────
```

Solve each problem.

A middle school has 255 students. A high school has 6 times as many students. How many children are there at the high school?

A train can carry 365 passengers. How many could it carry on

four trips?

six trips?

Multiplying by one-digit numbers

Find each product. Remember to regroup.

$$\begin{array}{r} {\scriptstyle 33} \\ 456 \\ \times 6 \\ \hline 2{,}736 \end{array}$$

$$\begin{array}{r} {\scriptstyle 12} \\ 823 \\ \times 8 \\ \hline 6{,}584 \end{array}$$

$$\begin{array}{r} {\scriptstyle 44} \\ 755 \\ \times 9 \\ \hline 6{,}795 \end{array}$$

Find each product.

$$\begin{array}{r} 394 \\ \times 7 \\ \hline \end{array}$$
$$\begin{array}{r} 736 \\ \times 7 \\ \hline \end{array}$$
$$\begin{array}{r} 827 \\ \times 8 \\ \hline \end{array}$$
$$\begin{array}{r} 943 \\ \times 9 \\ \hline \end{array}$$

$$\begin{array}{r} 643 \\ \times 6 \\ \hline \end{array}$$
$$\begin{array}{r} 199 \\ \times 6 \\ \hline \end{array}$$
$$\begin{array}{r} 821 \\ \times 7 \\ \hline \end{array}$$
$$\begin{array}{r} 547 \\ \times 8 \\ \hline \end{array}$$

$$\begin{array}{r} 501 \\ \times 7 \\ \hline \end{array}$$
$$\begin{array}{r} 377 \\ \times 8 \\ \hline \end{array}$$
$$\begin{array}{r} 843 \\ \times 8 \\ \hline \end{array}$$
$$\begin{array}{r} 222 \\ \times 9 \\ \hline \end{array}$$

$$\begin{array}{r} 471 \\ \times 9 \\ \hline \end{array}$$
$$\begin{array}{r} 223 \\ \times 8 \\ \hline \end{array}$$
$$\begin{array}{r} 606 \\ \times 6 \\ \hline \end{array}$$
$$\begin{array}{r} 513 \\ \times 7 \\ \hline \end{array}$$

$$\begin{array}{r} 500 \\ \times 9 \\ \hline \end{array}$$
$$\begin{array}{r} 800 \\ \times 9 \\ \hline \end{array}$$
$$\begin{array}{r} 900 \\ \times 8 \\ \hline \end{array}$$
$$\begin{array}{r} 200 \\ \times 9 \\ \hline \end{array}$$

Solve each problem.

A crate holds 550 apples. How many apples are there in 8 crates?

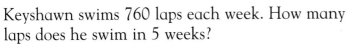

Keyshawn swims 760 laps each week. How many laps does he swim in 5 weeks?

Division with remainders

Find each quotient.

$$2\overline{)361} \quad 180\,r\,1$$
$$\underline{2}$$
$$16$$
$$\underline{16}$$
$$1$$

$$3\overline{)424} \quad 141\,r\,1$$
$$\underline{3}$$
$$12$$
$$\underline{12}$$
$$4$$
$$\underline{3}$$
$$1$$

$$4\overline{)235} \quad 58\,r\,3$$
$$\underline{20}$$
$$35$$
$$\underline{32}$$
$$3$$

Find each quotient.

$$2\overline{)413} \qquad 4\overline{)643} \qquad 3\overline{)572}$$

$$4\overline{)951} \qquad 2\overline{)365} \qquad 3\overline{)200}$$

$$4\overline{)737} \qquad 3\overline{)851} \qquad 4\overline{)203}$$

Write the answer in the box.

What is 563 divided by 2?   Divide 293 by 5.

What is 374 divided by 3?   Divide 767 by 4.

Division with remainders

Find each quotient.

$$\begin{array}{r} 62\,r\,6 \\ 9\overline{)564} \\ 54 \\ \hline 24 \\ 18 \\ \hline 6 \end{array}$$

$$\begin{array}{r} 66\,r\,1 \\ 7\overline{)463} \\ 42 \\ \hline 43 \\ 42 \\ \hline 1 \end{array}$$

Find each quotient.

$7\overline{)403}$　　　　　$8\overline{)655}$　　　　　$9\overline{)205}$

$9\overline{)574}$　　　　　$6\overline{)431}$　　　　　$7\overline{)121}$

$9\overline{)217}$　　　　　$9\overline{)404}$　　　　　$6\overline{)777}$

Write the answer in the box.

What is 759 divided by 7?　　　　　Divide 941 by 9.

What is 463 divided by 8?　　　　　Divide 232 by 6.

Real-life problems

Find the answer to each problem.

Jacob spent $4.68 at the store and had $4.77 left.
How much did he have to start with?

$9.45

$$
\begin{array}{r}
{\scriptstyle 1\ 1} \\
4.77 \\
+\ 4.68 \\
\hline
9.45
\end{array}
$$

Tracy receives a weekly allowance of $3.00 a week.
How much will she have if she saves all of it for 8 weeks?

$24.00

$$
\begin{array}{r}
3.00 \\
\times\ \ \ 8 \\
\hline
24.00
\end{array}
$$

Find the answer to each problem.

A theater charges $4 for each matinee ticket. If it sells 360 tickets for a matinee performance, how much does it take in?

David has saved $9.59. His sister has $3.24 less. How much does she have?

The cost for 9 children to go to a theme park is $72. How much does each child pay? If only 6 children go, what will the cost be?

Paul has $3.69. His sister gives him another $5.25, and he goes out and buys a CD single for $3.99. How much does he have left?

Ian has $20 in savings. He decides to spend $\frac{1}{4}$ of it. How much will he have left?

86

Real-life problems

Find the answer to each problem.

Nina has an hour to do her homework. She plans to spend $\frac{1}{3}$ of her time on math. How many minutes will she spend doing math?

20 minutes

1 hour is 60 minutes

$$3 \overline{)60}^{20}$$

In gym class, David makes 2 long jumps of 1.78 m and 2.19 m. How far does he jump altogether?

3.97 m

$$\begin{array}{r} 1 \\ 1.78 \text{ m} \\ + 2.19 \text{ m} \\ \hline 3.97 \text{ m} \end{array}$$

Find the answer to each problem.

Moishe has a can of lemonade containing 400 ml. He drinks $\frac{1}{4}$ of it. How much is left?

David ran 40 m in 8 seconds. At that speed, how far did he run in 1 second?

A large jar of coffee contains 1.75 kg. If 1.48 kg is left in the jar, how much has been used?

A worker can fill 145 boxes of tea in 15 minutes. How many boxes can he fill in 1 hour?

Jennifer's computer is 41.63 cm wide and her printer is 48.37 cm wide. How much space does she have for books if her desk is 1.5 m wide?

Perimeters of squares and rectangles

Find the perimeter of this rectangle.

To find the perimeter of a rectangle or a square, add the lengths of the four sides.

6 in. + 6 in. + 4 in. + 4 in. = 20 in.

You can also do this with multiplication.

(2 x 6) in. + (2 x 4) in.
= 12 in. + 8 in. = 20 in.

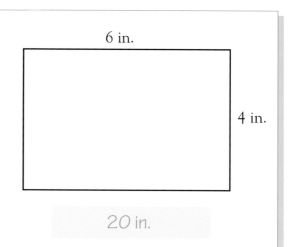

6 in.

4 in.

20 in.

Find the perimeters of these rectangles and squares.

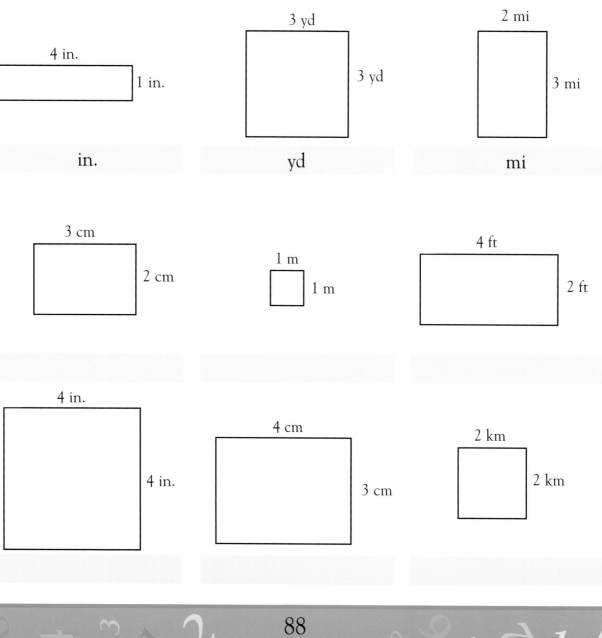

4 in.

1 in.

in.

3 yd

3 yd

yd

2 mi

3 mi

mi

3 cm

2 cm

1 m

1 m

4 ft

2 ft

4 in.

4 in.

4 cm

3 cm

2 km

2 km

Problems involving time

Find the answer to each problem.

Caitlin spends 35 minutes on her homework each day. How many minutes does she spend on her homework in one week from Monday through Friday?

175 minutes

$$\begin{array}{r} \overset{2}{35} \\ \times\ 5 \\ \hline 175 \end{array}$$

Jenny spends 175 minutes on her homework from Monday through Friday. How much time does she spend on homework each day?

35 minutes

$$5\overline{)175} = 35$$

Find the answer to each problem.

Amy works from 9 A.M. until 5 P.M. She has a lunch break from noon until 1 P.M. How many hours does she work in a 5-day week?

School children have a 15-minute break in the morning and a 10-minute break in the afternoon. How many minutes of break do they have in a week?

It takes 2 hours for one person to do a job. If John shares the work with 3 of his friends, how long will it take?

Mr. Tambo spent 7 days building a patio. If he worked a total of 56 hours and he divided the work evenly among the seven days, how long did he work each day?

It took Ben 45 hours to build a remote-controlled airplane. If he spent 5 hours a day working on it:

How many days did it take?

How many hours per day would he have needed to finish it in 5 days?

Using bar graphs

Use the graph to answer the questions.

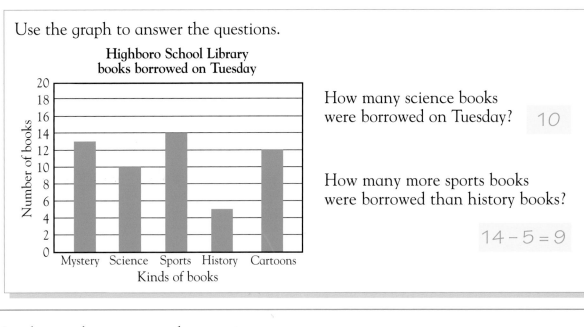

Highboro School Library books borrowed on Tuesday

How many science books were borrowed on Tuesday? **10**

How many more sports books were borrowed than history books?

14 − 5 = 9

Use the graphs to answer the questions.

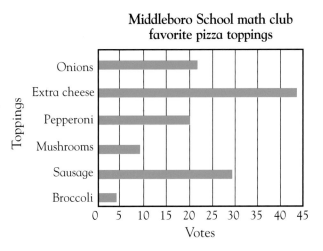

Middleboro School math club favorite pizza toppings

Which topping is the most popular?

Which topping got 8 votes?

About how many more votes did sausage receive than pepperoni?

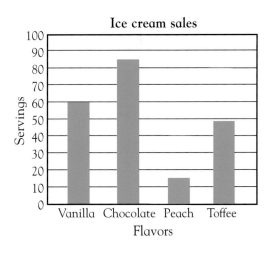

Ice cream sales

About how many servings of toffee ice cream were sold?

About how many more servings of chocolate were sold than vanilla?

Which flavor sold more than 40 servings but fewer than 50?

Congruency

Congruent triangles are triangles that are exactly the same shape and size. Triangles are congruent if the corresponding sides are the same and the three corresponding angles are the same.

Which triangles are congruent?

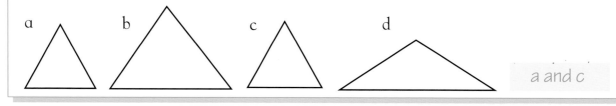

a   b   c   d

a and c

Which triangles are congruent?

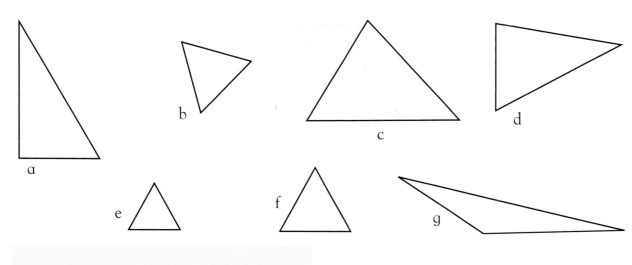

a b c d e f g

Which triangles are congruent?

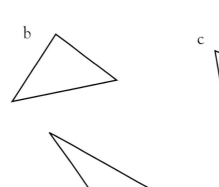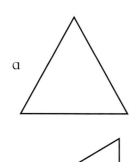

a b c d e f g

Lines of symmetry

How many lines of
symmetry does this figure have?   6

Six lines can be drawn each of
which divide the figure exactly in half.

How many lines of symmetry do these figures have?

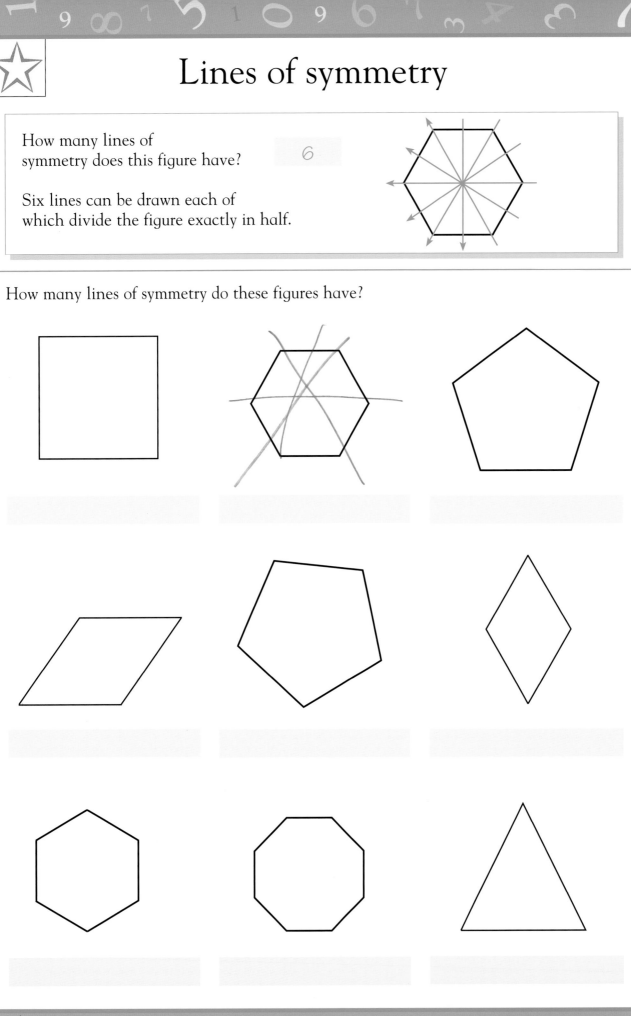

92

Writing equivalent number sentences ☆

Write a multiplication sentence that goes with $24 \div 6 = 4$.

$6 \times 4 = 24$ or $4 \times 6 = 24$

Write a related subtraction sentence for $5 + 12 = 17$.

$17 - 5 = 12$ or $17 - 12 = 5$

Write a related subtraction sentence for each sentence.

$25 + 12 = 37$

$35 + 8 = 43$

$13 + 9 = 22$

Write a related addition sentence for each sentence.

$35 - 24 = 11$

$82 - 23 = 59$

$45 - 20 = 25$

Write a related multiplication sentence for each sentence.

$36 \div 4 = 9$

$32 \div 2 = 16$

$72 \div 9 = 8$

Write a related division sentence for each sentence.

$8 \times 6 = 48$

$7 \times 12 = 84$

$9 \times 5 = 45$

Multiplying and dividing

Write the answer in the box.

26 x 10 = 260   26 x 100 = 2,600

400 ÷ 10 = 40   400 ÷ 100 = 4

Write the product in the box.

33 x 10 =   21 x 10 =   42 x 10 =

94 x 100 =   36 x 100 =   81 x 100 =

416 x 10 =   204 x 10 =   513 x 10 =

767 x 100 =   821 x 100 =   245 x 100 =

Write the quotient in the box.

120 ÷ 10 =   260 ÷ 10 =   470 ÷ 10 =

300 ÷ 100 =   800 ÷ 100 =   400 ÷ 100 =

20 ÷ 10 =   30 ÷ 10 =   70 ÷ 10 =

500 ÷ 100 =   100 ÷ 100 =   900 ÷ 100 =

Write the number that has been multiplied by 100.

_____ x 100 = 5,900   _____ x 100 = 71,400

_____ x 100 = 72,100   _____ x 100 = 23,400

_____ x 100 = 1,100   _____ x 100 = 47,000

_____ x 100 = 8,400   _____ x 100 = 44,100

Write the number that has been divided by 100.

_____ ÷ 100 = 2   _____ ÷ 100 = 8

_____ ÷ 100 = 21   _____ ÷ 100 = 18

_____ ÷ 100 = 86   _____ ÷ 100 = 21

_____ ÷ 100 = 10   _____ ÷ 100 = 59

Ordering sets of measures

Write these amounts in order, from least to greatest.

70 cm	300 mm	2 km	6 m	500 mm
300 mm	500 mm	70 cm	6 m	2 km

Write these amounts in order, from least to greatest.

500¢	$4.00	$5.50	350¢	640¢

2 qt	1 gal	12 pt	2 gal	10 qt

125 min	2 h	$3\frac{1}{2}$ h	200 min	$\frac{3}{4}$ h

2,500 m	2 km	1,000 cm	20 m	1,000 m

$240	3,500¢	$125.00	4,600¢	$50.00

1 yd	9 ft	24 in.	72 in.	7 ft

6 qt	8 pt	3 gal	1 qt	4 pt

2 h	75 min	$1\frac{1}{2}$ h	100 min	150 min

44 mm	4 cm	4 m	4 km	40 cm

4 yd	36 in.	2 ft	20 in.	2 yd

Decimal models

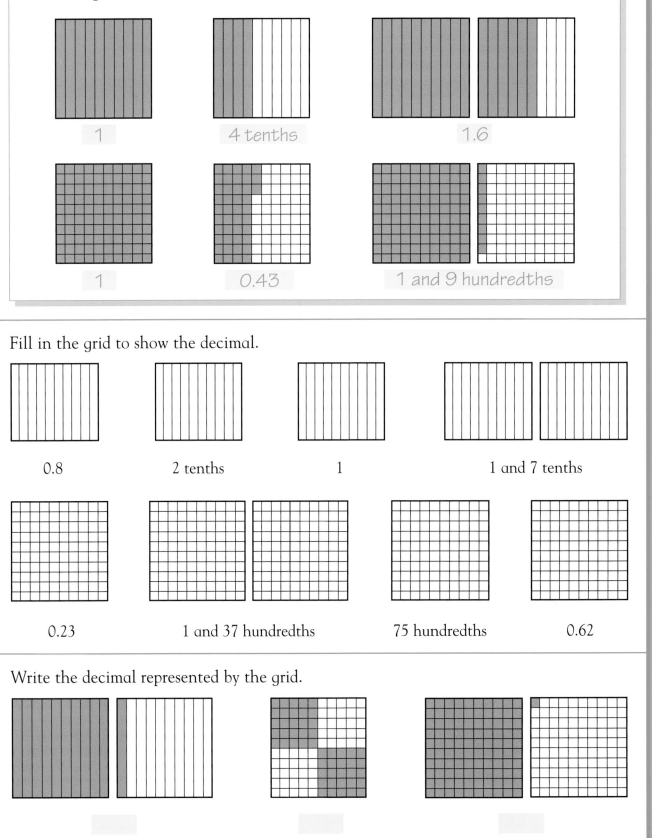

Fill in the grid to show the decimal.

1   4 tenths   1.6

1   0.43   1 and 9 hundredths

Fill in the grid to show the decimal.

0.8   2 tenths   1   1 and 7 tenths

0.23   1 and 37 hundredths   75 hundredths   0.62

Write the decimal represented by the grid.

Identifying patterns

Continue each pattern.

Steps of 2:	$\frac{1}{2}$	$2\frac{1}{2}$	$4\frac{1}{2}$	$6\frac{1}{2}$	$8\frac{1}{2}$	$10\frac{1}{2}$
Steps of 5:	3.5	8.5	13.5	18.5	23.5	28.5

Continue each pattern.

$5\frac{1}{2}$	$10\frac{1}{2}$	$15\frac{1}{2}$			
$1\frac{1}{4}$	$3\frac{1}{4}$	$5\frac{1}{4}$			
$8\frac{1}{3}$	$9\frac{1}{3}$	$10\frac{1}{3}$		$12\frac{1}{3}$	
$55\frac{3}{4}$	$45\frac{3}{4}$	$35\frac{3}{4}$			
$42\frac{1}{2}$	$38\frac{1}{2}$	$34\frac{1}{2}$			$22\frac{1}{2}$
7.5	6.5	5.5			
28.4	25.4	22.4		16.4	
81.6	73.6	65.6			
6.3	10.3	14.3			
12.1	13.1	14.1			17.1
14.6	21.6	28.6			
$11\frac{1}{2}$	$10\frac{1}{2}$	$9\frac{1}{2}$			
8.4	11.4	14.4		20.4	
$7\frac{3}{4}$	$13\frac{3}{4}$	$19\frac{3}{4}$			$37\frac{3}{4}$
57.5	48.5	39.5			

★ Products with odd and even numbers

Find the products of these numbers.

3 and 4   The product of 3 and 4 is 12.   6 and 8   The product of 6 and 8 is 48.

Find the products of these odd and even numbers.

5 and 6 _____   3 and 2 _____

7 and 4 _____   8 and 3 _____

6 and 3 _____   2 and 9 _____

10 and 3 _____   12 and 5 _____

What do you notice about your answers? _____

_____

Find the products of these odd numbers.

5 and 7 _____   3 and 9 _____

5 and 11 _____   7 and 3 _____

9 and 5 _____   11 and 7 _____

13 and 3 _____   1 and 5 _____

What do you notice about your answers? _____

_____

Find the products of these even numbers.

2 and 4 _____   4 and 6 _____

6 and 2 _____   4 and 8 _____

10 and 2 _____   4 and 10 _____

6 and 10 _____   6 and 8 _____

What do you notice about your answers? _____

_____

Can you write a rule for the products with odd and even numbers?

_____

Squares of numbers

Find the square of 2.

$2 \times 2 = 4$

What is the area of this square?

2 in.

2 in.

$2 \times 2 = 4$

Area = 4 in.²

Find the square of these numbers.

3		1		6	
7		8		5	
9		4		10	

Now try these.

| 13 | | 20 | | 40 | |
| 11 | | 12 | | 30 | |

What are the areas of these squares?

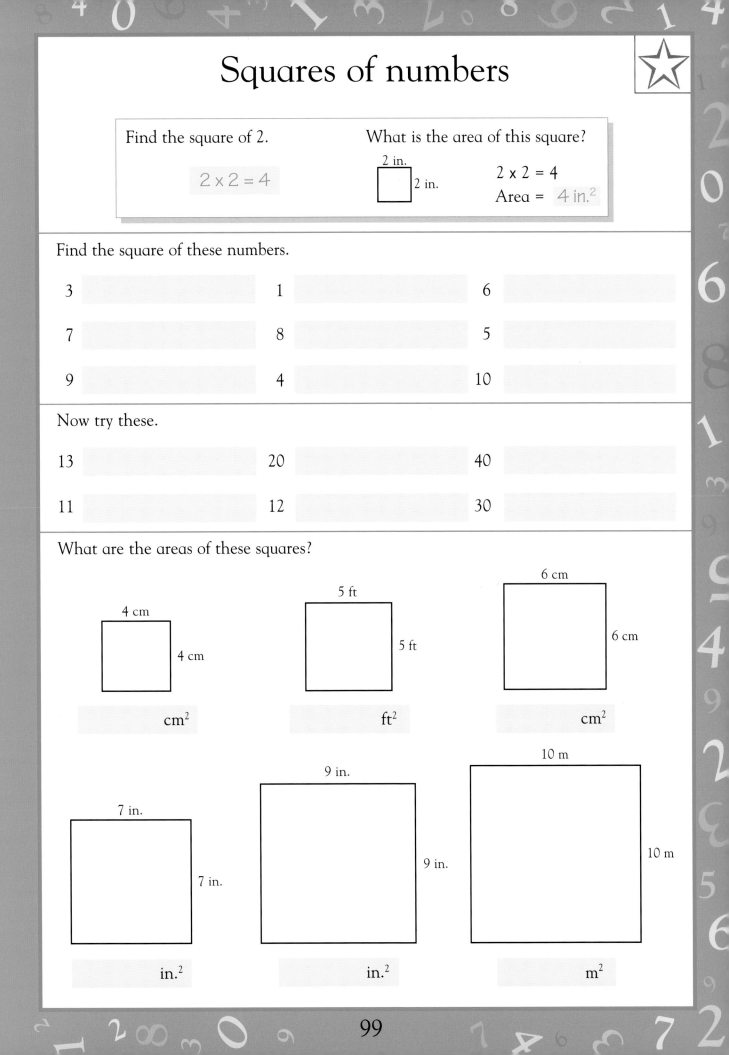

4 cm

4 cm

cm²

5 ft

5 ft

ft²

6 cm

6 cm

cm²

7 in.

7 in.

in.²

9 in.

9 in.

in.²

10 m

10 m

m²

⭐ Factors of numbers from 66 to 100

The factors of 66 are   1   2   3   6   11   22   33   66

Circle the factors of 94.   (1)   (2)   28   32   43   (47)   71   86   (94)

Write the factors of each number in the box.

The factors of 70 are

The factors of 85 are

The factors of 69 are

The factors of 83 are

The factors of 75 are

The factors of 96 are

The factors of 63 are

The factors of 99 are

The factors of 72 are

Circle the factors of 68.

    1   2   3   4   5   6   7   8   9   11   12   17   34   35   62   68

Circle the factors of 95.

    1   2   3   4   5   15   16   17   19   24   37   85   90   95   96

Circle the factors of 88.

    1   2   3   4   5   6   8   10   11   15   22   25   27   44   87   88

Circle the factors of 73.

    1   2   4   5   6   8   9   10   12   13   14   15   30   60   73

A prime number only has two factors, 1 and itself.
Write all the prime numbers between 66 and 100 in the box.

Renaming fractions

Rename these improper fractions as mixed numbers in simplest form.

$$\frac{17}{10} = 1\frac{7}{10} \qquad\qquad \frac{25}{6} = 4\frac{1}{6}$$

Rename this improper fraction as a mixed number in simplest form.

$$\frac{16}{10} = 1\frac{\cancel{6}^{3}}{\cancel{10}_{5}} = 1\frac{3}{5}$$

Rename these improper fractions as mixed numbers in simplest form.

$\frac{15}{4} =$	$\frac{13}{10} =$	$\frac{29}{5} =$
$\frac{19}{12} =$	$\frac{22}{9} =$	$\frac{17}{6} =$
$\frac{19}{6} =$	$\frac{24}{5} =$	$\frac{13}{3} =$
$\frac{13}{4} =$	$\frac{21}{2} =$	$\frac{14}{9} =$
$\frac{9}{8} =$	$\frac{11}{6} =$	$\frac{15}{7} =$
$\frac{17}{8} =$	$\frac{43}{4} =$	$\frac{11}{5} =$
$\frac{16}{10} =$	$\frac{36}{8} =$	$\frac{18}{8} =$
$\frac{45}{10} =$	$\frac{22}{6} =$	$\frac{24}{20} =$
$\frac{26}{8} =$	$\frac{20}{8} =$	$\frac{16}{12} =$
$\frac{25}{15} =$	$\frac{18}{4} =$	$\frac{20}{14} =$
$\frac{28}{24} =$	$\frac{32}{6} =$	$\frac{26}{10} =$
$\frac{18}{12} =$	$\frac{46}{4} =$	$\frac{30}{9} =$

Ordering sets of decimals

Write these decimals in order, from least to greatest.

5.63	2.14	5.6	3.91	1.25	4.63

9.39	0.24	7.63	8.25	7.49	9.40

1.05	2.36	1.09	2.41	7.94	1.50

3.92	5.63	2.29	4.62	5.36	2.15

28.71	21.87	27.18	21.78	28.17	27.81

Write these measures in order, from least to greatest.

$56.25	$32.40	$11.36	$32.04	$55.26	$36.19

94.21 km	87.05 km	76.91 km	94.36 km	65.99 km	110.75 km

$26.41	$47.23	$26.14	$35.23	$49.14	$35.32

19.51 m	16.15 m	15.53 m	12.65 m	24.24 m	16.51 m

7.35 l	8.29 l	5.73 l	8.92 l	10.65 l	4.29 l

Symmetry

How many lines of symmetry does each figure have?

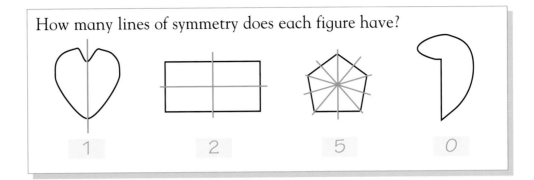

| 1 | 2 | 5 | 0 |

Is the dashed line a line symmetry? Write yes or no.

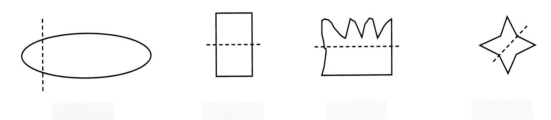

Draw the lines of symmetry. Write how many there are.

 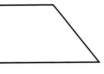

Draw the lines of symmetry. Write how many there are.

Draw the lines of symmetry. Write how many there are.

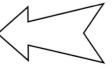

Comparing areas

Write how many units are in each figure.

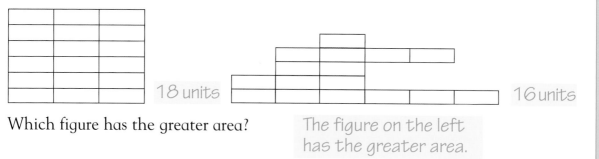

18 units   16 units

Which figure has the greater area?   The figure on the left has the greater area.

Write how many units are in each figure. Then circle the figure with the greatest area in each group.

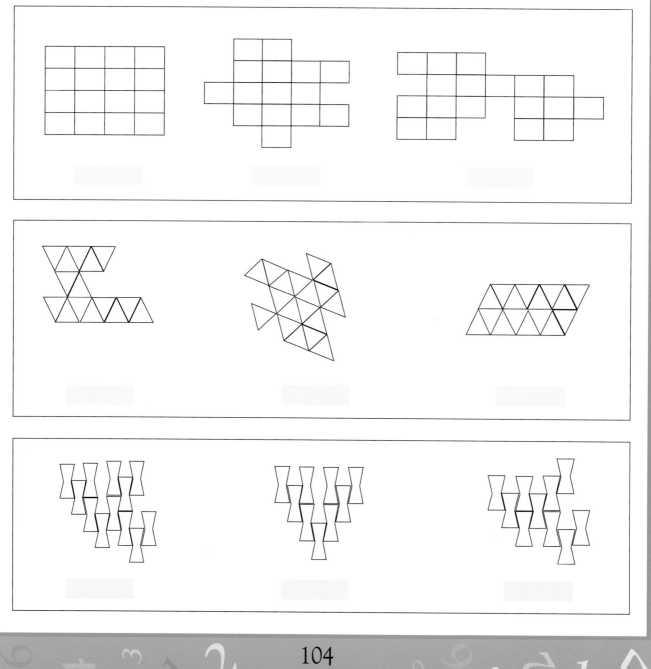

Probability

Use the table to answer the questions.

**Pairs of socks in
Mr. O' Neill's drawer**

color	number
red	2
blue	5
green	3
yellow	2
black	6

If Mr. O' Neill picks a pair of socks without looking, which color is he most likely to pick? black

Which color is Mr. O' Neill as likely to pick as red? yellow

Use the table to answer the questions.

Marbles in Margaret's bag

orange	blue	white	yellow
卌 卌 卌	卌 ‖	卌 卌	卌 卌 卌 卌

If Margaret picks a marble without looking, is she more likely to pick an orange marble or a yellow marble?

Which color is she least likely to pick?

Use the graph to answer the questions.

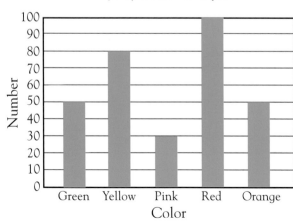

Jellybeans in a jar

If you pick a jellybean without looking, which color will you most probably pick?

Are you more likely to pick a pink jellybean or a yellow jellybean?

Which color jellybean are you as likely to pick as an orange one?

Column addition

Find these sums.

₁ ₁	₁ ₂₁
$327	1,374 km
$644	2,362 km
$923	1,690 km
+ $455	+ 4,216 km
$2,349	9,642 km

Find these sums.

539 yd	206 yd	481 yd	735 yd
965 yd	812 yd	604 yd	234 yd
774 yd	619 yd	274 yd	391 yd
+ 347 yd	+ 832 yd	+ 976 yd	+ 863 yd

746 lb	817 lb	944 lb	763 lb
201 lb	591 lb	835 lb	861 lb
432 lb	685 lb	391 lb	608 lb
+ 309 lb	+ 245 lb	+ 105 lb	+ 671 lb

6,329 m	5,245 m	6,431 m	8,690 m
3,251 m	2,845 m	7,453 m	5,243 m
2,642 m	1,937 m	4,650 m	6,137 m
+ 4,823 m	+ 5,610 m	+ 3,782 m	+ 5,843 m

$4,721	$3,654	$8,172	$4,352
$1,711	$5,932	$1,475	$3,920
$8,342	$6,841	$7,760	$8,439
+ $2,365	+ $4,736	+ $8,102	+ $1,348

1,573 mi	4,902 mi	3,756 mi	8,010 mi
6,231 mi	7,547 mi	1,150 mi	7,793 mi
2,112 mi	8,463 mi	5,535 mi	1,641 mi
+ 2,141 mi	+ 6,418 mi	+ 3,852 mi	+ 7,684 mi

Column addition

Find these sums.

1 11		2 21
3,461 km		$3,645
2,100 km		$4,231
3,522 km		$8,560
4,159 km		$7,213
+ 3,614 km		+ $9,463
16,856 km		$33,112

Find these sums.

3,144 m	2,510 m	3,276 m	1,475 m
2,345 m	1,734 m	1,593 m	2,653 m
8,479 m	5,421 m	6,837 m	2,765 m
1,004 m	3,205 m	1,769 m	3,742 m
+ 6,310 m	+ 2,365 m	+ 3,846 m	+ 5,905 m

$1,480	$4,527	$3,063	$8,741
$6,366	$8,309	$8,460	$6,334
$1,313	$6,235	$2,712	$3,231
$3,389	$4,487	$3,756	$6,063
+ $4,592	+ $4,065	+ $5,650	+ $4,096

8,644 km	3,823 km	8,636 km	8,618 km
3,353 km	9,275 km	8,986 km	3,453 km
6,400 km	3,669 km	5,367 km	4,404 km
5,768 km	2,998 km	6,863 km	4,361 km
+ 1,092 km	+ 7,564 km	+ 3,605 km	+ 5,641 km

$3,742	$8,596	$2,739	$8,463
$2,785	$5,430	$6,517	$5,641
$7,326	$8,379	$6,014	$9,430
$1,652	$2,943	$7,115	$8,204
+ $5,753	+ $1,081	+ $2,704	+ $6,326

Adding fractions

Write the sum in simplest form.

$\frac{1}{3} + \frac{1}{3} = \underline{}$

$\frac{2}{9} + \frac{4}{9} = \underline{} = \underline{}$

$\frac{1}{4} + \frac{1}{4} = \underline{} = \underline{}$

$\frac{5}{7} + \frac{1}{7} = \underline{}$

$\frac{2}{3} + \frac{2}{3} = \underline{} = \underline{}$

$\frac{1}{12} + \frac{3}{12} = \underline{} = \underline{}$

$\frac{3}{7} + \frac{5}{7} = \underline{} = \underline{}$

$\frac{5}{11} + \frac{9}{11} = \underline{} = \underline{}$

$\frac{2}{5} + \frac{4}{5} = \underline{} = \underline{}$

$\frac{5}{18} + \frac{4}{18} = \underline{} = \underline{}$

$\frac{5}{16} + \frac{7}{16} = \underline{} = \underline{}$

$\frac{5}{9} + \frac{5}{9} = \underline{} = \underline{}$

$\frac{3}{8} + \frac{5}{8} = \underline{} =$

$\frac{4}{15} + \frac{7}{15} = \underline{}$

$\frac{7}{13} + \frac{8}{13} = \underline{} = \underline{}$

$\frac{2}{5} + \frac{1}{5} = \underline{}$

$\frac{5}{16} + \frac{7}{16} = \underline{} = \underline{}$

$\frac{1}{6} + \frac{5}{6} = \underline{} =$

$\frac{9}{10} + \frac{7}{10} = \underline{} = \underline{} = \underline{}$

$\frac{3}{4} + \frac{3}{4} = \underline{} = \underline{} = \underline{}$

$\frac{4}{5} + \frac{3}{5} = \underline{} = \underline{}$

$\frac{1}{8} + \frac{5}{8} = \underline{} = \underline{}$

$\frac{7}{12} + \frac{5}{12} = \underline{} =$

$\frac{3}{10} + \frac{9}{10} = \underline{} = \underline{} = \underline{}$

$\frac{3}{11} + \frac{5}{11} = \underline{}$

$\frac{9}{15} + \frac{11}{15} = \underline{} = \underline{} = \underline{}$

$\frac{8}{14} + \frac{5}{14} = \underline{}$

$\frac{1}{20} + \frac{6}{20} = \underline{}$

Adding fractions

Write the sum in simplest form.

$$\frac{1}{12} + \frac{3}{4} = \frac{1}{12} + \frac{9}{12} = \frac{10}{12} = \frac{5}{6}$$

$$\frac{3}{5} + \frac{7}{10} = \frac{6}{10} + \frac{7}{10} = \frac{13}{10} = 1\frac{3}{10}$$

Write the sum in simplest form.

$$\frac{1}{6} + \frac{2}{3} = \frac{\quad}{\quad} + \frac{\quad}{\quad} = \frac{\quad}{\quad}$$

$$\frac{7}{12} + \frac{7}{36} = \frac{\quad}{\quad} + \frac{\quad}{\quad} = \frac{\quad}{\quad} = \frac{\quad}{\quad}$$

$$\frac{1}{3} + \frac{2}{6} = \frac{\quad}{\quad} + \frac{\quad}{\quad} = \frac{\quad}{\quad} = \frac{\quad}{\quad}$$

$$\frac{6}{10} + \frac{7}{30} = \frac{\quad}{\quad} + \frac{\quad}{\quad} = \frac{\quad}{\quad} = \frac{\quad}{\quad}$$

$$\frac{8}{12} + \frac{5}{24} = \frac{\quad}{\quad} + \frac{\quad}{\quad} = \frac{\quad}{\quad} = \frac{\quad}{\quad}$$

$$\frac{7}{12} + \frac{5}{6} = \frac{\quad}{\quad} + \frac{\quad}{\quad} = \frac{\quad}{\quad} = \frac{\quad}{\quad}$$

$$\frac{5}{7} + \frac{7}{14} = \frac{\quad}{\quad} + \frac{\quad}{\quad} = \frac{\quad}{\quad} = \frac{\quad}{\quad}$$

$$\frac{9}{25} + \frac{1}{5} = \frac{\quad}{\quad} + \frac{\quad}{\quad} = \frac{\quad}{\quad}$$

$$\frac{5}{6} + \frac{9}{12} = \frac{\quad}{\quad} + \frac{\quad}{\quad} = \frac{\quad}{\quad} = \frac{\quad}{\quad}$$

$$\frac{6}{16} + \frac{1}{4} = \frac{\quad}{\quad} + \frac{\quad}{\quad} = \frac{\quad}{\quad} = \frac{\quad}{\quad}$$

$$\frac{4}{5} + \frac{3}{10} = \frac{\quad}{\quad} + \frac{\quad}{\quad} = \frac{\quad}{\quad} = \frac{\quad}{\quad}$$

$$\frac{5}{15} + \frac{5}{30} = \frac{\quad}{\quad} + \frac{\quad}{\quad} = \frac{\quad}{\quad} = \frac{\quad}{\quad}$$

$$\frac{3}{8} + \frac{5}{24} = \frac{\quad}{\quad} + \frac{\quad}{\quad} = \frac{\quad}{\quad} = \frac{\quad}{\quad}$$

$$\frac{7}{8} + \frac{1}{2} = \frac{\quad}{\quad} + \frac{\quad}{\quad} = \frac{\quad}{\quad} = \frac{\quad}{\quad}$$

$$\frac{4}{9} + \frac{2}{3} = \frac{\quad}{\quad} + \frac{\quad}{\quad} = \frac{\quad}{\quad} = \frac{\quad}{\quad}$$

$$\frac{2}{3} + \frac{7}{15} = \frac{\quad}{\quad} + \frac{\quad}{\quad} = \frac{\quad}{\quad} = \frac{\quad}{\quad}$$

$$\frac{7}{8} + \frac{3}{16} = \frac{\quad}{\quad} + \frac{\quad}{\quad} = \frac{\quad}{\quad} = \frac{\quad}{\quad}$$

$$\frac{5}{14} + \frac{9}{28} = \frac{\quad}{\quad} + \frac{\quad}{\quad} = \frac{\quad}{\quad}$$

$$\frac{3}{10} + \frac{7}{20} = \frac{\quad}{\quad} + \frac{\quad}{\quad} = \frac{\quad}{\quad}$$

$$\frac{3}{33} + \frac{5}{11} = \frac{\quad}{\quad} + \frac{\quad}{\quad} = \frac{\quad}{\quad} = \frac{\quad}{\quad}$$

Subtracting fractions

Write the answer in simplest form.

$$\frac{5}{6} - \frac{4}{6} = \boxed{\frac{1}{6}} \qquad \frac{5}{8} - \frac{3}{8} = \frac{\cancel{2}^{1}}{\cancel{8}_{4}} = \boxed{\frac{1}{4}}$$

Write the answer in simplest form.

$$\frac{2}{3} - \frac{1}{3} = \underline{\quad} \qquad\qquad \frac{7}{9} - \frac{4}{9} = \underline{\quad} = \underline{\quad}$$

$$\frac{1}{4} - \frac{1}{4} = \boxed{} \qquad\qquad \frac{5}{7} - \frac{1}{7} = \underline{\quad}$$

$$\frac{7}{12} - \frac{5}{12} = \underline{\quad} = \underline{\quad} \qquad\qquad \frac{5}{11} - \frac{3}{11} = \underline{\quad}$$

$$\frac{6}{7} - \frac{5}{7} = \underline{\quad} \qquad\qquad \frac{9}{12} - \frac{5}{12} = \underline{\quad} = \underline{\quad}$$

$$\frac{18}{30} - \frac{15}{30} = \underline{\quad} = \underline{\quad} \qquad\qquad \frac{4}{5} - \frac{2}{5} = \underline{\quad}$$

$$\frac{3}{6} - \frac{1}{6} = \underline{\quad} = \underline{\quad} \qquad\qquad \frac{7}{8} - \frac{1}{8} = \underline{\quad} = \underline{\quad}$$

$$\frac{11}{16} - \frac{7}{16} = \underline{\quad} = \underline{\quad} \qquad\qquad \frac{5}{9} - \frac{2}{9} = \underline{\quad} = \underline{\quad}$$

$$\frac{7}{13} - \frac{5}{13} = \underline{\quad} \qquad\qquad \frac{14}{15} - \frac{4}{15} = \underline{\quad} = \underline{\quad}$$

$$\frac{12}{13} - \frac{8}{13} = \underline{\quad} \qquad\qquad \frac{4}{5} - \frac{1}{5} = \underline{\quad}$$

$$\frac{9}{10} - \frac{7}{10} = \underline{\quad} = \underline{\quad} \qquad\qquad \frac{5}{6} - \frac{1}{6} = \underline{\quad} = \underline{\quad}$$

$$\frac{8}{17} - \frac{4}{17} = \underline{\quad} \qquad\qquad \frac{11}{18} - \frac{8}{18} = \underline{\quad} = \underline{\quad}$$

$$\frac{4}{5} - \frac{3}{5} = \underline{\quad} \qquad\qquad \frac{7}{12} - \frac{1}{12} = \underline{\quad} = \underline{\quad}$$

$$\frac{9}{11} - \frac{5}{11} = \underline{\quad} \qquad\qquad \frac{8}{14} - \frac{5}{14} = \underline{\quad}$$

$$\frac{7}{8} - \frac{5}{8} = \underline{\quad} = \underline{\quad} \qquad\qquad \frac{9}{10} - \frac{3}{10} = \underline{\quad} = \underline{\quad}$$

$$\frac{3}{16} - \frac{2}{16} = \underline{\quad} \qquad\qquad \frac{17}{20} - \frac{7}{20} = \underline{\quad} = \underline{\quad}$$

Subtracting fractions

Write the answer in simplest form.

$$\frac{3}{4} - \frac{1}{12} = \frac{9}{12} - \frac{1}{12} = \frac{8}{12} = \frac{2}{3}$$

$$\frac{3}{5} - \frac{4}{10} = \frac{6}{10} - \frac{4}{10} = \frac{2}{10} = \frac{1}{5}$$

Write the answer in simplest form.

$$\frac{5}{6} - \frac{9}{12} = \underline{\quad} - \underline{\quad} = \underline{\quad}$$

$$\frac{6}{10} - \frac{7}{?} = \underline{\quad} - \underline{\quad} = \underline{\quad}$$

$$\frac{6}{14} - \frac{9}{28} = \underline{\quad} - \underline{\quad} = \underline{\quad}$$

$$\frac{1}{3} - \frac{2}{6} = \underline{\quad} - \underline{\quad} = \underline{\quad}$$

$$\frac{7}{8} - \frac{6}{16} = \underline{\quad} - \underline{\quad} = \underline{\quad} = \underline{\quad}$$

$$\frac{5}{15} - \frac{5}{30} = \underline{\quad} - \underline{\quad} = \underline{\quad} = \underline{\quad}$$

$$\frac{1}{2} - \frac{5}{12} = \underline{\quad} - \underline{\quad} = \underline{\quad}$$

$$\frac{8}{9} - \frac{2}{3} = \underline{\quad} - \underline{\quad} = \underline{\quad}$$

$$\frac{6}{16} - \frac{1}{4} = \underline{\quad} - \underline{\quad} = \underline{\quad} = \underline{\quad}$$

$$\frac{6}{7} - \frac{7}{14} = \underline{\quad} - \underline{\quad} = \underline{\quad}$$

$$\frac{7}{9} - \frac{7}{36} = \underline{\quad} - \underline{\quad} = \underline{\quad} = \underline{\quad}$$

$$\frac{2}{5} - \frac{4}{15} = \underline{\quad} - \underline{\quad} = \underline{\quad}$$

$$\frac{8}{12} - \frac{3}{24} = \underline{\quad} - \underline{\quad} = \underline{\quad}$$

$$\frac{3}{10} - \frac{3}{20} = \underline{\quad} - \underline{\quad} = \underline{\quad}$$

$$\frac{7}{8} - \frac{1}{2} = \underline{\quad} - \underline{\quad} = \underline{\quad}$$

$$\frac{7}{12} - \frac{2}{6} = \underline{\quad} - \underline{\quad} = \underline{\quad} = \underline{\quad}$$

$$\frac{5}{7} - \frac{1}{21} = \underline{\quad} - \underline{\quad} = \underline{\quad} = \underline{\quad}$$

$$\frac{14}{18} - \frac{5}{9} = \underline{\quad} - \underline{\quad} = \underline{\quad} = \underline{\quad}$$

$$\frac{3}{4} - \frac{3}{20} = \underline{\quad} - \underline{\quad} = \underline{\quad} = \underline{\quad}$$

$$\frac{1}{2} - \frac{3}{8} = \underline{\quad} - \underline{\quad} = \underline{\quad}$$

$$\frac{8}{21} - \frac{2}{7} = \underline{\quad} - \underline{\quad} = \underline{\quad}$$

$$\frac{3}{5} - \frac{6}{15} = \underline{\quad} - \underline{\quad} = \underline{\quad} = \underline{\quad}$$

Multiplying by two-digit numbers

Write the product for each problem.

$$
\begin{array}{r} {}^{1}_{1}56 \\ \times\ 32 \\ \hline 1\ 1\ 2 \\ 1{,}680 \\ \hline \underline{1{,}792} \end{array}
\qquad
\begin{array}{r} {}^{2}_{1}45 \\ \times\ 43 \\ \hline 135 \\ 1{,}800 \\ \hline \underline{1{,}935} \end{array}
$$

Write the product for each problem.

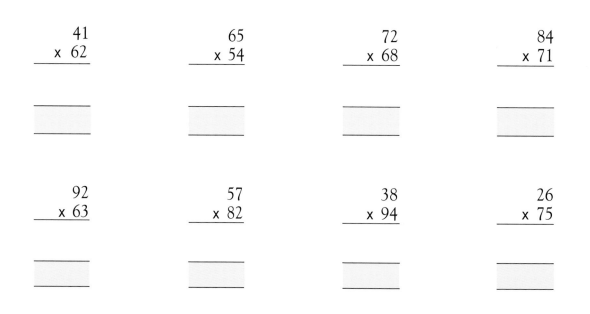

$$
\begin{array}{r} 56 \\ \times\ 23 \\ \hline \end{array}
\qquad
\begin{array}{r} 23 \\ \times\ 24 \\ \hline \end{array}
\qquad
\begin{array}{r} 47 \\ \times\ 25 \\ \hline \end{array}
\qquad
\begin{array}{r} 84 \\ \times\ 22 \\ \hline \end{array}
$$

$$
\begin{array}{r} 73 \\ \times\ 34 \\ \hline \end{array}
\qquad
\begin{array}{r} 52 \\ \times\ 35 \\ \hline \end{array}
\qquad
\begin{array}{r} 64 \\ \times\ 33 \\ \hline \end{array}
\qquad
\begin{array}{r} 51 \\ \times\ 32 \\ \hline \end{array}
$$

Write the product for each problem.

$$
\begin{array}{r} 41 \\ \times\ 62 \\ \hline \end{array}
\qquad
\begin{array}{r} 65 \\ \times\ 54 \\ \hline \end{array}
\qquad
\begin{array}{r} 72 \\ \times\ 68 \\ \hline \end{array}
\qquad
\begin{array}{r} 84 \\ \times\ 71 \\ \hline \end{array}
$$

$$
\begin{array}{r} 92 \\ \times\ 63 \\ \hline \end{array}
\qquad
\begin{array}{r} 57 \\ \times\ 82 \\ \hline \end{array}
\qquad
\begin{array}{r} 38 \\ \times\ 94 \\ \hline \end{array}
\qquad
\begin{array}{r} 26 \\ \times\ 75 \\ \hline \end{array}
$$

Multiplying by two-digit numbers

Write the product for each problem.

$$
\begin{array}{r}
7 \\
6 \\
39 \\
\times\ 87 \\
\hline
273 \\
3{,}120 \\
\hline
3{,}393
\end{array}
\qquad
\begin{array}{r}
7 \\
6 \\
68 \\
\times\ 98 \\
\hline
544 \\
6{,}120 \\
\hline
6{,}664
\end{array}
$$

Write the product for each problem.

87 x 98	76 x 78	99 x 69	85 x 98
88 x 95	67 x 76	94 x 69	89 x 47

Write the product for each problem.

87 x 79	46 x 67	58 x 59	73 x 98
95 x 67	58 x 88	78 x 97	96 x 79

Dividing by one-digit numbers

Find the quotient. Estimate your answer first.

3 x 100 = 300, so the quotient will be less than 100.
3 x 80 = 240 and 3 x 90 = 270,
so the quotient will be between 80 and 90.

$$\begin{array}{r} 85\,r\,2 \\ 3\overline{)257} \\ 24 \\ \hline 17 \\ 15 \\ \hline 2 \end{array}$$

Find the quotients. Remember to estimate your answers first.

2)571   4)823   3)604   4)925

2)147   3)259   4)725   5)811

2)593   4)406   3)739   5)591

114

Dividing by one-digit numbers

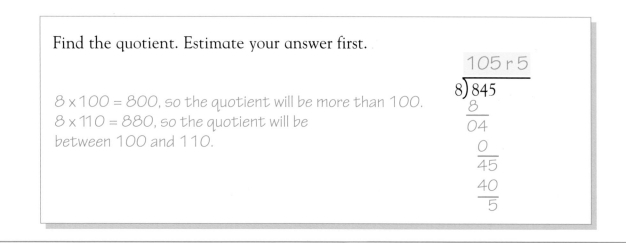

Find the quotient. Estimate your answer first.

$8 \times 100 = 800$, so the quotient will be more than 100.
$8 \times 110 = 880$, so the quotient will be between 100 and 110.

```
        105 r 5
     8)845
        8
        04
         0
        45
        40
         5
```

Find the quotients. Remember to estimate your answers first.

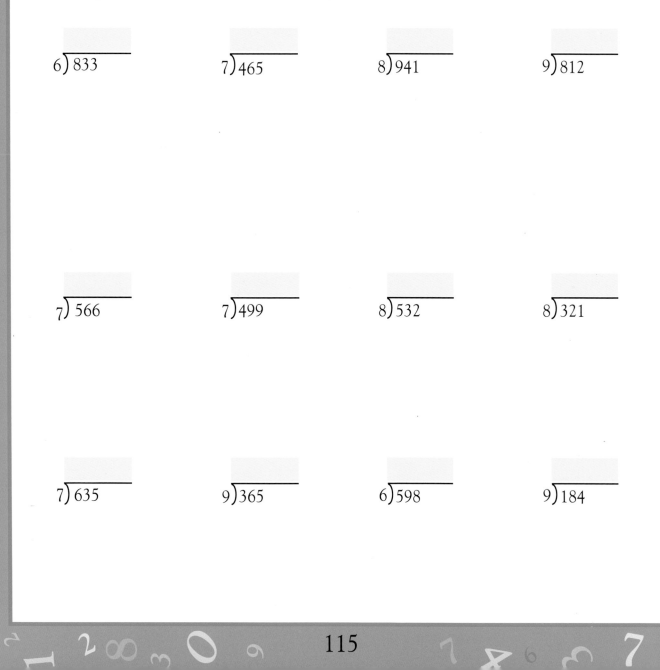

6)833   7)465   8)941   9)812

7)566   7)499   8)532   8)321

7)635   9)365   6)598   9)184

Real-life problems

Find the answer to each problem.

Tim spends $26.54 on holiday gifts for his family. His sister spends $32.11. How much more does she spend than Tim?

$5.57

```
  1110
  2 1011
  32.11
-  26.54
   5.57
```

A school spends $99 per class on new books. If there are 16 classes in the school, how much is spent?

$1,584

```
    99
 ×  16
   594
   990
 1,584
```

Mr. Brown has $4,762 in stocks and $2,247 in his bank. How much does he have altogether?

A shop in Chicago takes in $9,651 on a Saturday. A smaller branch in Evanston takes in $3,247. How much more does the Chicago shop take in?

A school raises money for charity. If 127 children brought in $2 each and 261 children brought in $3 each, how much did the school raise altogether?

David has to fill a pond that holds 66 gallons. If his bucket holds 3 gallons how many buckets of water will he need to fill the pond?

Samantha has $25. She spends $14.25 on an aquarium, $3.75 on gravel, and $2.50 on aquarium ornaments.
How much did she spend?
How much money does she have left?

A man regularly saves $1,200 each year. How much will he save in 5 years?

Real-life problems

Find the answer to each problem.

Jaime runs round a field 8 times.
If he runs a total of 944 yards,
what is the perimeter of the field?

118 yd

$$\begin{array}{r} 118 \\ 8\overline{)944} \\ \underline{8} \\ 14 \\ \underline{8} \\ 64 \\ \underline{64} \\ 0 \end{array}$$

Mr. and Mrs. Green's living room is 5.75 m
long and their dining room is 4.37 m long.
If they knock out the wall between them to
make one room, how long will it be?

10.12 m

$$\begin{array}{r} {\scriptstyle 1\ 1} \\ 5.75 \\ + 4.37 \\ \hline 10.12 \end{array}$$

A family's car trip took 5 hours. If they travelled 50 miles each hour, how far did they travel?

Two men weigh $218\frac{1}{2}$ lb and 173 lb.
What is the difference between their weights?

An electrictian uses 480 yd of electrician wire in 6 apartments. If he uses the same amount in each, how much does he use per house?

A jar of coffee weighs 36 oz.
How much will 7 jars weigh?

A box of pencils is 2 in. wide. How many can be stored on a shelf 1 yd long?

Maria spends 32 hours working on a school project. If she spreads the work evenly over 8 days, how many hours does she work each day?

Sean runs 143.26 m in 40 seconds. Malik runs 97.92 m in the same time. How much farther does Sean run than Malik?

Problems involving time

Find the answer to each problem.

A yard sale began at 12 P.M. and ended at 4:35 P.M. How long did it last?

Fred's watch says 2:27. What time will it say in 1h 26 min?

```
12:00 → 4:00 = 4 h
4:00 → 4:35 = 35 min
Total = 4 h 35 min
```

```
2:27 + 1 h = 3:27
3.27 + 26 min = 3:53
```

4 h 35 min

3:53

Rachel begins painting fences at 12:15 P.M. and finishes at 4:45 P.M. If she paints 3 fences, how long does each one take?

Joy works from 9 A.M. until 5 P.M. every day. If she takes an hour's lunch break, how many hours does she work altogether from Monday through Friday?

A train leaves at 2:29 P.M. and arrives at 10:47 P.M. How long does the trip take?

A castle has a 24-hour guard on the gate. Three soldiers share the work equally. If the first soldier starts his duty at 2:30 P.M., what times will the other two soldiers start their duties?

Soldier 2

Soldier 3

Kobe wants to videotape a program that starts at 3:30 P.M. and finishes at 5 P.M. If the program is on every day for the next five days, how many hours will he videotape?

Looking at graphs

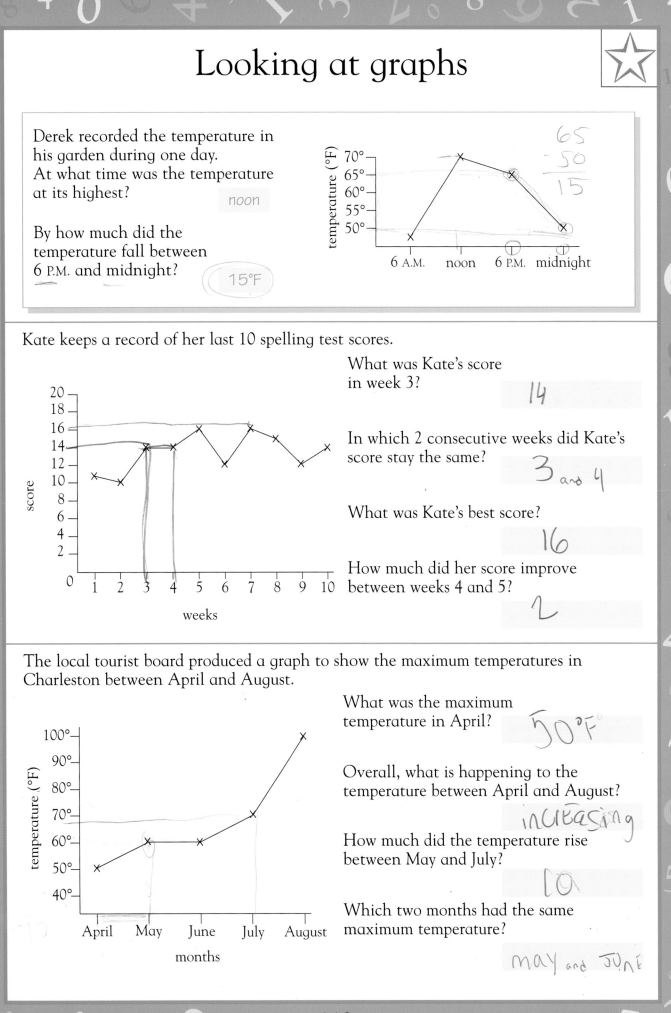

Derek recorded the temperature in his garden during one day.
At what time was the temperature at its highest?

noon

By how much did the temperature fall between 6 P.M. and midnight?

15°F

65
-50
15

Kate keeps a record of her last 10 spelling test scores.

What was Kate's score in week 3?

14

In which 2 consecutive weeks did Kate's score stay the same?

3 and 4

What was Kate's best score?

16

How much did her score improve between weeks 4 and 5?

2

The local tourist board produced a graph to show the maximum temperatures in Charleston between April and August.

What was the maximum temperature in April?

50°F

Overall, what is happening to the temperature between April and August?

increasing

How much did the temperature rise between May and July?

10

Which two months had the same maximum temperature?

may and june

Place value for whole numbers

Write the value of 7 in 573 in standard form and word form.

70   seventy

What happens to the value of 247 if you change the 2 to a 3?

The value of the number increases by 100.

Write the value of the 6 in these numbers in standard form and word form.

26   162   36,904   12,612

Circle the numbers that have a 7 with a value of seventy.

457,682   67,974   870,234   372,987

177,079   767,777   79,875   16,757

Write what happens to the value of each number.

Change the 6 in 3,586 to 3.

Change the 9 in 1,921 to 8.

Change the 7 in 7,246 to 9.

Change the 1 in 817 to 9.

Change the 5 in 50,247 to 1.

Change the 2 in 90,205 to 9.

Place value for decimals

Write the value of 5 in 7.53 in standard form and word form.

     0.5   *5 tenths*

What happens to the value of 2.48 if you change the 8 to a 1?

     The value of the number decreases by 0.07.

Write the value of the 9 in these numbers in standard form and written form.

  2.9   0.19   975.04   9.12

  0.89   591.65   19.85   3.96

Write what happens to the value of each number.

Change the 8 in 35.86 to 7.

Change the 2 in 1.02 to 6.

Change the 3 in 3,460 to 9.

Change the 1 in 8.17 to 6.

Change the 5 in 8.35 to 1.

Circle the numbers that have an 8 with a value of 8 tenths.

  457.68   1.8   8.09   35.85   388.1

Circle the numbers that have a 5 with a value of 5 hundredths.

  550.7   5.25   99.95   16.53   68.95

Circle the numbers that have a 3 with a value of 3 tenths.

  3,603.3   0.93   32.45   5.33   23.53

Reading tally charts

Use the chart to answer the questions.

Club members' pets

Pet	Number
dog	卌 卌 IIII
cat	卌 卌 卌 I
fish	卌 III

What is the most popular pet for club members? *cats*

How many more club members have cats than have fish?

16 − 8 = 8,   8 members

Use the chart to answer the questions.

Birds seen at feeder

sparrow	junco	blue jay	chickadee
卌 卌 卌 III	卌 III	卌 卌 I	卌 卌 卌 卌

What kinds of birds were seen
at the feeder more than 12 times?

What is the total number of
sparrows and chickadees seen at the feeder?

How many more blue jays than juncos were seen?

Use the chart to answer the questions.

Snacks chosen by students

carrots	chips	cookies	pretzels
IIII	卌 卌 III	卌 卌 卌 II	卌 卌 卌 卌 II

What snack did fewer than 10 students choose?

What is the most popular snack for students?

Was the total number of students who chose chips and cookies greater
than or less than the total number who chose carrots and pretzels?

Volumes of cubes

This cube is 1 cm long, 1 cm high, and 1 cm wide. We say it has a volume of 1 cubic centimeter (1 cm³).

1 cm
1 cm
1 cm

If we put 4 of these cubes together the new shape has a volume of 4 cm³.

These shapes are made of 1 cm³ cubes. What are their volumes?

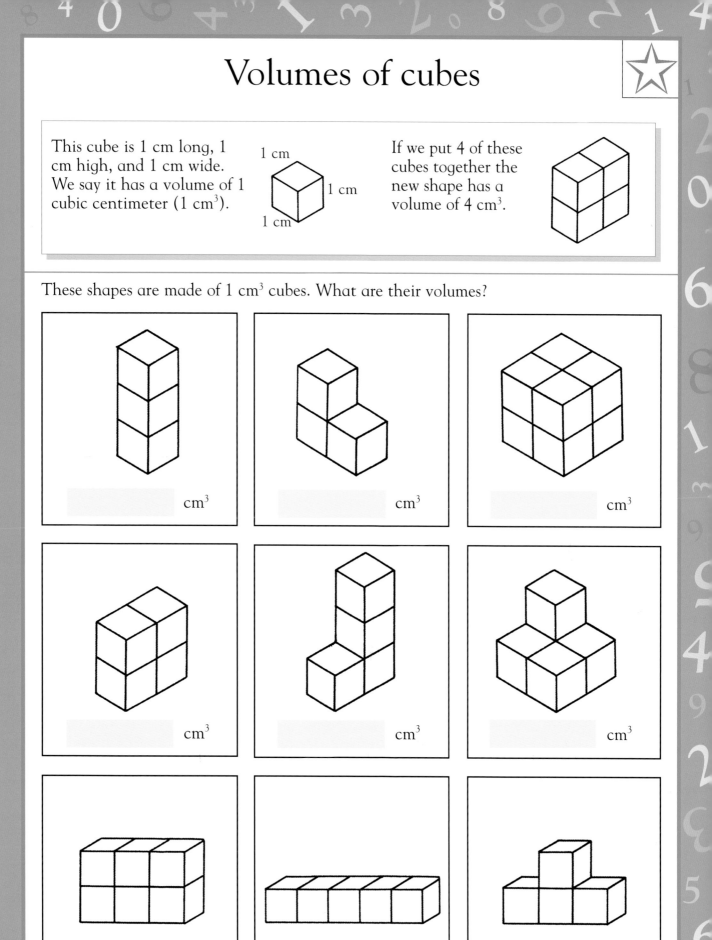

_____ cm³

_____ cm³

_____ cm³

_____ cm³

_____ cm³

_____ cm³

_____ cm³

_____ cm³

_____ cm³

Acute and obtuse angles

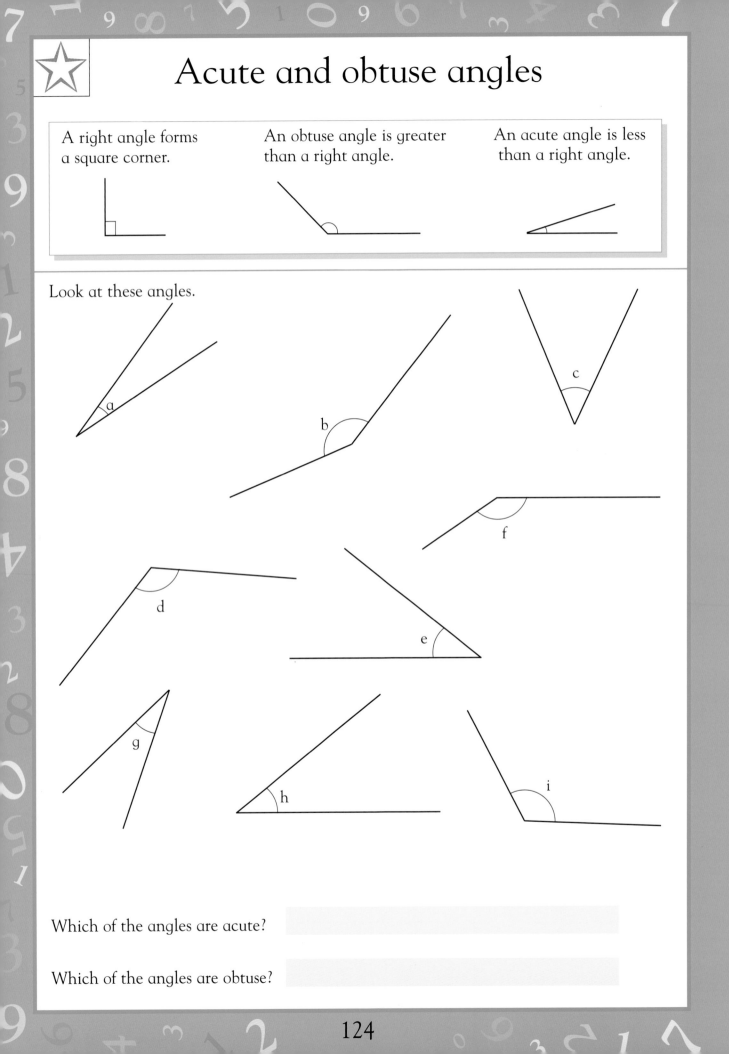

A right angle forms a square corner.

An obtuse angle is greater than a right angle.

An acute angle is less than a right angle.

Look at these angles.

Which of the angles are acute?

Which of the angles are obtuse?

Acute and obtuse angles

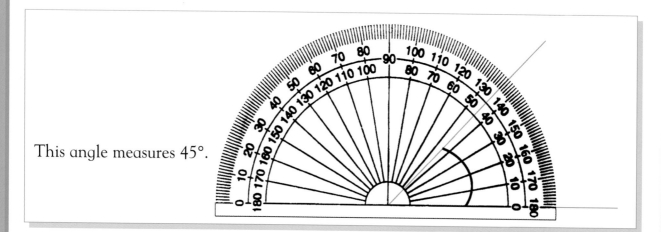

This angle measures 45°.

Use a protractor to measure these angles.

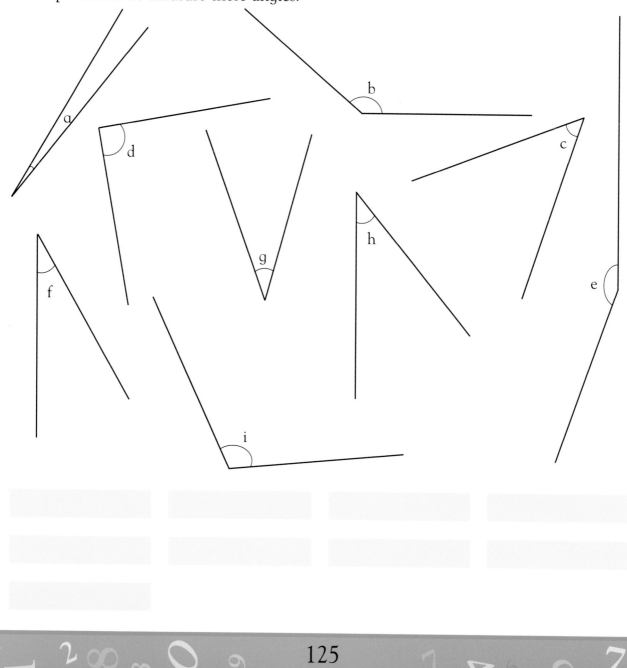

Addition fact families

Circle the number sentence that is in the same fact family.

12 − 5 = 7
5 + 7 = 12   12 − 4 = 8   (7 + 5 = 12)   12 + 12 = 24

10 − 8 = 2
8 + 2 =10   8 − 6 = 2   (2 + 8 = 10)   8 − 2 = 6

Circle the number sentence that is in the same fact family.

7 + 8 = 15
8 + 7 = 15   7 + 5 = 12   15 − 8 = 7   8 − 7 = 1

17 − 6 = 11
11 + 6 = 17   17 − 11 = 6   17 + 6 = 23   5 + 6 = 11

14 − 5 = 9
14 − 9 = 5   9 − 3 = 6   14 + 9 = 23   5 + 9 = 14

9 + 7 = 16
7 + 9 = 16   16 − 9 = 7   16 + 7 = 23   9 − 7 = 2

19 − 9 = 10
19 − 10 = 9   9 + 3 = 12   9 + 10 = 19   18 − 8 = 10

4 + 7 = 11
11 − 4 = 7   11 + 4 = 15   7 + 4 = 11   7 + 7 = 14

Write the fact family for each group of numbers.

5, 6, 11   6, 10, 4   5, 13, 8

Odds and evens

Write the answer in the box.

$3 + 3 =$ 6 $\qquad$ $4 + 6 =$ 10 $\qquad$ $7 + 3 =$ 10 $\qquad$ $2 + 6 =$ 8

Add the even numbers to the even numbers.

$4 + 8 =$ $\qquad$ $12 + 6 =$ $\qquad$ $10 + 6 =$ $\qquad$ $8 + 14 =$

$20 + 14 =$ $\qquad$ $14 + 12 =$ $\qquad$ $16 + 10 =$ $\qquad$ $30 + 20 =$

$14 + 16 =$ $\qquad$ $18 + 6 =$ $\qquad$ $22 + 8 =$ $\qquad$ $20 + 40 =$

What do you notice about each answer? _____

Add the odd numbers to the odd numbers.

$7 + 9 =$ $\qquad$ $5 + 7 =$ $\qquad$ $11 + 5 =$ $\qquad$ $9 + 5 =$

$7 + 7 =$ $\qquad$ $9 + 3 =$ $\qquad$ $15 + 5 =$ $\qquad$ $13 + 7 =$

$11 + 3 =$ $\qquad$ $17 + 9 =$ $\qquad$ $15 + 9 =$ $\qquad$ $13 + 15 =$

What do you notice about each answer? _____

Add the odd numbers to the even numbers.

$3 + 8 =$ $\qquad$ $9 + 12 =$ $\qquad$ $5 + 18 =$ $\qquad$ $7 + 14 =$

$11 + 4 =$ $\qquad$ $13 + 10 =$ $\qquad$ $15 + 6 =$ $\qquad$ $21 + 4 =$

$7 + 20 =$ $\qquad$ $13 + 30 =$ $\qquad$ $11 + 16 =$ $\qquad$ $17 + 6 =$

What do you notice about each answer? _____

Add the even numbers to the odd numbers.

$6 + 7 =$ $\qquad$ $8 + 5 =$ $\qquad$ $10 + 9 =$ $\qquad$ $2 + 17 =$

$10 + 29 =$ $\qquad$ $14 + 3 =$ $\qquad$ $8 + 13 =$ $\qquad$ $12 + 5 =$

$14 + 7 =$ $\qquad$ $8 + 51 =$ $\qquad$ $16 + 9 =$ $\qquad$ $30 + 17 =$

What do you notice about each answer? _____

Word problems

Write the answer in the box.

A number multiplied by 7 equals 35. What is the number?

I divide a number by 10 and the answer is 3. What number did I divide?

I multiply a number by 4 and the answer is 20. What is the number I multiplied?

After dividing a piece of wood into four equal sections, each section is
4 in. long. How long was the piece of wood I started with?

A number multiplied by 6 gives the answer 24. What is the number?

Some money is divided into five equal amounts. Each amount is 10 cents.
How much money was there before it was divided?

I multiply a number by 9 and the result is 45. What number was multiplied?

A number divided by 6 is 3. What number was divided?

Three children share 18 peanuts equally among themselves.
How many peanuts does each child receive?

A number divided by 4 is 8. What is the number?

I multiply a number by 6 and the answer is 30. What is the number?

Four sets of a number equal 16. What is the number?

A number divided by 5 is 5. What is the number?

A child divides a number by 8 and gets 2. What number was divided?

Three groups of a number equal 27. What is the number?

I multiply a number by 10 and the result is 100. What is the number?

Word problems

Write the answer in the box.

A child is given four dimes. How much money does she have altogether? 40¢

Write the answer in the box.

A box contains 6 eggs. How many boxes would I need to buy to have 18 eggs?

A boy is given three bags of candy. There are 20 pieces in each bag. How many pieces of candy does the boy have in total?

Four lifeboats carry a total of 100 people. How many people are in each boat?

A shepherd had 200 sheep but 70 were lost in a snowstorm. How many sheep does the shepherd have left?

Three women win the lottery and share $900 equally among themselves. How much does each woman receive?

A truck contains 50 barrels of oil. It delivers 27 barrels to one garage. How many barrels are left on the truck?

Andrej has a collection of 150 baseball cards. He sells 30 of them to a friend. How many cards does he have left?

When Peter multiplies his apartment number by 3, the result is 75. What is his apartment number?

One photograph costs $1.80. How much will two photographs cost?

A dog buries 20 bones on Monday, 30 bones on Tuesday, and 40 bones on Wednesday. How many bones has the dog buried altogether?

A car trip is supposed to be 70 miles long but the car breaks down half-way. How far has the car gone when it breaks down?

A teacher has 32 children in her class. 13 children are out with the flu. How many children are left in class?

Multiples

Circle the multiples of 3.

| 4 | 7 | (9) | 14 | 20 | (24) |

Circle the multiples of 3.

4	7	10	15	21	30	35	50
2	4	6	8	10	12	14	16
1	3	5	7	9	11	13	15
2	5	8	11	14	17	20	23
5	10	15	20	25	30	35	40
0	3	6	9	12	15	18	21
10	20	30	40	50	60	70	80
5	8	11	14	17	20	23	26
2	7	13	17	21	25	33	60

Circle the multiples of 4.

2	7	11	15	19	23	28	31
2	4	6	8	10	12	14	16
1	3	5	7	9	11	13	15
3	6	9	12	15	18	21	24
4	12	14	18	22	24	28	34
5	10	15	20	25	30	35	40
3	5	12	17	24	26	32	80
1	5	9	13	18	20	60	100
10	20	30	40	50	60	70	80

Factors

Write the factors of each number.

6   1, 2, 3, 6   8   1, 2, 4, 8

Write the factors of each number.

4	10	14
9	3	12
7	15	17
5	20	19
2	24	11
13	30	16

Write the factors of each number.

1	4	16
25	36	49
64	81	100

Do you notice anything about the number of factors each of the numbers has?

_____

Do you know the name for these special numbers? _____

Write the factors of each number.

2	3	5
7	11	13
17	19	23
29	31	37

Do you notice anything about the number of factors each of the numbers has?

_____

Do you know the name for these special numbers? _____

Fractions

Write the answer in the box.

$1\frac{1}{2} + \frac{1}{4} = \boxed{1\frac{3}{4}}$ $2\frac{1}{2} + 3\frac{1}{2} = \boxed{6}$ $1\frac{1}{4} + 2\frac{1}{2} = \boxed{3\frac{3}{4}}$

Write the answer in the box.

$2\frac{1}{4} + 1\frac{1}{4} =$ $1\frac{1}{2} + 1\frac{1}{2} =$ $1\frac{1}{4} + \frac{1}{4} =$

$3\frac{1}{2} + 1 =$ $3\frac{1}{2} + 1\frac{1}{4} =$ $2\frac{1}{4} + 4 =$

$4\frac{1}{2} + 1\frac{1}{4} =$ $2\frac{1}{2} + 1\frac{1}{2} =$ $5 + 1\frac{1}{2} =$

$3\frac{1}{4} + 1\frac{1}{2} =$ $2 + 3\frac{1}{2} =$ $7 + \frac{1}{2} =$

$3 + \frac{1}{4} =$ $4\frac{1}{4} + \frac{1}{4} =$ $5 + 4\frac{1}{2} =$

Write the answer in the box.

$1\frac{1}{3} + 2\frac{1}{3} =$ $3\frac{1}{3} + 4\frac{2}{3} =$ $1\frac{2}{3} + 5 =$

$3\frac{2}{3} + 2 =$ $4\frac{1}{3} + 1\frac{2}{3} =$ $2\frac{2}{3} + 1\frac{2}{3} =$

$1\frac{2}{3} + 1\frac{2}{3} =$ $4\frac{1}{3} + 2\frac{1}{3} =$ $3 + 2\frac{1}{3} =$

$6 + 2\frac{2}{3} =$ $2\frac{1}{3} + 3\frac{2}{3} =$ $3\frac{1}{3} + 1\frac{1}{3} =$

$5\frac{2}{3} + 2\frac{2}{3} =$ $7 + \frac{1}{3} =$ $2\frac{2}{3} + 5\frac{2}{3} =$

Write the answer in the box.

$2\frac{1}{5} + 2\frac{2}{5} =$ $3\frac{1}{5} + 2\frac{3}{5} =$ $1\frac{4}{5} + 6 =$

$3\frac{1}{5} + 3\frac{2}{5} =$ $4 + 2\frac{2}{5} =$ $5\frac{3}{5} + 1\frac{1}{5} =$

$\frac{3}{5} + \frac{3}{5} =$ $3\frac{2}{5} + \frac{4}{5} =$ $3\frac{2}{5} + \frac{2}{5} =$

Fractions and decimals

Write each fraction as a decimal.

$1 \frac{1}{10}$ = 1.1 $1 \frac{2}{10}$ = 1.2 $1 \frac{7}{10}$ = 1.7

Write each decimal as a fraction.

2.5 = $2\frac{1}{2}$ 1.9 = $1\frac{9}{10}$ 3.2 = $3\frac{2}{10}$

Write each fraction as a decimal.

$2 \frac{1}{2}$ $3 \frac{1}{10}$ $4 \frac{3}{10}$ $1 \frac{1}{2}$

$5 \frac{1}{10}$ $2 \frac{3}{10}$ $8 \frac{1}{10}$ $5 \frac{1}{2}$

$7 \frac{8}{10}$ $2 \frac{4}{10}$ $6 \frac{1}{2}$ $8 \frac{1}{2}$

$7 \frac{6}{10}$ $9 \frac{1}{2}$ $6 \frac{7}{10}$ $10 \frac{1}{2}$

Write each decimal as a fraction.

3.2	4.5	1.7	1.2
6.5	2.7	5.2	5.5
7.2	8.5	9.7	10.2
11.5	12.7	13.2	14.5
15.7	16.2	17.5	18.7

Write each fraction as a decimal.

$\frac{1}{2}$ = $\frac{2}{10}$ = $\frac{3}{10}$ =

Write each decimal as a fraction.

0.5 = —   0.2 = —   0.7 = —

Real-life problems

Write the answer in the box.

A number multiplied by 8 is 56.
What is the number?

7

I divide a number by 9 and the result is 6.
What is the number?

54

Write the answer in the box.

A number multiplied by 6 is 42.
What is the number?

I divide a number by 4 and the
result is 7. What is the number?

I divide a number by 8 and the
result is 6. What number did I
begin with?

A number multiplied by itself
gives the answer 25. What is
the number?

I divide a number by 7 and the
result is 7. What number did I
begin with?

A number multiplied by itself
gives the answer 49. What is
the number?

When I multiply a number by 7
I end up with 56. What
number did I begin with?

Seven times a number is 63.
What is the number?

What do I have to multiply 8
by to get the result 72?

Nine times a number is 81.
What is the number?

When 6 is multiplied by a
number the result is 42. What
number was 6 multiplied by?

A number divided by 8 gives
the answer 10. What was the
starting number?

I multiply a number by 9 and
end up with 45. What number
did I multiply?

I multiply a number by 9 and
the result is 81. What number
did I begin with?

Symmetry

The dotted line is a mirror line. Complete each shape.

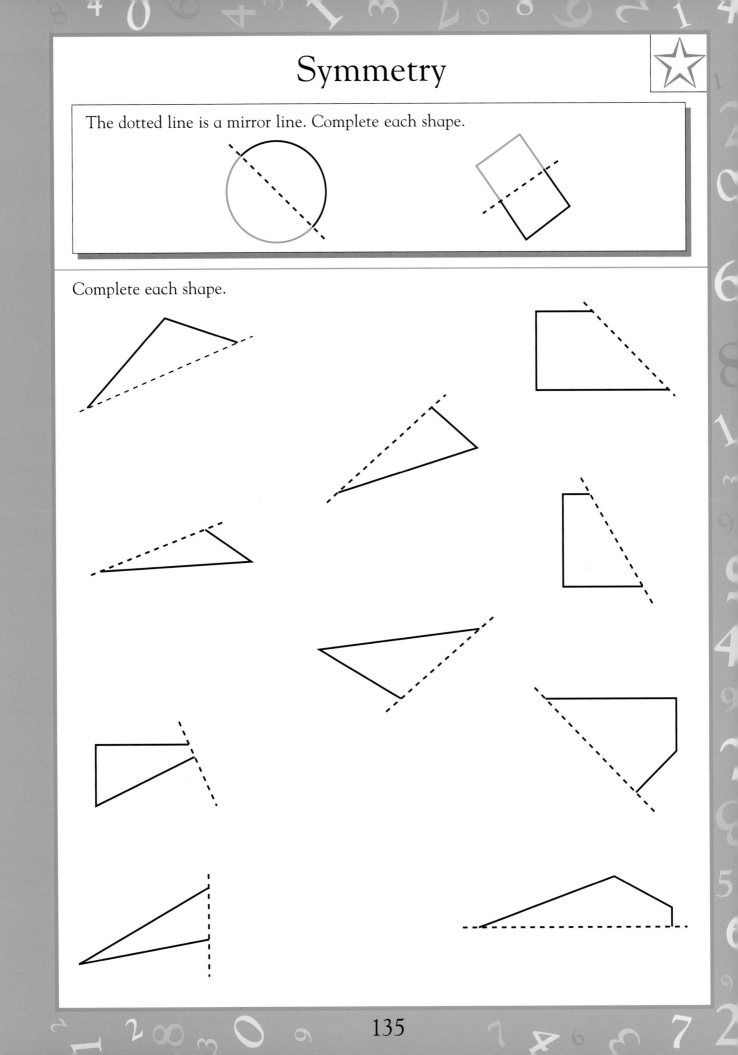

Complete each shape.

Fractions and decimals

Write each fraction as a decimal.

$\frac{1}{2}$ = 0.5 $\frac{1}{10}$ = 0.1

Write each decimal as a fraction.

0.25 = $\frac{1}{4}$ 0.4 = $\frac{4}{10}$

Write each fraction as a decimal.

$\frac{1}{10}$	$\frac{1}{2}$	$\frac{3}{10}$	$\frac{5}{10}$
$\frac{2}{10}$	$\frac{9}{10}$	$\frac{6}{10}$	$\frac{1}{10}$
$\frac{2}{10}$	$\frac{3}{10}$	$\frac{4}{10}$	$\frac{5}{10}$
$\frac{6}{10}$	$\frac{7}{10}$	$\frac{8}{10}$	$\frac{9}{10}$

Write each decimal as a fraction.

0.8	0.5	0.3	0.4
0.25	0.7	0.2	0.75
0.2	0.6	0.5	0.8
0.1	0.4	0.6	0.9

Write the answer in the box.

Which two of the fractions above are the same as 0.5?

Which two of the fractions above are the same as 0.8?

Which two of the fractions above are the same as 0.6?

Which two of the fractions above are the same as 0.2?

Which two of the fractions above are the same as 0.4?

Fractions of shapes

Shade $\frac{3}{5}$ of each shape.

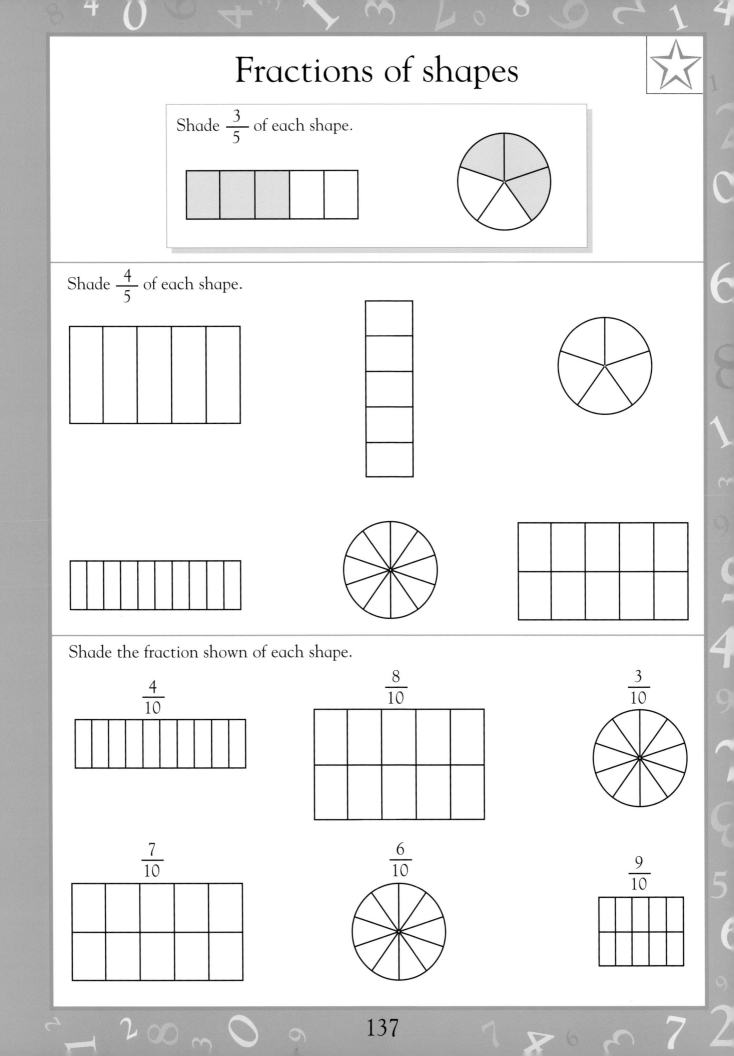

Shade $\frac{4}{5}$ of each shape.

Shade the fraction shown of each shape.

$\frac{4}{10}$

$\frac{8}{10}$

$\frac{3}{10}$

$\frac{7}{10}$

$\frac{6}{10}$

$\frac{9}{10}$

Fractions

Color $\frac{3}{4}$ of each shape.

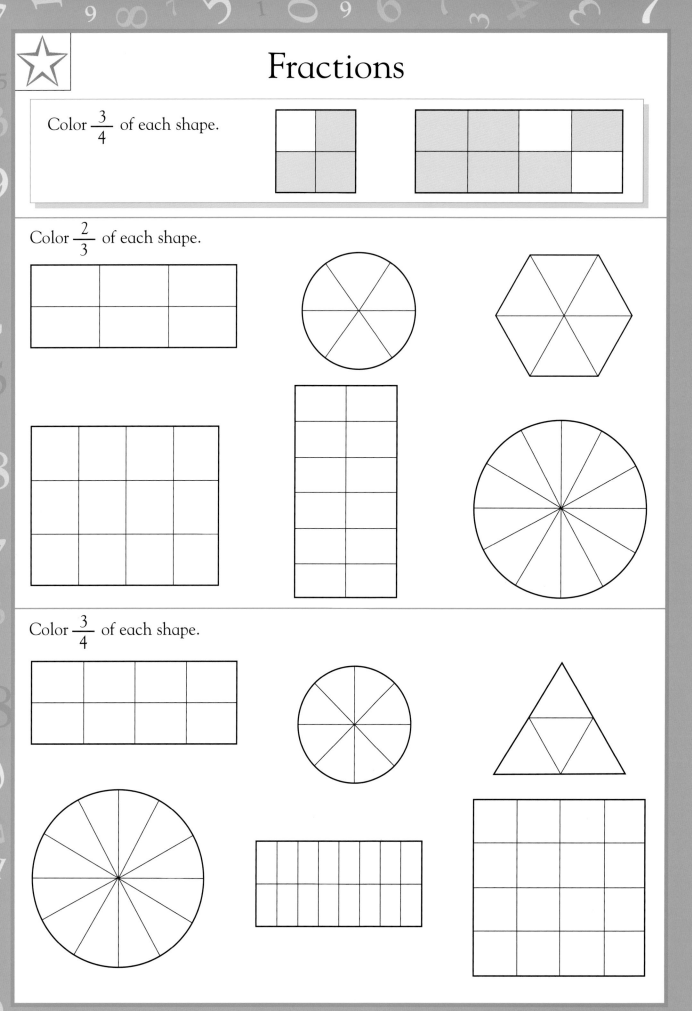

Color $\frac{2}{3}$ of each shape.

Color $\frac{3}{4}$ of each shape.

Reading timetables

	Frostburg	Elmhusrt	Badger Farm	Winchester
Redline Bus	8:00	8:05	8:15	8:25
Blueline tram	8:05	No stop	8:12	8:20
City taxi	8:30	8:35	8:45	8:55
Greenline Trolley	8:07	No stop	No stop	8:15

The timetable shows the times it takes to travel using different transport companies between Frostburg and Winchester.

Write the answer in the box.

How long does Redline take between Frostburg and Winchester?

When does the tram arrive at Badger Farm?

Where does the trolley not stop?

Where is City taxi at 8.35?

Does the tram stop at Elmhurst?

How long does the bus take to travel between Badger Farm and Winchester?

Which is the fastest trip between Frostburg and Winchester?

Which service arrives at five minutes to nine?

How long does City taxi take between Frostburg and Badger Farm?

Where is the tram at twelve minutes past eight?

Averages

Write the average of this row in the box.

4	2	2	2	6	3	2

The average is 3 .

Write the average of each row in the box.

2	3	7	4	2	7	2	5	
7	4	5	4	8	5	3	4	
5	3	5	3	5	2	4	5	
7	5	9	7	2	4	8	6	
4	3	4	3	4	3	4	7	
1	4	2	7	3	8	2	5	
3	2	1	2	2	3	2	1	
8	3	6	3	8	2	8	2	

Write the average of each row in the box.

4	8	6	3	9	6	6	
5	9	2	6	9	1	3	
6	3	8	6	1	5	6	
3	8	6	7	5	9	4	
1	8	3	4	2	6	4	
9	5	8	7	4	7	9	
1	3	2	3	1	2	2	
6	3	7	4	5	8	2	

Multiplying larger numbers by ones

Write the product for each problem.

1 3
529
x 4
2,116

1 3 1
1273
x 5
6,365

Write the product for each problem.

724
x 2
_____

831
x 3
_____

126
x 3
_____

455
x 4
_____

161
x 4
_____

282
x 5
_____

349
x 5
_____

253
x 6
_____

328
x 6
_____

465
x 6
_____

105
x 4
_____

562
x 4
_____

Write the product for each problem.

4,261
x 3
_____

1,582
x 3
_____

3,612
x 4
_____

4,284
x 4
_____

5,907
x 5
_____

1,263
x 5
_____

1,303
x 6
_____

1,467
x 6
_____

6,521
x 6
_____

8,436
x 6
_____

1,599
x 6
_____

3,761
x 6
_____

5,837
x 4
_____

6,394
x 5
_____

8,124
x 6
_____

3,914
x 6
_____

⭐ Multiplying larger numbers by ones

Write the product for each problem.

14	1 7 4
417	2,185
x 7	x 9
2,919	19,665

Write the product for each problem.

419	604	715	327
x 7	x 7	x 8	x 7

425	171	682	246
x 8	x 9	x 8	x 8

436	999	319	581
x 8	x 9	x 9	x 9

Write the product for each problem.

4,331	2,816	1,439	2,617
x 7	x 7	x 8	x 8

3,104	4,022	3,212	2,591
x 8	x 8	x 9	x 9

1,710	3,002	2,468	1,514
x 9	x 8	x 7	x 8

4,624	2,993	3,894	4,361
x 7	x 8	x 8	x 9

Real-life multiplication problems

There are 157 apples in a box.
How many will there be in three boxes?

471 apples

$$\begin{array}{r} \overset{1\ 2}{157} \\ \times \quad 3 \\ \hline 471 \end{array}$$

A stamp album can hold 550 stamps.
How many stamps will 5 albums hold?

A train can take 425 passengers.
How many can it take in four trips?

Mr Jenkins puts $256 a month into the bank.
How much will he have put in after six months?

SAVINGS BANK

A theater can seat 5,524 people. If a play runs for 7 days, what is the maximum number of people who will be able to see it?

A car costs $9,956. How much will it cost a company to buy nine cars for its people?

Installing a new window for a house costs $435. How much will it cost to install 8 windows of the same size?

An airplane flies at a steady speed of 550 mph.
How far will it travel in 7 hours?

Area of rectangles and squares

Find the area of this rectangle

To find the area of a rectangle or square, we multiply length (l) by width (w).

Area = 800 in.²

(w) 25 in.

←(1)→

32 in.

$$\begin{array}{r} \overset{1}{32} \\ \times\,25 \\ \hline {}^{1}160 \\ +640 \\ \hline 800 \text{ in.}^2 \end{array}$$

Find the area of these rectangles and squares.
You may need to do your work on a separate sheet.

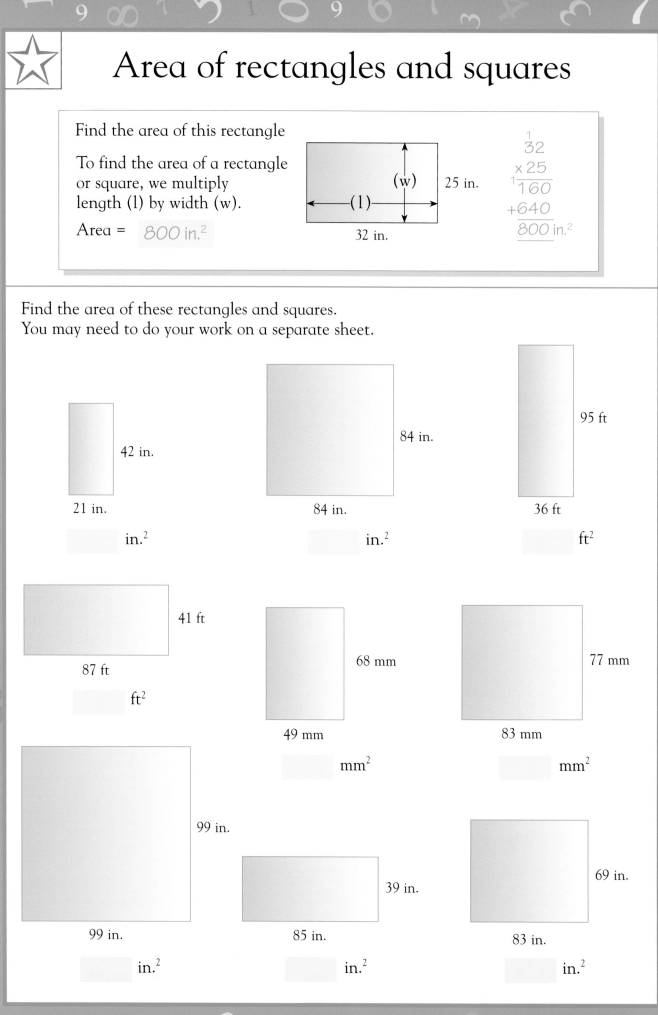

42 in.

21 in.

_____ in.²

84 in.

84 in.

_____ in.²

95 ft

36 ft

_____ ft²

41 ft

87 ft

_____ ft²

68 mm

49 mm

_____ mm²

77 mm

83 mm

_____ mm²

99 in.

99 in.

_____ in.²

39 in.

85 in.

_____ in.²

69 in.

83 in.

_____ in.²

Perimeter of shapes

Find the perimeter of this rectangle.

To find the perimeter of
a rectangle or square, we
add the two lengths and
the two widths together.

12.4 in.

27.3 in.

```
  1 1
 27.3 in.
 27.3 in.
 12.4 in.
+12.4 in.
 79.4 in.
```

79.4 in.

Find the perimeter of these rectangles and squares.

You may need to do your work on a separate sheet.

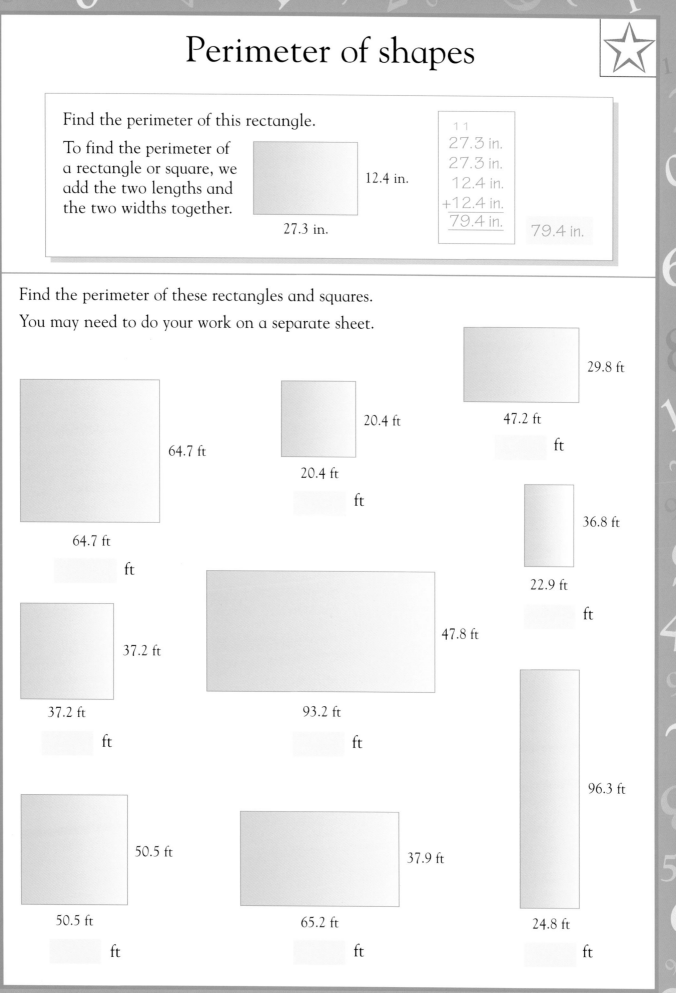

64.7 ft

64.7 ft

_____ ft

20.4 ft

20.4 ft

_____ ft

29.8 ft

47.2 ft

_____ ft

37.2 ft

37.2 ft

_____ ft

47.8 ft

93.2 ft

_____ ft

36.8 ft

22.9 ft

_____ ft

50.5 ft

50.5 ft

_____ ft

37.9 ft

65.2 ft

_____ ft

96.3 ft

24.8 ft

_____ ft

Adding fractions

Work out the answer to the problem.

$$\frac{1}{5} + \frac{3}{5} = \boxed{\frac{4}{5}} \qquad\qquad \frac{4}{9} + \frac{2}{9} = \frac{{}^2\cancel{6}}{\cancel{9}_3} = \boxed{\frac{2}{3}}$$

Remember to reduce to simplest form if you need to.

Work out the answer to each sum. Reduce to simplest form if you need to.

$$\frac{2}{7} + \frac{3}{7} = \frac{}{7} \qquad\qquad \frac{2}{9} + \frac{5}{9} = \frac{}{9} \qquad\qquad \frac{1}{3} + \frac{1}{3} = \frac{}{3}$$

$$\frac{3}{10} + \frac{4}{10} = \frac{}{10} \qquad\qquad \frac{1}{8} + \frac{2}{8} = \frac{}{8} \qquad\qquad \frac{2}{9} + \frac{3}{9} = \frac{}{9}$$

$$\frac{2}{5} + \frac{1}{5} = \underline{} \qquad\qquad \frac{1}{7} + \frac{5}{7} = \underline{} \qquad\qquad \frac{4}{9} + \frac{1}{9} = \frac{}{9}$$

$$\frac{3}{20} + \frac{4}{20} = \underline{} \qquad\qquad \frac{3}{100} + \frac{8}{100} = \underline{} \qquad\qquad \frac{7}{10} + \frac{2}{10} = \underline{}$$

$$\frac{1}{6} + \frac{2}{6} = \underline{} = \underline{} \qquad\qquad \frac{31}{100} + \frac{19}{100} = \underline{} = \underline{} \qquad\qquad \frac{11}{20} + \frac{4}{20} = \underline{} = \underline{}$$

$$\frac{3}{10} + \frac{3}{10} = \underline{} = \underline{} \qquad\qquad \frac{1}{12} + \frac{5}{12} = \underline{} = \underline{} \qquad\qquad \frac{2}{6} + \frac{2}{6} = \underline{} = \underline{}$$

$$\frac{3}{8} + \frac{3}{8} = \underline{} = \underline{} \qquad\qquad \frac{3}{8} + \frac{1}{8} = \underline{} = \underline{} \qquad\qquad \frac{5}{12} + \frac{3}{12} = \underline{} = \underline{}$$

$$\frac{1}{4} + \frac{1}{4} = \underline{} = \underline{} \qquad\qquad \frac{3}{20} + \frac{2}{20} = \underline{} = \underline{} \qquad\qquad \frac{2}{6} + \frac{2}{6} = \underline{} = \underline{}$$

$$\frac{2}{7} + \frac{4}{7} = \underline{} \qquad\qquad \frac{2}{9} + \frac{2}{9} = \underline{} \qquad\qquad \frac{13}{20} + \frac{5}{20} = \underline{} = \underline{}$$

$$\frac{81}{100} + \frac{9}{100} = \underline{} = \underline{} \qquad\qquad \frac{7}{20} + \frac{6}{20} = \underline{} \qquad\qquad \frac{3}{8} + \frac{2}{8} = \underline{}$$

$$\frac{6}{10} + \frac{2}{10} = \underline{} = \underline{} \qquad\qquad \frac{29}{100} + \frac{46}{100} = \underline{} = \underline{} \qquad\qquad \frac{73}{100} + \frac{17}{100} = \underline{} = \underline{}$$

Adding fractions

Write the answer to each problem.

$$\frac{3}{8} + \frac{5}{8} = \frac{8}{8} = 1 \qquad \frac{3}{4} + \frac{3}{4} = \frac{\cancel{6}}{\cancel{4}} = \frac{3}{2} = 1\frac{1}{2}$$

Write the answer to each problem.

$\dfrac{7}{10} + \dfrac{6}{10} = \dfrac{}{10} = 1\dfrac{}{10}$ $\qquad$ $\dfrac{6}{7} + \dfrac{5}{7} = \dfrac{}{7} = 1\dfrac{}{7}$ $\qquad$ $\dfrac{2}{3} + \dfrac{2}{3} = \dfrac{}{3} = 1\dfrac{}{3}$

$\dfrac{5}{10} + \dfrac{6}{10} = \dfrac{}{} = $ $\qquad$ $\dfrac{8}{13} + \dfrac{5}{13} = \dfrac{}{} = $ $\qquad$ $\dfrac{7}{8} + \dfrac{4}{8} = \dfrac{}{} = $

$\dfrac{7}{8} + \dfrac{5}{8} = \dfrac{}{} = \dfrac{}{} = $ $\qquad$ $\dfrac{2}{5} + \dfrac{3}{5} = \dfrac{}{} = $ $\qquad$ $\dfrac{5}{8} + \dfrac{5}{8} = \dfrac{}{} = \dfrac{}{} = $

$\dfrac{10}{20} + \dfrac{15}{20} = \dfrac{}{} = \dfrac{}{} = $ $\qquad$ $\dfrac{2}{3} + \dfrac{1}{3} = \dfrac{}{} = $ $\qquad$ $\dfrac{5}{6} + \dfrac{5}{6} = \dfrac{}{} = \dfrac{}{} = $

$\dfrac{5}{6} + \dfrac{3}{6} = \dfrac{}{} = \dfrac{}{} = $ $\qquad$ $\dfrac{6}{12} + \dfrac{7}{12} = \dfrac{}{} = $ $\qquad$ $\dfrac{8}{10} + \dfrac{6}{10} = \dfrac{}{} = \dfrac{}{} = $

$\dfrac{12}{20} + \dfrac{10}{20} = \dfrac{}{} = \dfrac{}{} = $ $\qquad$ $\dfrac{3}{10} + \dfrac{7}{10} = \dfrac{}{} = $ $\qquad$ $\dfrac{75}{100} + \dfrac{75}{100} = \dfrac{}{} = \dfrac{}{} = $

$\dfrac{10}{20} + \dfrac{16}{20} = \dfrac{}{} = \dfrac{}{} = $ $\qquad$ $\dfrac{4}{5} + \dfrac{4}{5} = \dfrac{}{} = $ $\qquad$ $\dfrac{11}{21} + \dfrac{17}{21} = \dfrac{}{} = \dfrac{}{} = $

Subtracting fractions

Write the answer to each problem.

$$\frac{4}{5} - \frac{2}{5} = \boxed{\frac{2}{5}} \qquad \frac{8}{9} - \frac{5}{9} = \frac{\cancel{3}^{1}}{\cancel{9}_{3}} = \boxed{\frac{1}{3}}$$

Reduce to simplest form if you need to.

Write the answer to each problem. Reduce to simplest form if you need to.

$$\frac{3}{5} - \frac{1}{5} = \frac{}{5} \qquad\qquad \frac{6}{7} - \frac{3}{7} = \frac{}{7} \qquad\qquad \frac{9}{10} - \frac{6}{10} = \frac{}{10}$$

$$\frac{7}{10} - \frac{4}{10} = \underline{} \qquad\qquad \frac{5}{9} - \frac{4}{9} = \underline{} \qquad\qquad \frac{2}{3} - \frac{1}{3} = \underline{}$$

$$\frac{7}{8} - \frac{3}{8} = \underline{} = \underline{} \qquad\qquad \frac{14}{20} - \frac{10}{20} = \underline{} = \underline{} \qquad\qquad \frac{5}{6} - \frac{1}{6} = \underline{} = \underline{}$$

$$\frac{11}{12} - \frac{5}{12} = \underline{} = \underline{} \qquad\qquad \frac{17}{20} - \frac{12}{20} = \underline{} = \underline{} \qquad\qquad \frac{9}{12} - \frac{3}{12} = \underline{} = \underline{}$$

$$\frac{8}{10} - \frac{6}{10} = \underline{} = \underline{} \qquad\qquad \frac{12}{12} - \frac{2}{12} = \underline{} = \underline{} \qquad\qquad \frac{9}{10} - \frac{3}{10} = \underline{} = \underline{}$$

$$\frac{8}{9} - \frac{2}{9} = \underline{} = \underline{} \qquad\qquad \frac{7}{8} - \frac{1}{8} = \underline{} = \underline{} \qquad\qquad \frac{9}{12} - \frac{3}{12} = \underline{} = \underline{}$$

$$\frac{3}{4} - \frac{2}{4} = \underline{} \qquad\qquad \frac{6}{8} - \frac{3}{8} = \underline{} \qquad\qquad \frac{18}{20} - \frac{8}{20} = \underline{} = \underline{}$$

$$\frac{4}{6} - \frac{2}{6} = \underline{} = \underline{} \qquad\qquad \frac{5}{12} - \frac{4}{12} = \underline{} \qquad\qquad \frac{3}{8} - \frac{2}{8} = \underline{}$$

$$\frac{5}{7} - \frac{1}{7} = \underline{} \qquad\qquad \frac{5}{16} - \frac{1}{16} = \underline{} = \underline{} \qquad\qquad \frac{90}{100} - \frac{80}{100} = \underline{} = \underline{}$$

Showing decimals

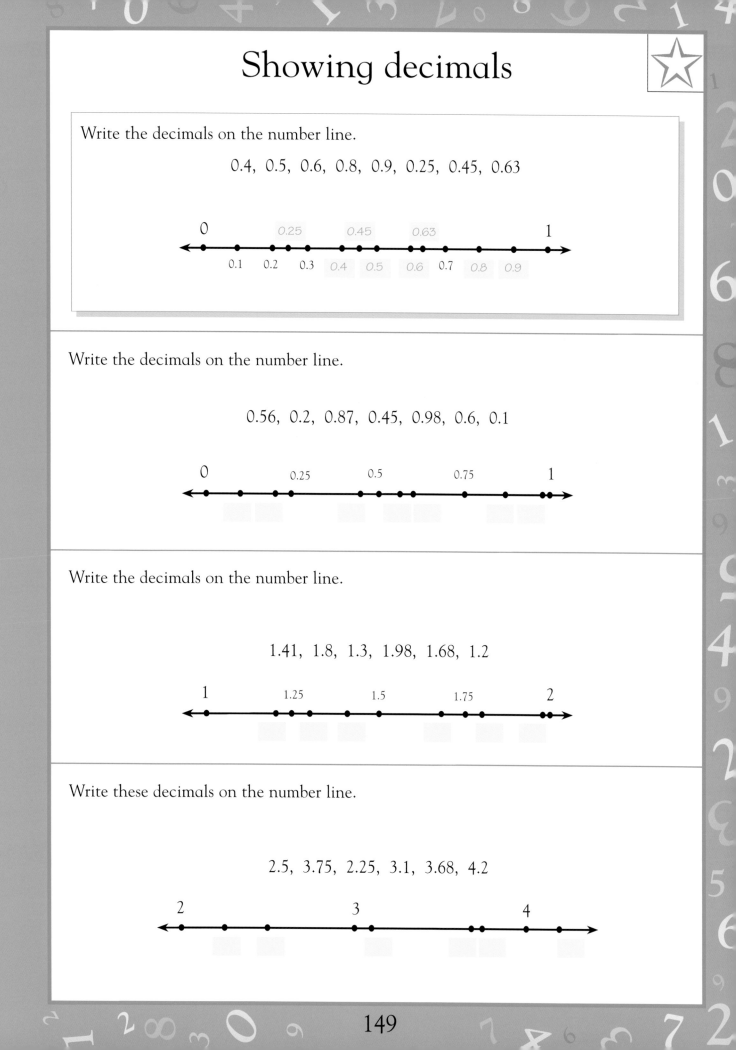

Write the decimals on the number line.

0.4, 0.5, 0.6, 0.8, 0.9, 0.25, 0.45, 0.63

0   0.25   0.45   0.63   1

0.1   0.2   0.3   0.4   0.5   0.6   0.7   0.8   0.9

Write the decimals on the number line.

0.56, 0.2, 0.87, 0.45, 0.98, 0.6, 0.1

0   0.25   0.5   0.75   1

Write the decimals on the number line.

1.41, 1.8, 1.3, 1.98, 1.68, 1.2

1   1.25   1.5   1.75   2

Write these decimals on the number line.

2.5, 3.75, 2.25, 3.1, 3.68, 4.2

2   3   4

Conversions: length

Units of length	
12 inches	1 foot
3 feet	1 yard
5,280 feet	1 mile
1,760 yards	1 mile

This conversion table shows how to convert inches, feet, yards, and miles.

Brian's rope is 60 inches long. How many feet long is it?

$60 \div 12 = 5$ 5 feet long

Neilika's rope is 3 yards long. How many inches long is it?

$3 \times 3 = 9$
$9 \times 12 = 108$ 9 feet long
108 inches long

Convert each measurement to feet.

36 inches	12 inches	48 inches	72 inches

Convert each measurement to yards.

6 feet	12 feet	27 feet	36 feet

Convert each measurement to inches.

4 feet	12 feet	8 feet	5 feet

Convert each measurement to feet.

6 yards	2 yards	7 yards	5 yards

Convert each measurement.

4 yards	5 yards	4 miles	1 mile
inches	inches	feet	inches

15,840 feet	31,680 feet	1,760 yards	3,520 yards
miles	miles	mile	miles

Conversions: capacity

Units of capacity	
8 fluid ounces	1 cup
2 cups	1 pint
2 pints	1 quart
4 quarts	1 gallon

This conversion table shows how to convert ounces, cups pints, quarts, and gallons.

Katya's thermos holds 8 pints. How many cups does it hold?

8 x 2 = 16   16 cups

Hannah's thermos holds 6 cups. How many pints does it hold?

6 ÷ 2 = 3   3 pints

Convert each measurement to cups.

32 fluid ounces	16 fluid ounces	96 fluid ounces	80 fluid ounces

Convert each measurement to pints.

6 cups	12 cups	36 cups	50 cups

4 quarts	12 quarts	30 quarts	6 quarts

Convert each measurement to gallons.

16 quarts	32 quarts	100 quarts	20 quarts

Convert each measurement.

3 gallons	5 quarts	36 cups	72 pints
pints	cups	quarts	gallons

1 quart	240 fluid ounces	7 quarts	11 gallons
fluid ounces	pints	cups	pints

Rounding money

Round to the nearest dollar.

$3.95 rounds to $4

$2.25 rounds to $2

Round to the nearest ten dollars.

$15.50 rounds to $20

$14.40 rounds to $10

Round to the nearest dollar.

$2.60 rounds to

$9.55 rounds to

$7.15 rounds to

$8.49 rounds to

$1.75 rounds to

$6.95 rounds to

$3.39 rounds to

$4.30 rounds to

$2.53 rounds to

Round to the nearest ten dollars.

$37.34 rounds to

$71.99 rounds to

$55.31 rounds to

$21.75 rounds to

$66.89 rounds to

$12.79 rounds to

$85.03 rounds to

$52.99 rounds to

$15.00 rounds to

Round to the nearest hundred dollars.

$307.12 rounds to

$860.55 rounds to

$739.10 rounds to

$175.50 rounds to

$417.13 rounds to

$249.66 rounds to

$115.99 rounds to

$650.15 rounds to

$367.50 rounds to

Estimating sums of money

Round to the leading digit. Estimate the sum.

$$
\begin{array}{r}
\$3.26 \rightarrow \quad \$3 \\
+ \$4.82 \rightarrow + \$5 \\
\hline
\text{is about} \quad \$8
\end{array}
\qquad
\begin{array}{r}
\$68.53 \rightarrow \quad \$70 \\
+ \$34.60 \rightarrow + \$30 \\
\hline
\text{is about} \quad \$100
\end{array}
$$

Round to the leading digit. Estimate the sum.

$$
\begin{array}{r}
\$52.61 \rightarrow \\
+ \$27.95 \rightarrow \underline{\qquad} \\
\hline
\text{is about} \quad \underline{\qquad}
\end{array}
\qquad
\begin{array}{r}
\$19.20 \rightarrow \\
+ \$22.13 \rightarrow \underline{\qquad} \\
\hline
\text{is about} \quad \underline{\qquad}
\end{array}
\qquad
\begin{array}{r}
\$70.75 \rightarrow \\
+ \$12.49 \rightarrow \underline{\qquad} \\
\hline
\text{is about} \quad \underline{\qquad}
\end{array}
$$

$$
\begin{array}{r}
\$701.34 \rightarrow \\
+ \$100.80 \rightarrow \underline{\qquad} \\
\hline
\text{is about} \quad \underline{\qquad}
\end{array}
\qquad
\begin{array}{r}
\$339.50 \rightarrow \\
+ \$422.13 \rightarrow \underline{\qquad} \\
\hline
\text{is about} \quad \underline{\qquad}
\end{array}
\qquad
\begin{array}{r}
\$160.07 \rightarrow \\
+ \$230.89 \rightarrow \underline{\qquad} \\
\hline
\text{is about} \quad \underline{\qquad}
\end{array}
$$

$$
\begin{array}{r}
\$25.61 \rightarrow \\
+ \$72.51 \rightarrow \underline{\qquad} \\
\hline
\text{is about} \quad \underline{\qquad}
\end{array}
\qquad
\begin{array}{r}
\$61.39 \rightarrow \\
+ \$19.50 \rightarrow \underline{\qquad} \\
\hline
\text{is about} \quad \underline{\qquad}
\end{array}
\qquad
\begin{array}{r}
\$18.32 \rightarrow \\
+ \$13.90 \rightarrow \underline{\qquad} \\
\hline
\text{is about} \quad \underline{\qquad}
\end{array}
$$

$$
\begin{array}{r}
\$587.35 \rightarrow \\
+ 251.89 \rightarrow \underline{\qquad} \\
\hline
\text{is about} \quad \underline{\qquad}
\end{array}
\qquad
\begin{array}{r}
\$109.98 \rightarrow \\
+ \$210.09 \rightarrow \underline{\qquad} \\
\hline
\text{is about} \quad \underline{\qquad}
\end{array}
\qquad
\begin{array}{r}
\$470.02 \rightarrow \\
+ \$203.17 \rightarrow \underline{\qquad} \\
\hline
\text{is about} \quad \underline{\qquad}
\end{array}
$$

Round to the leading digit. Estimate the sum.

$\$75.95 + \$17.95 \rightarrow$ \qquad\qquad $\$41.67 + \$20.35 \rightarrow$

$\$49.19 + \$38.70 \rightarrow$ \qquad\qquad $\$784.65 + \$101.05 \rightarrow$

$\$516.50 + \$290.69 \rightarrow$ \qquad\qquad $\$58.78 + \$33.25 \rightarrow$

$\$82.90 + \$11.79 \rightarrow$ \qquad\qquad $\$90.09 + \$14.50 \rightarrow$

Estimating differences of money

Round the numbers to the leading digit. Estimate the differences.

$8.75 → $9
− $5.10 → −$5
is about $4

$61.47 → $60
+ $35.64 → −$40
is about $20

Round the numbers to the leading digit. Estimate the differences.

$17.90 →
− $12.30 → _____
is about _____

$6.40 →
− $3.75 → _____
is about _____

$87.45 →
− $54.99 → _____
is about _____

$34.90 →
− $12.60 → _____
is about _____

$8.68 →
− $4.39 → _____
is about _____

$363.24 →
− $127.66 → _____
is about _____

$78.75 →
+ $24.99 → _____
is about _____

$64.21 →
− $28.56 → _____
is about _____

$723.34 →
− $487.12 → _____
is about _____

Round the numbers to the leading digit. Estimate the differences.

$8.12 − $1.35

→   =

$49.63 − $27.85

→   =

$7.50 − $3.15

→   =

$85.15 − $42.99

→   =

$5.85 − $4.75

→   =

$634.60 − $267.25

→   =

$37.35 − $16.99

→   =

$842.17 − $169.54

→   =

$56.95 − $20.58

→   =

$628.37 − $252.11

→   =

Estimating sums and differences

Round the numbers to the leading digit. Estimate the sum or difference.

$$\begin{array}{r} 3{,}576 \rightarrow \;\;4{,}000 \\ + \;1{,}307 \rightarrow +1{,}000 \\ \hline \text{is about} \quad 5{,}000 \end{array}$$

$$\begin{array}{r} 198{,}248 \rightarrow \;\;200{,}000 \\ - \;116{,}431 \rightarrow -100{,}000 \\ \hline \text{is about} \quad 100{,}000 \end{array}$$

Round the numbers to the leading digit. Estimate the sum or difference.

$$\begin{array}{r} 685 \rightarrow \\ + \;489 \rightarrow \\ \hline \text{is about} \end{array}$$

$$\begin{array}{r} 21{,}481 \rightarrow \\ - \;12{,}500 \rightarrow \\ \hline \text{is about} \end{array}$$

$$\begin{array}{r} 7{,}834 \rightarrow \\ + \;3{,}106 \rightarrow \\ \hline \text{is about} \end{array}$$

$$\begin{array}{r} 682{,}778 \rightarrow \\ + \;130{,}001 \rightarrow \\ \hline \text{is about} \end{array}$$

$$\begin{array}{r} 58{,}499 \rightarrow \\ - \;22{,}135 \rightarrow \\ \hline \text{is about} \end{array}$$

$$\begin{array}{r} 902{,}276 \rightarrow \\ - \;615{,}999 \rightarrow \\ \hline \text{is about} \end{array}$$

$$\begin{array}{r} 46{,}801 \rightarrow \\ + \;34{,}700 \rightarrow \\ \hline \text{is about} \end{array}$$

$$\begin{array}{r} 9{,}734 \rightarrow \\ - \;8{,}306 \rightarrow \\ \hline \text{is about} \end{array}$$

$$\begin{array}{r} 65{,}606 \rightarrow \\ + \;85{,}943 \rightarrow \\ \hline \text{is about} \end{array}$$

$$\begin{array}{r} 5{,}218 \rightarrow \\ - \;3{,}673 \rightarrow \\ \hline \text{is about} \end{array}$$

$$\begin{array}{r} 745 \rightarrow \\ + \;451 \rightarrow \\ \hline \text{is about} \end{array}$$

$$\begin{array}{r} 337{,}297 \rightarrow \\ - \;168{,}931 \rightarrow \\ \hline \text{is about} \end{array}$$

Write < or > for each problem.

329 + 495   800   11,569 – 6,146   6,000

563 – 317   300   8,193 – 6,668   1,000

41,924 – 12,445   50,000   634,577 + 192,556   800,000

18,885 + 12,691   30,000   713,096 – 321,667   400,000

Conversion tables

Draw a table to convert dollars to cents.

$	cents
1	100
2	200
3	300

Complete the conversion chart below.

Weeks	Days
1	7
2	
	28
10	70

If there are 60 minutes in 1 hour, make a conversion chart for up to 10 hours.

Hours	Minutes

Answer Section with Parents' Notes
Grade 4 Workbook

This section provides answers to all the activities in the book. These pages will enable you to mark your children's work, or they can be used by your children if they prefer to do their own marking.

The notes for each page help to explain common errors and problems and, where appropriate, indicate the kind of practice needed to ensure that your children understand where and how they have made errors.

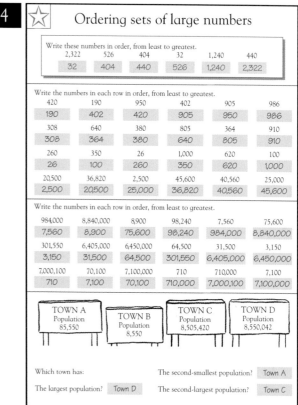

☆ **Reading and writing numbers**

264,346 in words is	Two hundred sixty-four thousand, three hundred forty-six
One million, three hundred twelve thousand, five hundred two is	1,312,502

Write each of these numbers in words.

326,208	Three hundred twenty-six thousand, two hundred eight
704,543	Seven hundred four thousand, five hundred forty-three
240,701	Two hundred forty thousand, seven hundred one
278,520	Two hundred seventy-eight thousand, five hundred twenty

Write each of these in numbers.

Five hundred seventeen thousand, forty-two	517,042
Six hundred ninety-four thousand, seven hundred eleven	694,711
Eight hundred nine thousand, two hundred three	809,203
Nine hundred thousand, four hundred four	900,404

Write each of these numbers in words.

9,307,012	Nine million, three hundred seven thousand, twelve
5,042,390	Five million, forty-two thousand, three hundred ninety
9,908,434	Nine million, nine hundred eight thousand, four hundred thirty-four
8,400,642	Eight million, four hundred thousand, six hundred forty-two

Write each of these in numbers.

Eight million, two hundred fifty-one	8,000,251
Two million, forty thousand, four hundred four	2,040,404
Seven million, three hundred two thousand, one hundred one	7,302,101
Two million, five hundred forty-one thousand, five	2,541,005

Children may use zeros incorrectly in numbers. In word form, zeros are omitted, but children should take care to include them when writing numbers in standard form.

3

Multiplying and dividing by 10 ☆

Write the answer in the box.
26 x 10 = 260
40 ÷ 10 = 4

Write the answer in the box.

76 x 10 = 760	43 x 10 = 430	93 x 10 = 930
66 x 10 = 660	13 x 10 = 130	47 x 10 = 470
147 x 10 = 1,470	936 x 10 = 9,360	284 x 10 = 2,840
364 x 10 = 3,640	821 x 10 = 8,210	473 x 10 = 4,730

Write the answer in the box.

30 ÷ 10 = 3	20 ÷ 10 = 2	70 ÷ 10 = 7
60 ÷ 10 = 6	50 ÷ 10 = 5	580 ÷ 10 = 58
310 ÷ 10 = 31	270 ÷ 10 = 27	100 ÷ 10 = 10
540 ÷ 10 = 54	890 ÷ 10 = 89	710 ÷ 10 = 71

Write the number that has been multiplied by 10.

37 x 10 = 370	64 x 10 = 640	74 x 10 = 740
81 x 10 = 810	10 x 10 = 100	83 x 10 = 830
714 x 10 = 7,140	307 x 10 = 3,070	529 x 10 = 5,290
264 x 10 = 2,640	829 x 10 = 8,290	648 x 10 = 6,480

Write the number that has been divided by 10.

30 ÷ 10 = 3	20 ÷ 10 = 2	90 ÷ 10 = 9
420 ÷ 10 = 42	930 ÷ 10 = 93	740 ÷ 10 = 74
570 ÷ 10 = 57	380 ÷ 10 = 38	860 ÷ 10 = 86

Children should realize that multiplying a whole number by 10 means writing a zero at the end of it. To divide a multiple of 10 by 10, simply take the final zero off the number. The two final sections can be solved by using the inverse operation.

☆ **Ordering sets of large numbers**

Write these numbers in order, from least to greatest.

2,322	526	404	32	1,240	440
32	404	440	526	1,240	2,322

Write the numbers in each row in order, from least to greatest.

420	190	950	402	905	986
190	402	420	905	950	986
308	640	380	805	364	910
308	364	380	640	805	910
260	350	26	1,000	620	100
26	100	260	350	620	1,000
20,500	36,820	2,500	45,600	40,560	25,000
2,500	20,500	25,000	36,820	40,560	45,600

Write the numbers in each row in order, from least to greatest.

984,000	8,840,000	8,900	98,240	7,560	75,600
7,560	8,900	75,600	98,240	984,000	8,840,000
301,550	6,405,000	6,450,000	64,500	31,500	3,150
3,150	31,500	64,500	301,550	6,405,000	6,450,000
7,000,100	70,100	7,100,000	710	710,000	7,100
710	7,100	70,100	710,000	7,000,100	7,100,000

TOWN A
Population
85,550

TOWN B
Population
8,550

TOWN C
Population
8,505,420

TOWN D
Population
8,550,042

Which town has:		The second-smallest population?	Town A
The largest population?	Town D	The second-largest population?	Town C

Some children may need help to identify the value of the significant digit of each number in a set. If the numbers are close in value, it will be necessary to compare the digits to the right of the significant digit.

Rounding numbers

Round each number.
36 to the nearest ten	40
124 to the nearest hundred	100
4,360 to the nearest thousand	4,000

Remember: If a number is halfway between, round it up.

Round each number to the nearest ten.

24	20	91	90	55	60	73	70
57	60	68	70	49	50	35	40
82	80	37	40	22	20	52	50
46	50	26	30	85	90	99	100
43	40	51	50	78	80	29	30

Round each number to the nearest hundred.

386	400	224	200	825	800	460	500
539	500	429	400	378	400	937	900
772	800	255	300	549	500	612	600
116	100	750	800	618	600	990	1,000
940	900	843	800	172	200	868	900

Round each number to the nearest thousand.

3,240	3,000	2,500	3,000	9,940	10,000	1,051	1,000
8,945	9,000	5,050	5,000	5,530	6,000	4,850	5,000
6,200	6,000	7,250	7,000	8,499	8,000	8,450	8,000
12,501	13,000	8,762	9,000	6,500	7,000	3,292	3,000
1,499	1,000	14,836	15,000	10,650	11,000	11,241	11,000

Children may have difficulty with numbers that have final digits of 5 or greater—for example, they may round 429 to 500 rather than 400. Make sure children understand which digit determines how to round the number.

Identifying patterns

Continue each pattern.

Steps of 9:	5	14	23	32	41	50
Steps of 14:	20	34	48	62	76	90

Continue each pattern.

21	38	55	72	89	106	123	140
13	37	61	85	109	133	157	181
7	25	43	61	79	97	115	133
32	48	64	80	96	112	128	144
12	31	50	69	88	107	126	145
32	54	76	98	120	142	164	186
24	64	104	144	184	224	264	304
4	34	64	94	124	154	184	214
36	126	216	306	396	486	576	666
12	72	132	192	252	312	372	432
25	45	65	85	105	125	145	165
22	72	122	172	222	272	322	372
25	100	175	250	325	400	475	550
60	165	270	375	480	585	690	795
8	107	206	305	404	503	602	701
10	61	112	163	214	265	316	367
26	127	228	329	430	531	632	733
48	100	152	204	256	308	360	412

Children should determine what number to add to the first number to make the second number, and double-check that adding the same number turns the second number into the third. They can then repeat the operation to continue the pattern.

Recognizing multiples of 6, 7, and 8

Circle the multiples of 6.

8 (12) 15 (18) 20 (24)

Circle the multiples of 6.

8	22	14	(18)	(36)	40
16	38	44	25	(30)	(60)
(6)	21	19	(54)	56	(24)
(12)	(48)	10	20	35	26
(42)	39	23	28	(36)	32

Circle the multiples of 7.

(7)	17	24	59	(42)	55
15	20	(21)	46	12	(70)
(14)	27	69	36	47	(49)
65	19	57	(28)	38	(63)
33	34	(35)	37	60	(56)

Circle the multiples of 8.

(40)	26	15	25	38	(56)
26	(8)	73	41	(64)	12
75	58	62	(24)	31	(72)
12	(80)	(32)	46	38	78
(16)	42	66	28	(48)	68

Circle the number that is a multiple of 6 and 7.

18 54 (42) 21 28 63

Circle the numbers that are multiples of 6 and 8.

16 (24) 36 (48) 54 42

Circle the number that is a multiple of 7 and 8.

24 32 40 28 42 (56)

Success on this page will basically depend on a knowledge of multiplication tables. Where children experience difficulty, multiplication table practice should be encouraged.

Factors of numbers from 1 to 30

The factors of 10 are 1 2 5 10

Circle the factors of 4. (1) (2) 3 (4)

Write all the factors of each number.

The factors of 26 are	1, 2, 13, 26
The factors of 30 are	1, 2, 3, 5, 6, 10, 15, 30
The factors of 9 are	1, 3, 9
The factors of 12 are	1, 2, 3, 4, 6, 12
The factors of 15 are	1, 3, 5, 15
The factors of 22 are	1, 2, 11, 22
The factors of 20 are	1, 2, 4, 5, 10, 20
The factors of 21 are	1, 3, 7, 21
The factors of 24 are	1, 2, 3, 4, 6, 8, 12, 24

Circle all the factors of each number.

Which numbers are factors of 14? (1) (2) 3 5 (7) 9 12 (14)
Which numbers are factors of 13? (1) 2 3 4 5 6 7 8 9 10 11 (13)
Which numbers are factors of 7? (1) 2 3 4 5 6 (7)
Which numbers are factors of 11? (1) 2 3 4 5 6 7 8 9 10 (11)
Which numbers are factors of 6? (1)(2)(3) 4 5 (6)
Which numbers are factors of 8? (1)(2) 3 (4) 5 6 7 (8)
Which numbers are factors of 17? (1) 2 5 7 12 14 16 (17)
Which numbers are factors of 18? (1)(2)(3) 4 5 (6) 8 (9) 10 12 (18)

Some numbers only have factors of 1 and themselves. They are called prime numbers. Write down all the prime numbers that are less than 30 in the box.

2, 3, 5, 7, 11, 13, 17, 19, 23, 29

Encourage a systematic approach such as starting at 1 and working toward the number that is half of the number in question. Children often forget that 1 and the number itself are factors. You may need to point out that 1 is not a prime number.

Recognizing equivalent fractions ☆

Make each pair of fractions equal by writing a number in the box.

$\frac{1}{2} = \frac{2}{4}$ $\frac{1}{3} = \frac{2}{6}$

Make each pair of fractions equal by writing a number in the box.

$\frac{1}{2} = \frac{5}{10}$	$\frac{3}{4} = \frac{6}{8}$	$\frac{1}{3} = \frac{3}{9}$
$\frac{2}{3} = \frac{8}{12}$	$\frac{6}{12} = \frac{3}{6}$	$\frac{4}{8} = \frac{1}{2}$
$\frac{1}{5} = \frac{2}{10}$	$\frac{4}{12} = \frac{2}{6}$	$\frac{3}{5} = \frac{6}{10}$
$\frac{1}{4} = \frac{2}{8}$	$\frac{6}{18} = \frac{1}{3}$	$\frac{3}{12} = \frac{1}{4}$
$\frac{3}{9} = \frac{1}{3}$	$\frac{4}{10} = \frac{2}{5}$	$\frac{3}{4} = \frac{9}{12}$
$\frac{4}{16} = \frac{1}{4}$	$\frac{15}{20} = \frac{3}{4}$	$\frac{6}{12} = \frac{1}{2}$
$\frac{3}{5} = \frac{6}{10}$	$\frac{3}{6} = \frac{1}{2}$	$\frac{9}{12} = \frac{3}{4}$

Make each row of fractions equal by writing a number in each box.

$\frac{1}{2} = \frac{2}{4} = \frac{3}{6} = \frac{4}{8} = \frac{5}{10} = \frac{6}{12}$

$\frac{1}{4} = \frac{2}{8} = \frac{3}{12} = \frac{4}{16} = \frac{5}{20} = \frac{6}{24}$

$\frac{3}{4} = \frac{6}{8} = \frac{9}{12} = \frac{12}{16} = \frac{15}{20} = \frac{18}{24}$

$\frac{1}{3} = \frac{2}{6} = \frac{3}{9} = \frac{4}{12} = \frac{5}{15} = \frac{12}{36}$

$\frac{1}{5} = \frac{2}{10} = \frac{3}{15} = \frac{4}{20} = \frac{5}{25} = \frac{6}{30}$

$\frac{2}{3} = \frac{4}{6} = \frac{6}{9} = \frac{8}{12} = \frac{10}{15} = \frac{14}{21}$

If children have problems with this page, point out that fractions remain the same as long as you multiply the numerator and denominator by the same number, or divide the numerator and denominator by the same number.

10

☆ Ordering sets of numbers

Write the numbers in order, from least to greatest.

$2 \quad 1\frac{1}{2} \quad \frac{1}{2} \quad \frac{1}{4} \quad 1\frac{3}{4}$

$\boxed{\frac{1}{4}} \quad \boxed{\frac{1}{2}} \quad \boxed{1\frac{1}{2}} \quad \boxed{1\frac{3}{4}} \quad \boxed{2}$

Write each row of numbers in order, from least to greatest.

4	$2\frac{1}{2}$	$1\frac{3}{4}$	$1\frac{1}{4}$	$3\frac{1}{2}$	$1\frac{1}{4}$	$1\frac{3}{4}$	$2\frac{1}{2}$	$3\frac{1}{2}$	4
2	$1\frac{1}{2}$	1	$2\frac{1}{4}$	3	1	$1\frac{1}{2}$	2	$2\frac{1}{4}$	3
2	$1\frac{1}{4}$	$3\frac{1}{2}$	$1\frac{1}{2}$	$2\frac{1}{2}$	$1\frac{1}{4}$	$1\frac{1}{2}$	2	$2\frac{1}{2}$	$3\frac{1}{2}$
$7\frac{1}{2}$	$3\frac{1}{4}$	$1\frac{1}{2}$	$1\frac{1}{4}$	$2\frac{3}{4}$	$1\frac{1}{4}$	$1\frac{1}{2}$	$2\frac{3}{4}$	$3\frac{1}{4}$	$7\frac{1}{2}$
$4\frac{1}{4}$	$3\frac{1}{2}$	$2\frac{3}{4}$	$2\frac{1}{2}$	$3\frac{1}{4}$	$2\frac{1}{2}$	$2\frac{3}{4}$	$3\frac{1}{4}$	$3\frac{1}{2}$	$4\frac{1}{4}$
$3\frac{3}{4}$	$3\frac{1}{3}$	$4\frac{1}{4}$	$3\frac{2}{3}$	$3\frac{1}{2}$	$3\frac{1}{3}$	$3\frac{1}{2}$	$3\frac{2}{3}$	$3\frac{3}{4}$	$4\frac{1}{4}$
$4\frac{2}{3}$	$4\frac{1}{2}$	$4\frac{3}{4}$	$4\frac{1}{3}$	$5\frac{1}{4}$	$4\frac{1}{3}$	$4\frac{1}{2}$	$4\frac{2}{3}$	$4\frac{3}{4}$	$5\frac{1}{4}$
$7\frac{1}{2}$	$6\frac{2}{3}$	$7\frac{3}{4}$	$7\frac{1}{4}$	$6\frac{1}{2}$	$6\frac{1}{2}$	$6\frac{2}{3}$	$7\frac{1}{4}$	$7\frac{1}{2}$	$7\frac{3}{4}$
$14\frac{1}{2}$	$15\frac{3}{4}$	$15\frac{1}{2}$	$14\frac{3}{4}$	$13\frac{3}{4}$	$13\frac{3}{4}$	$14\frac{1}{2}$	$14\frac{3}{4}$	$15\frac{1}{2}$	$15\frac{3}{4}$
$7\frac{1}{3}$	$8\frac{1}{2}$	$7\frac{3}{4}$	$8\frac{1}{5}$	$7\frac{2}{3}$	$7\frac{1}{3}$	$7\frac{2}{3}$	$7\frac{3}{4}$	$8\frac{1}{5}$	$8\frac{1}{2}$

The most likely area of difficulty will be ordering fractions such as $\frac{3}{4}$ and $\frac{2}{3}$. If children experience difficulty, refer to the previous page or use two index cards, cut into quarters and into thirds, to allow comparison.

Rounding decimals ☆

Round each decimal to the nearest whole number.

3.4 → 3

5.7 → 6

4.5 → 5

If the whole number has 5 after it, round it to the whole number above.

Round each decimal to the nearest whole number.

6.2	6	2.5	3	1.5	2	3.8	4
5.5	6	2.8	3	3.2	3	8.5	9
5.4	5	7.9	8	3.7	4	2.3	2
1.1	1	8.6	9	8.3	8	9.2	9
4.7	5	6.3	6	7.3	7	8.7	9

Round each decimal to the nearest whole number.

14.4	14	42.3	42	74.1	74	59.7	60
29.9	30	32.6	33	63.5	64	96.4	96
18.2	18	37.5	38	39.6	40	76.3	76
40.1	40	28.7	29	26.9	27	12.5	13
29.5	30	38.5	39	87.2	87	41.6	42

Round each decimal to the nearest whole number.

137.6	138	423.5	424	426.2	426	111.8	112
641.6	642	333.5	334	805.2	805	246.8	247
119.5	120	799.6	800	562.3	562	410.2	410
682.4	682	759.6	760	531.5	532	829.9	830
743.4	743	831.1	831	276.7	277	649.3	649

If children experience difficulty, you might want to use a number line showing tenths. Errors often occur when a number with 9 in the ones column is rounded up. Children also often neglect to alter the tens digit in a number such as 19.7.

☆ Adding two numbers

Find each sum.

$\begin{array}{r} 271 \\ + 524 \\ \hline 795 \end{array}$ $\begin{array}{r} 483 \\ + 571 \\ \hline 1,054 \end{array}$

Remember to regroup if you need to.

Find each sum.

$\begin{array}{r} 334 \\ + 265 \\ \hline 599 \end{array}$ $\begin{array}{r} 352 \\ + 127 \\ \hline 479 \end{array}$ $\begin{array}{r} 723 \\ + 345 \\ \hline 1,068 \end{array}$ $\begin{array}{r} 843 \\ + 291 \\ \hline 1,134 \end{array}$

$\begin{array}{r} 385 \\ + 606 \\ \hline 991 \end{array}$ $\begin{array}{r} 363 \\ + 147 \\ \hline 510 \end{array}$ $\begin{array}{r} 535 \\ + 187 \\ \hline 722 \end{array}$ $\begin{array}{r} 392 \\ + 488 \\ \hline 880 \end{array}$

Write the answer in the box.

$213 + 137 = 350$ $535 + 167 = 702$

Write the missing number in the box.

$\begin{array}{r} 3\,6\,2 \\ + 4\,1\,9 \\ \hline 7\,8\,1 \end{array}$ $\begin{array}{r} 2\,5\,6 \\ + 5\,8\,1 \\ \hline 8\,3\,7 \end{array}$ $\begin{array}{r} 7\,2\,1 \\ + 2\,6\,4 \\ \hline 9\,8\,5 \end{array}$ $\begin{array}{r} 7\,3\,9 \\ + 2\,4\,0 \\ \hline 9\,7\,9 \end{array}$

Find each sum.

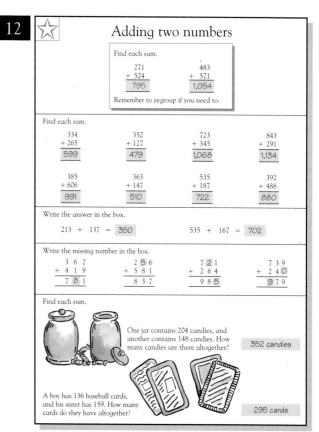

One jar contains 204 candies, and another contains 148 candies. How many candies are there altogether?

352 candies

A boy has 136 baseball cards, and his sister has 159. How many cards do they have altogether?

295 cards

The questions on this page involve straightforward addition work. If children have difficulty with the horizontal sums, suggest that they rewrite them in vertical form. Some errors may result from neglecting to regroup.

13

Adding two numbers

Find each sum.

$$\begin{array}{r}{}^{1\ 1}\\ 4,321 \\ +\,2,465 \\ \hline 6,786 \end{array} \qquad \begin{array}{r}{}^{1\ 1}\\ 3,794 \\ +\,5,325 \\ \hline 9,119 \end{array}$$

Remember to carry if you need to.

Find each sum.

$$\begin{array}{r} 2,642 \\ +\,3,241 \\ \hline 5,883 \end{array} \qquad \begin{array}{r} 4,325 \\ +\,2,653 \\ \hline 6,978 \end{array} \qquad \begin{array}{r} 2,471 \\ +\,4,238 \\ \hline 6,709 \end{array}$$

$$\begin{array}{r} 3,749 \\ +\,2,471 \\ \hline 6,220 \end{array} \qquad \begin{array}{r} 5,764 \\ +\,3,915 \\ \hline 9,679 \end{array} \qquad \begin{array}{r} 8,482 \\ +\,1,349 \\ \hline 9,831 \end{array}$$

Write the answer in the box.

1,342 + 1,264 = 2,606   2,531 + 4,236 = 6,767

2,013 + 3,642 = 5,655   1,738 + 4,261 = 5,999

Write the missing number in the box.

$$\begin{array}{r} 3,7\ 4\ 1 \\ +\,2,9\ 4\ \boxed{3} \\ \hline 6,\ 6\ 8\ 4 \end{array} \qquad \begin{array}{r} 1,\ 6\ 5\ 2 \\ +\,3,\ 2\ 7\ 4 \\ \hline 4,\ 9\ 2\ 6 \end{array} \qquad \begin{array}{r} 3,\ 6\ 4\ 2 \\ +\,4,\ 8\ 3\ 1 \\ \hline 8,\ 4\ 7\ 3 \end{array}$$

Find each sum.

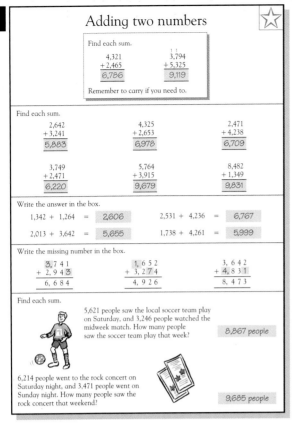

5,621 people saw the local soccer team play on Saturday, and 3,246 people watched the midweek match. How many people saw the soccer team play that week?   8,867 people

6,214 people went to the rock concert on Saturday night, and 3,471 people went on Sunday night. How many people saw the rock concert that weekend?   9,685 people

This page is similar to the previous page, with larger numbers. If children have difficulty with the section on missing numbers, have them try various digits until they find the correct one.

14

Subtracting three-digit numbers

Write the difference between the lines.

$$\begin{array}{r} 364 \\ -\,223 \\ \hline 141 \end{array} \qquad \begin{array}{r}{}^{6\ 11}\\ 47\!\!\not{4}\ \text{cm} \\ -\,252\ \text{cm} \\ \hline 219\ \text{cm} \end{array}$$

Write the difference between the lines.

$$\begin{array}{r} 263 \\ -\,151 \\ \hline 112 \end{array} \quad \begin{array}{r} 478 \\ -\,234 \\ \hline 244 \end{array} \quad \begin{array}{r} 845 \\ -\,624 \\ \hline 221 \end{array} \quad \begin{array}{r} 793 \\ -\,581 \\ \hline 212 \end{array}$$

$$\begin{array}{r} 580\ \text{ft} \\ -\,230\ \text{ft} \\ \hline 350\ \text{ft} \end{array} \quad \begin{array}{r} 659\ \text{m} \\ -\,318\ \text{m} \\ \hline 341\ \text{m} \end{array} \quad \begin{array}{r} 850\ \text{yd} \\ -\,740\ \text{yd} \\ \hline 110\ \text{yd} \end{array} \quad \begin{array}{r} 372\ \text{m} \\ -\,262\ \text{m} \\ \hline 110\ \text{m} \end{array}$$

Write the difference in the box.

365 − 123 = 242   799 − 354 = 445

$876 − $515 = $361 $940 − $730 = $210

$684 − $574 = $110 $220 − $120 = $100

Write the difference between the lines.

$$\begin{array}{r} 363 \\ -\,145 \\ \hline 218 \end{array} \quad \begin{array}{r} 484 \\ -\,237 \\ \hline 247 \end{array} \quad \begin{array}{r} 561 \\ -\,342 \\ \hline 219 \end{array} \quad \begin{array}{r} 394 \\ -\,185 \\ \hline 209 \end{array}$$

$$\begin{array}{r} 937 \\ -\,719 \\ \hline 218 \end{array} \quad \begin{array}{r} 568 \\ -\,209 \\ \hline 359 \end{array} \quad \begin{array}{r} 225 \\ -\,116 \\ \hline 109 \end{array} \quad \begin{array}{r} 752 \\ -\,329 \\ \hline 423 \end{array}$$

Find the answer to each problem.

A grocer has 234 apples. He sells 127. How many apples does he have left?   107 apples

A store has 860 videos to rent. 420 are rented. How many are left in the store?   440 videos

There are 572 children in a school. 335 are girls. How many are boys?   237 boys

In some of these problems, children may incorrectly subtract the smaller digit from the larger one, when they should be subtracting the larger digit from the smaller one. In such cases, point out that children should regroup.

15

Subtracting three-digit numbers

Write the difference between the lines.

$$\begin{array}{r}{}^{3\ 11}\\ 4\!\!\not{1}\!\not{5} \\ -\,152 \\ \hline 263 \end{array} \qquad \begin{array}{r}{}^{6\ \not{2}\ 11}\\ 7\!\!\not{X}\!\!\not{X}\ \text{m} \\ -\,392\ \text{m} \\ \hline 319\ \text{m} \end{array}$$

Write the difference between the lines.

$$\begin{array}{r} 524\ \text{m} \\ -\,263\ \text{m} \\ \hline 261\ \text{m} \end{array} \quad \begin{array}{r} 319\ \text{m} \\ -\,137\ \text{m} \\ \hline 182\ \text{m} \end{array} \quad \begin{array}{r} 647\ \text{ft} \\ -\,456\ \text{ft} \\ \hline 191\ \text{ft} \end{array} \quad \begin{array}{r} 915\ \text{yd} \\ -\,193\ \text{yd} \\ \hline 722\ \text{yd} \end{array}$$

$$\begin{array}{r} 714 \\ -\,407 \\ \hline 307 \end{array} \quad \begin{array}{r} 926 \\ -\,827 \\ \hline 99 \end{array} \quad \begin{array}{r} 421 \\ -\,355 \\ \hline 66 \end{array} \quad \begin{array}{r} 815 \\ -\,786 \\ \hline 29 \end{array}$$

Write the difference in the box.

512 − 304 = 208   648 − 239 = 409

831 − 642 = 189   377 − 198 = 179

Write the difference between the lines.

$$\begin{array}{r} 423 \\ -\,136 \\ \hline 287 \end{array} \quad \begin{array}{r} 615 \\ -\,418 \\ \hline 197 \end{array} \quad \begin{array}{r} 312 \\ -\,113 \\ \hline 199 \end{array} \quad \begin{array}{r} 924 \\ -\,528 \\ \hline 396 \end{array}$$

Write the missing number in the box.

$$\begin{array}{r} 7\ 2\ 3 \\ -\,1\ 2\ \boxed{8} \\ \hline 5\ 9\ 5 \end{array} \quad \begin{array}{r} 5\ \boxed{6}\ 2 \\ -\,3\ 1\ 7 \\ \hline 2\ 4\ 5 \end{array} \quad \begin{array}{r} 8\ 3\ 4 \\ -\,2\ 5\ 7 \\ \hline 5\ 7\ 7 \end{array} \quad \begin{array}{r} 5\ 3\ 2 \\ -\,1\ \boxed{8}\ 5 \\ \hline 3\ 4\ 7 \end{array}$$

Find the answer to each problem.

A theater holds 645 people. 257 people buy tickets. How many seats are empty?   388 seats

There are 564 people in a park. 276 are boating on the lake. How many are taking part in other activities?   288 people

Some children may have difficulty with the section on missing numbers. Have them use trial and error until they find the correct number, or encourage them to use addition and subtraction fact families to find the number.

Adding decimals

Write the answer between the lines.

$$\begin{array}{r} \$5.25 \\ +\,\$2.40 \\ \hline \$7.65 \end{array} \qquad \begin{array}{r} 2.25\ \text{m} \\ +\,3.50\ \text{m} \\ \hline 5.75\ \text{m} \end{array}$$

Write the answer between the lines.

$$\begin{array}{r} \$2.25 \\ +\,\$4.50 \\ \hline \$6.75 \end{array} \quad \begin{array}{r} \$7.50 \\ +\,\$2.25 \\ \hline \$9.75 \end{array} \quad \begin{array}{r} \$3.35 \\ +\,\$1.50 \\ \hline \$4.85 \end{array}$$

$$\begin{array}{r} \$6.45 \\ +\,\$2.35 \\ \hline \$8.80 \end{array} \quad \begin{array}{r} \$3.15 \\ +\,\$4.75 \\ \hline \$7.90 \end{array} \quad \begin{array}{r} \$1.50 \\ +\,\$3.95 \\ \hline \$5.45 \end{array}$$

$$\begin{array}{r} 5.50\ \text{m} \\ +\,2.35\ \text{m} \\ \hline 7.85\ \text{m} \end{array} \quad \begin{array}{r} 3.60\ \text{m} \\ +\,4.15\ \text{m} \\ \hline 7.75\ \text{m} \end{array} \quad \begin{array}{r} 7.30\ \text{m} \\ +\,1.65\ \text{m} \\ \hline 8.95\ \text{m} \end{array}$$

$$\begin{array}{r} 6.15\ \text{m} \\ +\,2.20\ \text{m} \\ \hline 8.35\ \text{m} \end{array} \quad \begin{array}{r} 3.30\ \text{m} \\ +\,6.55\ \text{m} \\ \hline 9.85\ \text{m} \end{array} \quad \begin{array}{r} 5.20\ \text{m} \\ +\,1.75\ \text{m} \\ \hline 6.95\ \text{m} \end{array}$$

Write the answer in the box.

$5.25 + $3.30 = $8.55   6.15 m + 1.50 m = 7.65 m $6.35 + $2.30 = $8.65

$5.20 + $2.55 = $7.75   2.45 m + 5.10 m = 7.55 m $7.45 + $1.50 = $8.95

Find the answer to each problem.

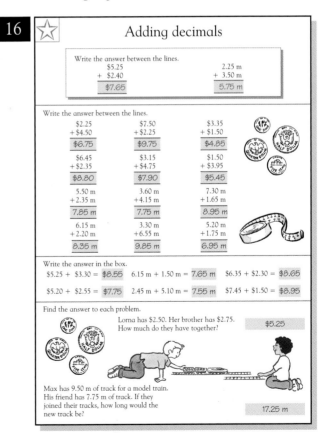

Lorna has $2.50. Her brother has $2.75. How much do they have together? $5.25

Max has 9.50 m of track for a model train. His friend has 7.75 m of track. If they joined their tracks, how long would the new track be?   17.25 m

Children may place the decimal point incorrectly in problems that are presented horizontally. Have them rewrite the problems in vertical form, lining up the decimal points. You may also need to remind children to regroup when necessary.

17

Adding decimals ⭐

Write the answer between the lines.

$3.35 + $5.55 **$8.90**	3.45 m + 1.25 m **4.70 m**

Write the answer between the lines.

$3.60 + $2.25 **$5.85**	$1.25 + $4.55 **$5.80**	$7.45 + $2.35 **$9.80**
$3.60 + $3.25 **$6.85**	$7.35 + $1.45 **$8.80**	$5.25 + $2.65 **$7.90**
3.45 m + 4.35 m **7.80 m**	8.55 m + 1.35 m **9.90 m**	1.75 m + 5.20 m **6.95 m**
2.40 m + 1.45 m **3.85 m**	7.15 m + 1.35 m **8.50 m**	3.85 m + 4.10 m **7.95 m**

Write the answer in the box.

$2.75 + $4.15 = **$6.90**   3.75 m + 2.75 m = **6.50 m** $3.65 + $1.50 = **$5.15**

$6.25 + $1.50 = **$7.75**   8.65 m + 2.55 m = **11.20 m** $3.45 + $1.55 = **$5.00**

Work out the answer to each sum.

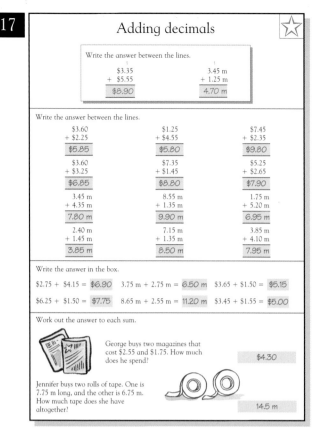

George buys two magazines that cost $2.55 and $1.75. How much does he spend?   **$4.30**

Jennifer buys two rolls of tape. One is 7.75 m long, and the other is 6.75 m. How much tape does she have altogether?   **14.5 m**

You may wish to discuss with children that when the final decimal place of a sum is zero, it can be written, but it can also be omitted—unless the sum is an amount of dollars.

18

⭐ Subtracting decimals

Write the difference between the lines.

$6.55 − $3.20 **$3.35**	4.70 m − 2.50 m **2.20 m**

Write the difference between the lines.

$7.45 − $3.30 **$4.15**	$9.60 − $7.20 **$2.40**	$5.55 − $2.40 **$3.15**
$8.35 − $3.25 **$5.10**	$3.95 − $1.75 **$2.20**	$6.55 − $2.40 **$4.15**

Write the difference between the lines.

3.90 m − 1.40 m **2.50 m**	4.75 m − 3.35 m **1.40 m**	9.20 m − 2.20 m **7.00 m**
7.55 m − 1.15 m **6.40 m**	2.15 m − 1.00 m **1.15 m**	3.35 m − 2.20 m **1.15 m**

Write the difference in the box.

$4.15 − $1.10 = **$3.05** $3.55 − $2.50 = **$1.05**

$9.75 − $4.30 = **$5.45** $8.85 − $6.05 = **$2.80**

7.55 m − 2.30 m = **5.25 m**   6.15 m − 4.05 m = **2.10 m**

Find the answer to each problem.

Mei-ling has $4.65 to spend. She buys a book for $3.45. How much money does she have left?   **$1.20**

Shawn is given $9.50 for his birthday. If he spends $3.20 at the mall, how much money will he have left?   **$6.30**

Some children are confused about subtracting decimals. Show them that once they line up the decimal points, they can simply subtract the digits, lining up the decimal point of the answer as well.

19

Subtracting decimals ⭐

Write the difference between the lines.

4 13 $5̶.3̶5 − $2.40 **$2.95**	6 13 7̶.3̶5 m − 1.65 m **5.70 m**

Write the difference between the lines.

$6.55 − $2.75 **$3.80**	$7.45 − $3.65 **$3.80**	$8.65 − $4.75 **$3.90**
$3.15 − $1.25 **$1.90**	$5.70 − $2.90 **$2.80**	$4.15 − $1.75 **$2.40**

Write the difference between the lines.

5.35 m − 2.55 m **2.80 m**	7.25 m − 2.55 m **4.70 m**	4.15 m − 2.25 m **1.90 m**
5.45 m − 2.55 m **2.90 m**	8.15 m − 2.20 m **5.95 m**	7.30 m − 3.50 m **3.80 m**

Write the difference in the box.

$6.25 − $2.50 = **$3.75** $4.35 − $2.55 = **$1.80**

$5.20 − $3.30 = **$1.90** $7.40 − $3.80 = **$3.60**

6.45 m − 2.55 m = **3.90 m**   7.35 m − 3.55 m = **3.80 m**

Find the answer to each problem.

Keisha has a piece of wood 4.55 m long. She cuts off a piece 1.65 m long. How long a piece of wood is left?   **2.90 m**

Eli's long-jump result is 2.35 m. Steven's is 1.40 m. How much longer is Eli's jump than Steven's?   **0.95 m**

This page follows from the previous page, but the subtraction involves regrouping. You may need to remind children that they can regroup across a decimal point in the same way as they would if the decimal point were not there.

20

⭐ Multiplying by one-digit numbers

Find each product.

32 x 2 **64**	26 x 3 **78**	34 x 4 **136**

Find each product.

27 x 2 **54**	32 x 3 **96**	16 x 4 **64**	19 x 2 **38**
22 x 3 **66**	25 x 4 **100**	18 x 6 **108**	33 x 5 **165**
39 x 2 **78**	26 x 2 **52**	41 x 2 **82**	38 x 3 **114**
29 x 3 **87**	45 x 2 **90**	28 x 3 **84**	16 x 6 **96**
10 x 5 **50**	40 x 2 **80**	20 x 4 **80**	50 x 3 **150**

Find the answer to each problem.

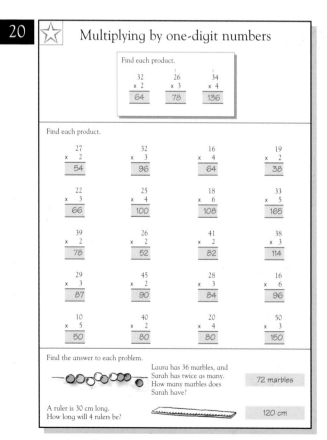

Laura has 36 marbles, and Sarah has twice as many. How many marbles does Sarah have?   **72 marbles**

A ruler is 30 cm long. How long will 4 rulers be?   **120 cm**

Errors made on this page generally highlight gaps in children's knowledge of the 2, 3, 4, 5 and 6 multiplication tables. Other errors can result from neglecting to regroup.

Multiplying by one-digit numbers

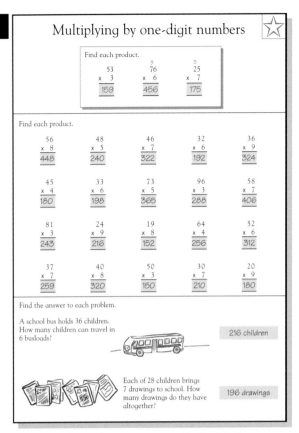

Find each product.

53	3 76	3 25
x 3	x 6	x 7
159	456	175

Find each product.

56	48	46	32	36
x 8	x 5	x 7	x 6	x 9
448	240	322	192	324

45	33	73	96	58
x 4	x 6	x 5	x 3	x 7
180	198	365	288	406

81	24	19	64	52
x 3	x 9	x 8	x 4	x 6
243	216	152	256	312

37	40	50	30	20
x 7	x 8	x 3	x 7	x 9
259	320	150	210	180

Find the answer to each problem.

A school bus holds 36 children. How many children can travel in 6 busloads? 216 children

Each of 28 children brings 7 drawings to school. How many drawings do they have altogether? 196 drawings

Errors made on this page generally highlight gaps in children's knowledge of the 6, 7, 8, and 9 times tables. As on the previous page, errors may result from neglecting to regroup.

22

Division with remainders

Find each quotient.

5 r 1	6 r 2
3)16	4)26
15	24
1	2

Find each quotient.

17 r 1	11 r 2	7 r 1	9 r 4
2)35	4)46	3)22	5)49
2	4	21	45
15	6	1	4
14	4		
1	2		

14 r 2	12 r 3	7 r 2	12 r 2
4)58	5)63	5)37	4)50
4	5	35	4
18	13	2	10
16	10		8
2	3		2

25 r 1	14 r 3	18 r 4	16 r 3
3)76	4)59	5)94	5)83
6	4	5	5
16	19	44	33
15	16	40	30
1	3	4	3

49 r 1	18 r 3	15 r 2	18 r 1
2)99	4)75	5)77	2)37
8	4	5	2
19	35	27	17
18	32	25	16
1	3	2	1

Write the answer in the box.

What is 27 divided by 4? 6 r 3 Divide 78 by 5. 15 r 3

What is 46 divided by 3? 15 r 1 Divide 63 by 2. 31 r 1

Children may have difficulty finding quotients with remainders. Have them perform long division until the remaining value to be divided is less than the divisor. That value is the remainder.

23

Division with remainders

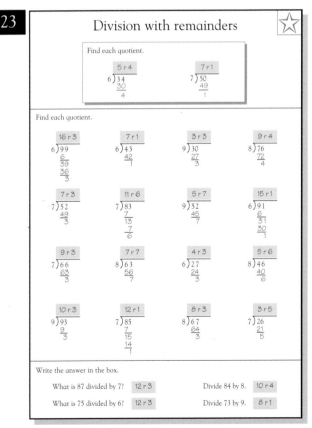

Find each quotient.

5 r 4	7 r 1
6)34	7)50
30	49
4	1

Find each quotient.

16 r 3	7 r 1	3 r 3	9 r 4
6)99	6)43	9)30	8)76
6	42	27	72
39	1	3	4
36			
3			

7 r 3	11 r 6	5 r 7	15 r 1
7)52	7)83	9)52	6)91
49	7	45	6
3	13	7	31
	7		30
	6		1

9 r 3	7 r 7	4 r 3	5 r 6
7)66	8)63	6)27	8)46
63	56	24	40
3	7	3	6

10 r 3	12 r 1	8 r 3	3 r 5
9)93	7)85	8)67	7)26
9	7	64	21
3	15	3	5
	14		
	1		

Write the answer in the box.

What is 87 divided by 7? 12 r 3 Divide 84 by 8. 10 r 4

What is 75 divided by 6? 12 r 3 Divide 73 by 9. 8 r 1

This page is similar to the previous page, but the divisors are numbers greater than 5, so children will need to know their times tables for numbers greater than 5.

Real-life problems

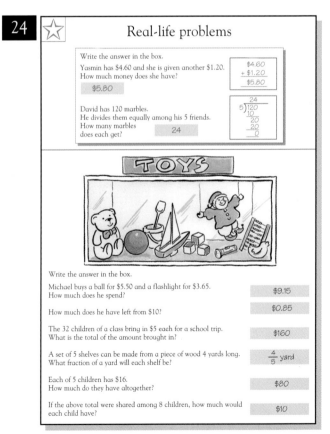

Write the answer in the box.

Yasmin has $4.60 and she is given another $1.20. How much money does she have?

$5.80

| $4.60 |
| + $1.20 |
| $5.80 |

David has 120 marbles. He divides them equally among his 5 friends. How many marbles does each get? 24

| 24 |
| 5)120 |
| 10 |
| 20 |
| 20 |
| 0 |

TOYS

Write the answer in the box.

Michael buys a ball for $5.50 and a flashlight for $3.65. How much does he spend? $9.15

How much does he have left from $10? $0.85

The 32 children of a class bring in $5 each for a school trip. What is the total of the amount brought in? $160

A set of 5 shelves can be made from a piece of wood 4 yards long. What fraction of a yard will each shelf be? $\frac{4}{5}$ yard

Each of 5 children has $16. How much do they have altogether? $80

If the above total were shared among 8 children, how much would each child have? $10

This page tests children's ability to choose operations required to solve real-life problems, mostly involving money. Discussing whether the answer will be larger or smaller than the question will help children decide what operation to use.

Real-life problems

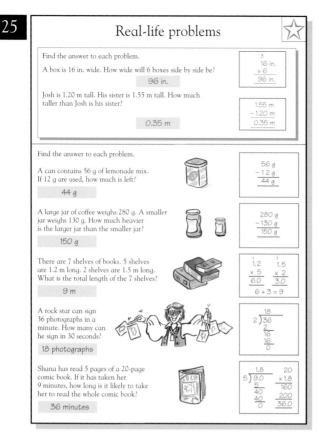

Find the answer to each problem.

A box is 16 in. wide. How wide will 6 boxes side by side be?

96 in.

$$\begin{array}{r} \overset{3}{16} \text{ in.} \\ \times\ 6 \\ \hline 96 \text{ in.} \end{array}$$

Josh is 1.20 m tall. His sister is 1.55 m tall. How much taller than Josh is his sister?

0.35 m

$$\begin{array}{r} 1.55 \text{ m} \\ -\ 1.20 \text{ m} \\ \hline 0.35 \text{ m} \end{array}$$

Find the answer to each problem.

A can contains 56 g of lemonade mix. If 12 g are used, how much is left?

44 g

$$\begin{array}{r} 56 \text{ g} \\ -\ 12 \text{ g} \\ \hline 44 \text{ g} \end{array}$$

A large jar of coffee weighs 280 g. A smaller jar weighs 130 g. How much heavier is the larger jar than the smaller jar?

150 g

$$\begin{array}{r} 280 \text{ g} \\ -\ 130 \text{ g} \\ \hline 150 \text{ g} \end{array}$$

There are 7 shelves of books. 5 shelves are 1.2 m long. 2 shelves are 1.5 m long. What is the total length of the 7 shelves?

9 m

$$\begin{array}{r} 1.2 \\ \times\ 5 \\ \hline 6.0 \end{array} \quad \begin{array}{r} 1.5 \\ \times\ 2 \\ \hline 3.0 \end{array}$$

$$6 + 3 = 9$$

A rock star can sign 36 photographs in a minute. How many can he sign in 30 seconds?

18 photographs

$$\begin{array}{r} 18 \\ 2)\overline{36} \\ \underline{2} \\ 16 \\ \underline{16} \\ 0 \end{array}$$

Shana has read 5 pages of a 20-page comic book. If it has taken her 9 minutes, how long is it likely to take her to read the whole comic book?

36 minutes

$$\begin{array}{r} 1.8 \\ 5)\overline{9.0} \\ \underline{5} \\ 40 \\ \underline{40} \\ 0 \end{array} \quad \begin{array}{r} 20 \\ \times\ 1.8 \\ \hline 160 \\ 200 \\ \hline 36.0 \end{array}$$

This page continues with real-life problems, but with units other than money. To solve the third problem children must perform three operations.

26

Areas of rectangles and squares

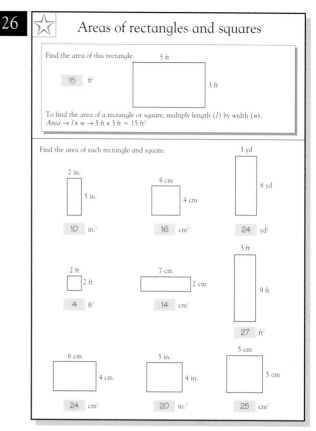

Find the area of this rectangle.

15 ft²

To find the area of a rectangle or square, multiply length (*l*) by width (*w*).
Area → *l* x *w* → 5 ft x 3 ft = 15 ft²

Find the area of each rectangle and square.

2 in. × 5 in. → **10** in.²

4 cm × 4 cm → **16** cm²

3 yd × 8 yd → **24** yd²

2 ft × 2 ft → **4** ft²

7 cm × 2 cm → **14** cm²

3 ft × 9 ft → **27** ft²

6 cm × 4 cm → **24** cm²

5 in. × 4 in. → **20** in.²

5 cm × 5 cm → **25** cm²

Children should understand that area is measured in square units, such as cm². They will reach incorrect answers if they add sides instead of multiplying them, or try to find the area of a square by doubling the length of one side.

27

Problems involving time

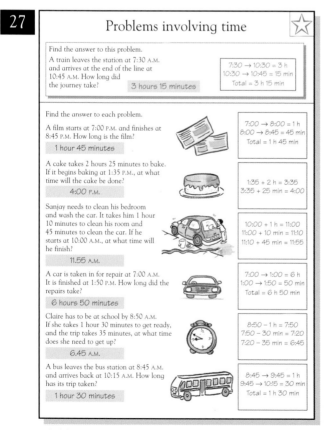

Find the answer to this problem.

A train leaves the station at 7:30 A.M. and arrives at the end of the line at 10:45 A.M. How long did the journey take?

3 hours 15 minutes

7:30 → 10:30 = 3 h
10:30 → 10:45 = 15 min
Total = 3 h 15 min

Find the answer to each problem.

A film starts at 7:00 P.M. and finishes at 8:45 P.M. How long is the film?

1 hour 45 minutes

7:00 → 8:00 = 1 h
8:00 → 8:45 = 45 min
Total = 1 h 45 min

A cake takes 2 hours 25 minutes to bake. If it begins baking at 1:35 P.M., at what time will the cake be done?

4:00 P.M.

1:35 + 2 h = 3:35
3:35 + 25 min = 4:00

Sanjay needs to clean his bedroom and wash the car. It takes him 1 hour 10 minutes to clean his room and 45 minutes to clean the car. If he starts at 10:00 A.M., at what time will he finish?

11.55 A.M.

10:00 + 1 h = 11:00
11:00 + 10 min = 11:10
11:10 + 45 min = 11:55

A car is taken in for repair at 7:00 A.M. It is finished at 1:50 P.M. How long did the repairs take?

6 hours 50 minutes

7:00 → 1:00 = 6 h
1:00 → 1:50 = 50 min
Total = 6 h 50 min

Claire has to be at school by 8:50 A.M. If she takes 1 hour 30 minutes to get ready, and the trip takes 35 minutes, at what time does she need to get up?

6.45 A.M.

8:50 – 1 h = 7:50
7:50 – 30 min = 7:20
7:20 – 35 min = 6:45

A bus leaves the bus station at 8:45 A.M. and arrives back at 10:15 A.M. How long has its trip taken?

1 hour 30 minutes

8:45 → 9:45 = 1 h
9:45 → 10:15 = 30 min
Total = 1 h 30 min

Children can reach the correct answers using a variety of methods. Sample methods are provided in the answers, but any method that children use to reach a correct answer is acceptable.

Bar graphs

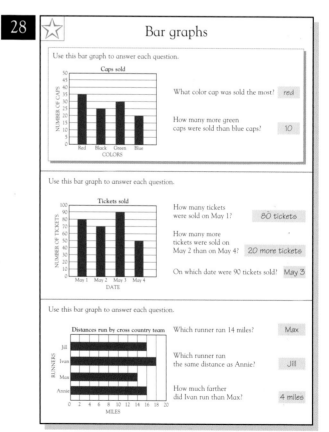

Use this bar graph to answer each question.

Caps sold

What color cap was sold the most? **red**

How many more green caps were sold than blue caps? **10**

Use this bar graph to answer each question.

Tickets sold

How many tickets were sold on May 1? **80 tickets**

How many more tickets were sold on May 2 than on May 4? **20 more tickets**

On which date were 90 tickets sold? **May 3**

Use this bar graph to answer each question.

Distances run by cross country team

Which runner ran 14 miles? **Max**

Which runner ran the same distance as Annie? **Jill**

How much farther did Ivan run than Max? **4 miles**

This page requires children to read information, to look for specific information, and to manipulate the information they read on a bar graph. They may need to be reassured that horizontal bar graphs can be read in much the same way as vertical graphs.

Probability

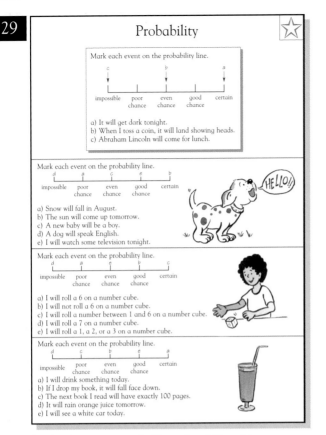

Mark each event on the probability line.

c   b   a

impossible | poor chance | even chance | good chance | certain

a) It will get dark tonight.
b) When I toss a coin, it will land showing heads.
c) Abraham Lincoln will come for lunch.

Mark each event on the probability line.

d   a   c   e   b

impossible | poor chance | even chance | good chance | certain

a) Snow will fall in August.
b) The sun will come up tomorrow.
c) A new baby will be a boy.
d) A dog will speak English.
e) I will watch some television tonight.

HELLO!!

Mark each event on the probability line.

d   a   e   b   c

impossible | poor chance | even chance | good chance | certain

a) I will roll a 6 on a number cube.
b) I will not roll a 6 on a number cube.
c) I will roll a number between 1 and 6 on a number cube.
d) I will roll a 7 on a number cube.
e) I will roll a 1, a 2, or a 3 on a number cube.

Mark each event on the probability line.

d   c   b   e   a

impossible | poor chance | even chance | good chance | certain

a) I will drink something today.
b) If I drop my book, it will fall face down.
c) The next book I read will have exactly 100 pages.
d) It will rain orange juice tomorrow.
e) I will see a white car today.

In the first section, children should be able to identify events categorically. As the second section is based on mathematical probability, the answers are not subjective. There may be some discussion of answers for the third section.

30

Triangles

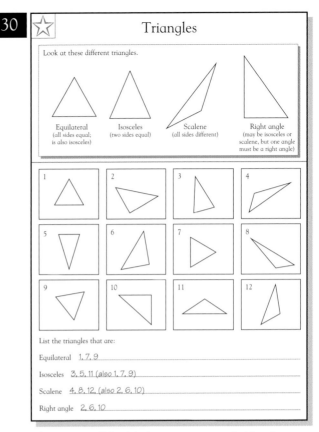

Look at these different triangles.

Equilateral (all sides equal; is also isosceles)   Isosceles (two sides equal)   Scalene (all sides different)   Right angle (may be isosceles or scalene, but one angle must be a right angle)

1	2	3	4
5	6	7	8
9	10	11	12

List the triangles that are:

Equilateral   1, 7, 9

Isosceles   3, 5, 11 (also 1, 7, 9)

Scalene   4, 8, 12, (also 2, 6, 10)

Right angle   2, 6, 10

This page will highlight any gaps in children's ability to recognize and name triangles. Make sure that children can identify triangles that have been rotated.

31

Expanded form

What is the value of 3 in 2,308?   300

Write 3,417 in expanded form.

(3 x 1,000) + (4 x 100) + (1 x 10) + (7 x 1)

3,000 + 400 + 10 + 7

What is the value of 5 in each of these numbers?

25   5   5,904   5,000   52   50   2,512   500   805   5

What is the value of 8 in each of these numbers?

8,300   8,000   982   80   1,805   800   768   8   19,873   800

Circle each number in which 7 has the value of 70.

7,682   927   (870)   (372)   707

(171)   767   (875)   7,057   70,000

Write each number in expanded form.

3,897
3,000 + 800 + 90 + 7

24,098
20,000 + 4,000 + 90 + 8

50,810
50,000 + 800 + 10

8,945
8,000 + 900 + 40 + 5

6,098
6,000 + 90 + 8

14,003
10,000 + 4,000 + 3

Errors may occur when children write numbers that include zeros in expanded form. When they work out the problems, they need not write 0 x 100 for a number such as 6,098. However, for a number such as 50,815, they should write 50 x 1,000.

Speed trials

Write the answers as fast as you can, but get them right!

4 x 10 = 40   8 x 2 = 16   6 x 5 = 30

Write the answers as fast as you can, but get them right!

3 x 2 = 6	0 x 5 = 0	3 x 10 = 30	0 x 3 = 0
5 x 2 = 10	10 x 5 = 50	5 x 10 = 50	10 x 3 = 30
1 x 2 = 2	8 x 5 = 40	1 x 10 = 10	8 x 3 = 24
4 x 2 = 8	6 x 5 = 30	4 x 10 = 40	6 x 3 = 18
7 x 2 = 14	2 x 5 = 10	7 x 10 = 70	2 x 3 = 6
2 x 2 = 4	7 x 5 = 35	2 x 10 = 20	7 x 3 = 21
6 x 2 = 12	4 x 5 = 20	6 x 10 = 60	4 x 3 = 12
8 x 2 = 16	1 x 5 = 5	8 x 10 = 80	1 x 3 = 3
10 x 2 = 20	5 x 5 = 25	10 x 10 = 100	5 x 3 = 15
0 x 2 = 0	3 x 5 = 15	0 x 10 = 0	3 x 3 = 9
9 x 2 = 18	5 x 3 = 15	9 x 10 = 90	6 x 4 = 24
2 x 7 = 14	5 x 8 = 40	10 x 7 = 70	3 x 4 = 12
2 x 1 = 2	5 x 6 = 30	10 x 1 = 10	7 x 4 = 28
2 x 4 = 8	5 x 9 = 45	10 x 4 = 40	4 x 4 = 16
3 x 7 = 21	5 x 7 = 35	10 x 7 = 70	10 x 4 = 40
2 x 5 = 10	5 x 4 = 20	10 x 5 = 50	8 x 4 = 32
2 x 9 = 18	5 x 1 = 5	10 x 9 = 90	0 x 4 = 0
2 x 6 = 12	4 x 7 = 28	10 x 6 = 60	9 x 4 = 36
2 x 8 = 16	5 x 10 = 50	10 x 8 = 80	5 x 4 = 20
2 x 3 = 6	5 x 2 = 10	10 x 3 = 30	2 x 4 = 8

All the 3s

You will need to know these:

$1 \times 3 = 3$ $2 \times 3 = 6$ $3 \times 3 = 9$ $4 \times 3 = 12$ $5 \times 3 = 15$ $10 \times 3 = 30$

How many altogether?

6 sets of three are 18   six threes are 18 $6 \times 3 =$ 18

How many altogether?

7 sets of three are 21   seven threes are 21 $7 \times 3 =$ 21

How many altogether?

8 sets of three are 24   eight threes are 24 $8 \times 3 =$ 24

How many altogether?

9 sets of three are 27   nine threes are 27 $9 \times 3 =$ 27

34

All the 3s again

You should know all of the three times table by now.

$1 \times 3 = 3$ $2 \times 3 = 6$ $3 \times 3 = 9$ $4 \times 3 = 12$ $5 \times 3 = 15$
$6 \times 3 = 18$ $7 \times 3 = 21$ $8 \times 3 = 24$ $9 \times 3 = 27$ $10 \times 3 = 30$

Say these to yourself a few times.

Cover the three times table with a sheet of paper so you can't see the numbers.
Write the answers. Be as fast as you can, but get them right!

$1 \times 3 =$ 3	$5 \times 3 =$ 15	$6 \times 3 =$ 18
$2 \times 3 =$ 6	$7 \times 3 =$ 21	$9 \times 3 =$ 27
$3 \times 3 =$ 9	$9 \times 3 =$ 27	$4 \times 3 =$ 12
$4 \times 3 =$ 12	$4 \times 3 =$ 12	$5 \times 3 =$ 15
$5 \times 3 =$ 15	$6 \times 3 =$ 18	$3 \times 7 =$ 21
$6 \times 3 =$ 18	$8 \times 3 =$ 24	$3 \times 4 =$ 12
$7 \times 3 =$ 21	$10 \times 3 =$ 30	$2 \times 3 =$ 6
$8 \times 3 =$ 24	$1 \times 3 =$ 3	$10 \times 3 =$ 30
$9 \times 3 =$ 27	$3 \times 3 =$ 9	$3 \times 9 =$ 27
$10 \times 3 =$ 30	$2 \times 3 =$ 6	$3 \times 6 =$ 18
$3 \times 1 =$ 3	$3 \times 5 =$ 15	$3 \times 5 =$ 15
$3 \times 2 =$ 6	$3 \times 7 =$ 21	$3 \times 8 =$ 24
$3 \times 3 =$ 9	$3 \times 9 =$ 27	$7 \times 3 =$ 21
$3 \times 4 =$ 12	$3 \times 4 =$ 12	$3 \times 2 =$ 6
$3 \times 5 =$ 15	$3 \times 6 =$ 18	$3 \times 10 =$ 30
$3 \times 6 =$ 18	$3 \times 8 =$ 24	$8 \times 3 =$ 24
$3 \times 7 =$ 21	$3 \times 10 =$ 30	$3 \times 0 =$ 0
$3 \times 8 =$ 24	$3 \times 1 =$ 3	$1 \times 3 =$ 3
$3 \times 9 =$ 27	$3 \times 0 =$ 0	$3 \times 3 =$ 9
$3 \times 10 =$ 30	$3 \times 2 =$ 6	$3 \times 9 =$ 27

35

All the 4s

You should know these:

$1 \times 4 = 4$ $2 \times 4 = 8$ $3 \times 4 = 12$ $4 \times 4 = 16$ $5 \times 4 = 20$ $10 \times 4 = 40$

How many altogether?

6 sets of four are 24   six fours are 24 $6 \times 4 =$ 24

How many altogether?

7 sets of four are 28   seven fours are 28 $7 \times 4 =$ 28

How many altogether?

8 sets of four are 32   eight fours are 32 $8 \times 4 =$ 32

How many altogether?

9 sets of four are 36   nine fours are 36 $9 \times 4 =$ 36

36

All the 4s again

You should know all of the four times table by now.

$1 \times 4 = 4$ $2 \times 4 = 8$ $3 \times 4 = 12$ $4 \times 4 = 16$ $5 \times 4 = 20$
$6 \times 4 = 24$ $7 \times 4 = 28$ $8 \times 4 = 32$ $9 \times 4 = 36$ $10 \times 4 = 40$

Say these to yourself the a few times.

Cover the four times table with a sheet of paper so you can't see the numbers.
Write the answers. Be as fast as you can, but get them right!

$1 \times 4 =$ 4	$5 \times 4 =$ 20	$6 \times 4 =$ 24
$2 \times 4 =$ 8	$7 \times 4 =$ 28	$9 \times 4 =$ 36
$3 \times 4 =$ 12	$9 \times 4 =$ 36	$4 \times 1 =$ 4
$4 \times 4 =$ 16	$3 \times 4 =$ 12	$5 \times 4 =$ 20
$5 \times 4 =$ 20	$6 \times 4 =$ 24	$4 \times 7 =$ 28
$6 \times 4 =$ 24	$8 \times 4 =$ 32	$3 \times 4 =$ 12
$7 \times 4 =$ 28	$10 \times 4 =$ 40	$2 \times 4 =$ 8
$8 \times 4 =$ 32	$1 \times 4 =$ 4	$10 \times 4 =$ 40
$9 \times 4 =$ 36	$4 \times 4 =$ 16	$4 \times 3 =$ 12
$10 \times 4 =$ 40	$2 \times 4 =$ 8	$4 \times 6 =$ 24
$4 \times 1 =$ 4	$4 \times 5 =$ 20	$4 \times 5 =$ 20
$4 \times 2 =$ 8	$4 \times 7 =$ 28	$4 \times 8 =$ 32
$4 \times 3 =$ 12	$4 \times 9 =$ 36	$7 \times 4 =$ 28
$4 \times 4 =$ 16	$4 \times 4 =$ 16	$4 \times 2 =$ 8
$4 \times 5 =$ 20	$4 \times 6 =$ 24	$4 \times 10 =$ 40
$4 \times 6 =$ 24	$4 \times 8 =$ 32	$8 \times 4 =$ 32
$4 \times 7 =$ 28	$4 \times 10 =$ 40	$4 \times 0 =$ 0
$4 \times 8 =$ 32	$4 \times 1 =$ 4	$1 \times 4 =$ 4
$4 \times 9 =$ 36	$4 \times 0 =$ 0	$4 \times 4 =$ 16
$4 \times 10 =$ 40	$4 \times 2 =$ 8	$4 \times 9 =$ 36

37 Speed trials

You should know all of the 1, 2, 3, 4, 5, and 10 times tables by now, but how quickly can you do them?
Ask someone to time you as you do this page.
Remember, you must be fast but also correct.

4 x 2 = 8	6 x 3 = 18	9 x 5 = 45
8 x 3 = 24	3 x 4 = 12	8 x 10 = 80
7 x 4 = 28	7 x 5 = 35	7 x 2 = 14
6 x 5 = 30	3 x 10 = 30	6 x 3 = 18
8 x 10 = 80	1 x 2 = 2	5 x 4 = 20
8 x 2 = 16	7 x 3 = 21	4 x 5 = 20
5 x 3 = 15	4 x 4 = 16	3 x 10 = 30
9 x 4 = 36	6 x 5 = 30	2 x 2 = 4
5 x 5 = 25	4 x 10 = 40	1 x 3 = 3
7 x 10 = 70	6 x 2 = 12	0 x 4 = 0
0 x 2 = 0	5 x 3 = 15	10 x 5 = 50
4 x 3 = 12	8 x 4 = 32	9 x 2 = 18
6 x 4 = 24	0 x 5 = 0	8 x 3 = 24
3 x 5 = 15	2 x 10 = 20	7 x 4 = 28
4 x 10 = 40	7 x 2 = 14	6 x 5 = 30
7 x 2 = 14	8 x 3 = 24	5 x 10 = 50
3 x 3 = 9	9 x 4 = 36	4 x 0 = 0
2 x 4 = 8	5 x 5 = 25	3 x 2 = 6
7 x 5 = 35	7 x 10 = 70	2 x 8 = 16
9 x 10 = 90	5 x 2 = 10	1 x 9 = 9

38 Some of the 6s

You should already know parts of the 6 times table because they are parts of the 1, 2, 3, 4, 5, and 10 times tables.
1 x 6 = 6   2 x 6 = 12   3 x 6 = 18
4 x 6 = 24   5 x 6 = 30   10 x 6 = 60
Find out if you can remember them quickly and correctly.

Cover the six times table with paper so you can't see the numbers.
Write the answers as quickly as you can.

What is three sixes?	18	What is ten sixes?	60
What is two sixes?	12	What is four sixes?	24
What is one six?	6	What is five sixes?	30

Write the answers as quickly as you can.

How many sixes make 12?	2	How many sixes make 6?	1
How many sixes make 30?	5	How many sixes make 18?	3
How many sixes make 24?	4	How many sixes make 60?	10

Write the answers as quickly as you can.

Multiply six by three.	18	Multiply six by ten.	60
Multiply six by two.	12	Multiply six by five.	30
Multiply six by one.	6	Multiply six by four.	24

Write the answers as quickly as you can.

4 x 6 = 24	2 x 6 = 12	10 x 6 = 60
5 x 6 = 30	1 x 6 = 6	3 x 6 = 18

Write the answers as quickly as you can.
A box contains six eggs. A man buys five boxes. How many eggs does he have? 30

A pack contains six sticks of gum.
How many sticks will there be in 10 packs? 60

39 The rest of the 6s

You need to learn these:
6 x 6 = 36   7 x 6 = 42   8 x 6 = 48   9 x 6 = 54

This work will help you remember the 6 times table.

Complete these sequences.

6   12   18   24   30   36   42   48   54   60

5 x 6 = 30   so   6 x 6 = 30 plus another 6 = 36

18   24   30   36   42   48   54   60

6 x 6 = 36   so   7 x 6 = 36 plus another 6 = 42

6   12   18   24   30   36   42   48   54   60

7 x 6 = 42   so   8 x 6 = 42 plus another 6 = 48

6   12   18   24   30   36   42   48   54   60

8 x 6 = 48   so   9 x 6 = 48 plus another 6 = 54

6   12   18   24   30   36   42   48   54   60

Test yourself on the rest of the 6 times table.
Cover the above part of the page with a sheet of paper.

What is six sixes?	36	What is seven sixes? 42
What is eight sixes?	48	What is nine sixes? 54

8 x 6 = 48   7 x 6 = 42   6 x 6 = 36   9 x 6 = 54

40 Practice the 6s

You should know all of the 6 times table now, but how quickly can you remember it?
Ask someone to time you as you do this page.
Remember, you must be fast but also correct.

1 x 6 = 6	2 x 6 = 12	7 x 6 = 42
2 x 6 = 12	4 x 6 = 24	3 x 6 = 18
3 x 6 = 18	6 x 6 = 36	9 x 6 = 54
4 x 6 = 24	8 x 6 = 48	6 x 4 = 24
5 x 6 = 30	10 x 6 = 60	1 x 6 = 6
6 x 6 = 36	1 x 6 = 6	6 x 2 = 12
7 x 6 = 42	3 x 6 = 18	6 x 8 = 48
8 x 6 = 48	5 x 6 = 30	0 x 6 = 0
9 x 6 = 54	7 x 6 = 42	6 x 3 = 18
10 x 6 = 60	9 x 6 = 54	5 x 6 = 30
6 x 1 = 6	6 x 3 = 18	6 x 7 = 42
6 x 2 = 12	6 x 5 = 30	2 x 6 = 12
6 x 3 = 18	6 x 7 = 42	6 x 9 = 54
6 x 4 = 24	6 x 9 = 54	4 x 6 = 24
6 x 5 = 30	6 x 2 = 12	8 x 6 = 48
6 x 6 = 36	6 x 4 = 24	10 x 6 = 60
6 x 7 = 42	6 x 6 = 36	6 x 5 = 30
6 x 8 = 48	6 x 8 = 48	6 x 0 = 0
6 x 9 = 54	6 x 10 = 60	6 x 1 = 6
6 x 10 = 60	6 x 0 = 0	6 x 6 = 36

Speed trials

You should know all of the 1, 2, 3, 4, 5, 6, and 10 times tables by now, but how quickly can you remember them?
Ask someone to time you as you do this page.
Remember, you must be fast but also correct.

4 x 6 = 24	6 x 3 = 18	9 x 6 = 54
5 x 3 = 15	8 x 6 = 48	8 x 6 = 48
7 x 3 = 21	6 x 6 = 36	7 x 3 = 21
6 x 5 = 30	3 x 10 = 30	6 x 6 = 36
6 x 10 = 60	6 x 2 = 12	5 x 4 = 20
8 x 2 = 16	7 x 3 = 21	4 x 6 = 24
5 x 3 = 15	4 x 6 = 24	3 x 6 = 18
9 x 6 = 54	6 x 5 = 30	2 x 6 = 12
5 x 5 = 25	6 x 10 = 60	6 x 3 = 18
7 x 6 = 42	6 x 2 = 12	0 x 6 = 0
0 x 2 = 0	5 x 3 = 15	10 x 5 = 50
6 x 3 = 18	8 x 4 = 32	6 x 2 = 12
6 x 6 = 36	0 x 6 = 0	8 x 3 = 24
3 x 5 = 15	5 x 10 = 50	7 x 6 = 42
4 x 10 = 40	7 x 6 = 42	6 x 5 = 30
7 x 10 = 70	8 x 3 = 24	5 x 10 = 50
3 x 6 = 18	9 x 6 = 54	6 x 0 = 0
2 x 4 = 8	5 x 5 = 25	3 x 10 = 30
6 x 9 = 54	7 x 10 = 70	2 x 8 = 16
9 x 10 = 90	5 x 6 = 30	1 x 8 = 8

Some of the 7s

You should already know parts of the 7 times table because they are parts of the 1, 2, 3, 4, 6 and 10 times tables.
1 x 7 = 7   2 x 7 = 14   3 x 7 = 21   4 x 7 = 28
5 x 7 = 35   6 x 7 = 42   10 x 7 = 70
Find out if you can remember them quickly and correctly.

Cover the seven times table with paper and write the answers to these questions as quickly as you can.

What is three sevens? 21	What is ten sevens? 70
What is two sevens? 14	What is four sevens? 28
What is six sevens? 42	What is five sevens? 35

Write the answers as quickly as you can.

How many sevens make 14? 2	How many sevens make 42? 6
How many sevens make 35? 5	How many sevens make 21? 3
How many sevens make 28? 4	How many sevens make 70? 10

Write the answers as quickly as you can.

Multiply seven by three. 21	Multiply seven by ten. 70
Multiply seven by two. 14	Multiply seven by five. 35
Multiply seven by six. 42	Multiply seven by four. 28

Write the answers as quickly as you can.

4 x 7 = 28	2 x 7 = 14	10 x 7 = 70
5 x 7 = 35	1 x 7 = 7	3 x 7 = 21

Write the answers as quickly as you can.

A bag has seven candies. Ann buys five bags. How many candies does she have? 35

How many days are there in six weeks? 42

The rest of the 7s

You should now know all of the 1, 2, 3, 4, 5, 6, and 10 times tables.
You need to learn only these parts of the seven times table.
7 x 7 = 49   8 x 7 = 56   9 x 7 = 63

This work will help you remember the 7 times table.

Complete these sequences.

7   14   21   28   35   42   49   56   63   70

6 x 7 = 42   so   7 x 7 = 42 plus another 7 = 49

21   28   35   42   49   56   63   70

7 x 7 = 49   so   8 x 7 = 49 plus another 7 = 56

7   14   21   28   35   42   49   56   63   70

8 x 7 = 56   so   9 x 7 = 56 plus another 7 = 63

7   14   21   28   35   42   49   56   63   70

Test yourself on the rest of the 7 times table.
Cover the section above with a sheet of paper.

What is seven sevens? 49	What is eight sevens? 56
What is nine sevens? 63	What is ten sevens? 70

8 x 7 = 56   7 x 7 = 49   9 x 7 = 63   10 x 7 = 70

How many days are there in eight weeks? 56

A package contains seven pens.
How many pens will there be in nine packets? 63

How many sevens make 56? 8

Practice the 7s

You should know all of the 7 times table now, but how quickly can you remember it?
Ask someone to time you as you do this page.
Remember, you must be fast but also correct.

1 x 7 = 7	2 x 7 = 14	7 x 6 = 42
2 x 7 = 14	4 x 7 = 28	3 x 7 = 21
3 x 7 = 21	6 x 7 = 42	9 x 7 = 63
4 x 7 = 28	8 x 7 = 56	7 x 4 = 28
5 x 7 = 35	10 x 7 = 70	1 x 7 = 7
6 x 7 = 42	1 x 7 = 7	7 x 2 = 14
7 x 7 = 49	3 x 7 = 21	7 x 8 = 56
8 x 7 = 56	5 x 7 = 35	0 x 7 = 0
9 x 7 = 63	7 x 7 = 49	7 x 3 = 21
10 x 7 = 70	9 x 7 = 63	5 x 7 = 35
7 x 1 = 7	7 x 3 = 21	7 x 7 = 49
7 x 2 = 14	7 x 5 = 35	2 x 7 = 14
7 x 3 = 21	7 x 7 = 49	7 x 9 = 63
7 x 4 = 28	7 x 9 = 63	4 x 7 = 28
7 x 5 = 35	7 x 2 = 14	8 x 7 = 56
7 x 6 = 42	7 x 4 = 28	10 x 7 = 70
7 x 7 = 49	7 x 6 = 42	7 x 5 = 35
7 x 8 = 56	7 x 8 = 56	7 x 0 = 0
7 x 9 = 63	7 x 10 = 70	7 x 1 = 7
7 x 10 = 70	7 x 0 = 0	6 x 7 = 42

Speed trials

You should know all of the 1, 2, 3, 4, 5, 6, 7, and 10 times tables by now, but how quickly can you remember them?
Ask someone to time you as you do this page.
Remember, you must be fast but also correct.

4 x 7 = 28	7 x 3 = 21	9 x 7 = 63
5 x 10 = 50	8 x 7 = 56	7 x 6 = 42
7 x 5 = 35	6 x 6 = 36	8 x 3 = 24
6 x 5 = 30	5 x 10 = 50	6 x 6 = 36
6 x 10 = 60	6 x 3 = 18	7 x 4 = 28
8 x 7 = 56	7 x 5 = 35	4 x 6 = 24
5 x 8 = 40	4 x 6 = 24	3 x 7 = 21
9 x 6 = 54	6 x 5 = 30	2 x 8 = 16
5 x 7 = 35	7 x 10 = 70	7 x 3 = 21
7 x 6 = 42	6 x 7 = 42	0 x 6 = 0
0 x 5 = 0	5 x 7 = 35	10 x 7 = 70
6 x 3 = 18	8 x 4 = 32	6 x 2 = 12
6 x 7 = 42	0 x 7 = 0	8 x 7 = 56
3 x 5 = 15	5 x 8 = 40	7 x 7 = 49
4 x 7 = 28	7 x 6 = 42	6 x 5 = 30
7 x 10 = 70	8 x 3 = 24	5 x 10 = 50
7 x 8 = 56	9 x 6 = 54	7 x 0 = 0
2 x 7 = 14	7 x 7 = 49	3 x 10 = 30
4 x 9 = 36	9 x 10 = 90	2 x 7 = 14
9 x 10 = 90	5 x 6 = 30	7 x 8 = 56

Some of the 8s

You should already know some of the 8 times table because it is part of the 1, 2, 3, 4, 5, 6, 7, and 10 times tables.
1 x 8 = 8   2 x 8 = 16   3 x 8 = 24   4 x 8 = 32
5 x 8 = 40   6 x 8 = 48   7 x 8 = 56   10 x 8 = 80
Find out if you can remember them quickly and correctly.

Cover the 8 times table with paper so you can't see the numbers.
Write the answers as quickly as you can.

What is three eights?	24	What is ten eights?	80
What is two eights?	16	What is four eights?	32
What is six eights?	48	What is five eights?	40

Write the answers as quickly as you can.

How many eights equal 16?	2	How many eights equal 40?	5
How many eights equal 32?	4	How many eights equal 24?	3
How many eights equal 56?	7	How many eights equal 48?	6

Write the answers as quickly as you can.

Multiply eight by three.	24	Multiply eight by ten.	80
Multiply eight by two.	16	Multiply eight by five.	40
Multiply eight by six.	48	Multiply eight by four.	32

Write the answers as quickly as you can.

6 x 8 = 48	2 x 8 = 16	10 x 8 = 80
5 x 8 = 40	7 x 8 = 56	3 x 8 = 24

Write the answers as quickly as you can.
A pizza has eight slices. John buys six pizzas.
How many slices does he have? 48
Which number multiplied by 8 gives the answer 56? 7

47

The rest of the 8s

You need to learn only these parts of the eight times table.
8 x 8 = 64   9 x 8 = 72

This work will help you remember the 8 times table.

Complete these sequences.

8   16   24   32   40   48   56   64   72   80

7 x 8 = 56   so   8 x 8 = 56 plus another 8 = 64

24   32   40   48   56   64   72   80

8 x 8 = 64   so   9 x 8 = 64 plus another 8 = 72

8   16   24   32   40   48   56   64   72   80

8   16   24   32   40   48   56   64   72   80

Test yourself on the rest of the 8 times table.
Cover the section above with a sheet of paper.

What is seven eights?	56	What is eight eights? 64
What is nine eights?	72	What is eight nines? 72

8 x 8 = 64   9 x 8 = 72   8 x 9 = 72   10 x 8 = 80

What number multiplied by 8 gives the answer 72? 9

A number multiplied by 8 gives the answer 80. What is the number? 10

David puts out building bricks in piles of 8.
How many bricks will there be in 10 piles? 80

What number multiplied by 5 gives the answer 40? 8

How many 8s make 72? 9

48

Practice the 8s

You should know all of the 8 times table now, but how quickly can you remember it?
Ask someone to time you as you do this page.
Be fast but also correct.

1 x 8 = 8	2 x 8 = 16	8 x 6 = 48
2 x 8 = 16	4 x 8 = 32	3 x 8 = 24
3 x 8 = 24	6 x 8 = 48	9 x 8 = 72
4 x 8 = 32	8 x 8 = 64	8 x 4 = 32
5 x 8 = 40	10 x 8 = 80	1 x 8 = 8
6 x 8 = 48	1 x 8 = 8	8 x 2 = 16
7 x 8 = 56	3 x 8 = 24	7 x 8 = 56
8 x 8 = 64	5 x 8 = 40	0 x 8 = 0
9 x 8 = 72	7 x 8 = 56	8 x 3 = 24
10 x 8 = 80	9 x 8 = 72	5 x 8 = 40
8 x 1 = 8	8 x 3 = 24	8 x 8 = 64
8 x 2 = 16	8 x 5 = 40	2 x 8 = 16
8 x 3 = 24	8 x 8 = 64	8 x 9 = 72
8 x 4 = 32	8 x 9 = 72	4 x 8 = 32
8 x 5 = 40	8 x 2 = 16	8 x 6 = 48
8 x 6 = 48	8 x 4 = 32	10 x 8 = 80
8 x 7 = 56	8 x 6 = 48	8 x 5 = 40
8 x 8 = 64	8 x 8 = 64	8 x 0 = 0
8 x 9 = 72	8 x 10 = 80	8 x 1 = 8
8 x 10 = 80	8 x 0 = 0	6 x 8 = 48

Speed trials ☆

You should know all of the 1, 2, 3, 4, 5, 6, 7, 8, and 10 times tables now, but how quickly can you remember them?
Ask someone to time you as you do this page.
Be fast but also correct.

4 x 8 = 32	7 x 8 = 56	9 x 8 = 72
5 x 10 = 50	8 x 7 = 56	7 x 6 = 42
7 x 8 = 56	6 x 8 = 48	8 x 3 = 24
8 x 5 = 40	8 x 10 = 80	8 x 8 = 64
6 x 10 = 60	6 x 3 = 18	7 x 4 = 28
8 x 7 = 56	7 x 7 = 49	4 x 8 = 32
5 x 8 = 40	5 x 6 = 30	3 x 7 = 21
9 x 8 = 72	6 x 7 = 42	2 x 8 = 16
8 x 8 = 64	7 x 10 = 70	7 x 3 = 21
7 x 6 = 42	6 x 9 = 54	0 x 8 = 0
7 x 5 = 35	5 x 8 = 40	10 x 8 = 80
6 x 8 = 48	8 x 4 = 32	6 x 2 = 12
6 x 7 = 42	0 x 8 = 0	8 x 6 = 48
5 x 7 = 35	5 x 9 = 45	7 x 8 = 56
8 x 4 = 32	7 x 6 = 42	6 x 5 = 30
7 x 10 = 70	8 x 3 = 24	8 x 10 = 80
2 x 8 = 16	9 x 6 = 54	8 x 7 = 56
4 x 7 = 28	8 x 6 = 48	5 x 10 = 50
6 x 9 = 54	9 x 10 = 90	8 x 2 = 16
9 x 10 = 90	6 x 6 = 36	8 x 9 = 72

☆ Some of the 9s

You should already know nearly all of the 9 times table because it is part of the 1, 2, 3, 4, 5, 6, 7, 8, and 10 times tables.
1 x 9 = 9   2 x 9 = 18   3 x 9 = 27   4 x 9 = 36   5 x 9 = 45
6 x 9 = 54   7 x 9 = 63   8 x 9 = 72   10 x 9 = 90
Find out if you can remember them quickly and correctly.

Cover the nine times table so you can't see the numbers.
Write the answers as quickly as you can.

What is three nines?	27	What is ten nines?	90
What is two nines?	18	What is four nines?	36
What is six nines?	54	What is five nines?	45
What is seven nines?	63	What is eight nines?	72

Write the answers as quickly as you can.

How many nines equal 18?	2	How many nines equal 54?	6
How many nines equal 90?	10	How many nines equal 27?	3
How many nines equal 72?	8	How many nines equal 36?	4
How many nines equal 45?	5	How many nines equal 63?	7

Write the answers as quickly as you can.

Multiply nine by seven.	63	Multiply nine by ten.	90
Multiply nine by two.	18	Multiply nine by five.	45
Multiply nine by six.	54	Multiply nine by four.	36
Multiply nine by three.	27	Multiply nine by eight.	72

Write the answers as quickly as you can.

6 x 9 = 54	2 x 9 = 18	10 x 9 = 90
5 x 9 = 45	3 x 9 = 27	8 x 9 = 72
0 x 9 = 0	7 x 9 = 63	4 x 9 = 36

The rest of the 9s ☆

You need to learn only this part of the nine times table.
9 x 9 = 81

This work will help you remember the 9 times table.
Complete these sequences.

9   18   27   36   45   54   63   72   81   90

8 x 9 = 72   so   9 x 9 = 72 plus another 9 = 81

27   36   45   54   63   72   81   90

9   18   27   36   45   54   63   72   81   90

9   18   27   36   45   54   63   72   81   90

Look for a pattern in the nine times table.

1	x	9	=	09
2	x	9	=	18
3	x	9	=	27
4	x	9	=	36
5	x	9	=	45
6	x	9	=	54
7	x	9	=	63
8	x	9	=	72
9	x	9	=	81
10	x	9	=	90

Write down any patterns you can see. (There is more than one.)
The digits in every answer have a sum of 9.
If we take the first number of every answer, from top to bottom, we get
0, 1, 2, 3, 4, 5, 6, 7, 8, 9.
If we take the second number of every answer, from bottom to top, we get
0, 1, 2, 3, 4, 5, 6, 7, 8, 9, again.
The first and last answers are opposites (09 and 90), the second and
the second last answers are opposites (18 and 81) and so on.

☆ Practice the 9s

You should know all of the 9 times table now, but how quickly can you remember it?
Ask someone to time you as you do this page.
Be fast and correct.

1 x 9 = 9	2 x 9 = 18	9 x 6 = 54
2 x 9 = 18	4 x 9 = 36	3 x 9 = 27
3 x 9 = 27	6 x 9 = 54	9 x 9 = 81
4 x 9 = 36	9 x 7 = 63	9 x 4 = 36
5 x 9 = 45	10 x 9 = 90	1 x 9 = 9
6 x 9 = 54	1 x 9 = 9	9 x 2 = 18
7 x 9 = 63	3 x 9 = 27	7 x 9 = 63
8 x 9 = 72	5 x 9 = 45	0 x 9 = 0
9 x 9 = 81	7 x 9 = 63	9 x 3 = 27
10 x 9 = 90	9 x 9 = 81	5 x 9 = 45
9 x 1 = 9	9 x 3 = 27	9 x 9 = 81
9 x 2 = 18	9 x 5 = 45	2 x 9 = 18
9 x 3 = 27	0 x 9 = 0	8 x 9 = 72
9 x 4 = 36	9 x 1 = 9	4 x 9 = 36
9 x 5 = 45	9 x 2 = 18	9 x 7 = 63
9 x 6 = 54	9 x 4 = 36	10 x 9 = 90
9 x 7 = 63	9 x 6 = 54	9 x 5 = 45
9 x 8 = 72	9 x 8 = 72	9 x 0 = 0
9 x 9 = 81	9 x 10 = 90	9 x 1 = 9
9 x 10 = 90	9 x 0 = 0	6 x 9 = 54

Encourage children to notice patterns. It does not matter how they express these. One pattern is to deduct 1 from the number being multiplied. This gives the first digit of the answer. Then deduct this first digit from 9 to get the second digit of the answer.

Speed trials

You should know all of the times tables by now, but how quickly can you remember them?
Ask someone to time you as you do this page.
Be fast and correct.

6 x 8 = 48	4 x 8 = 32	8 x 10 = 80
9 x 10 = 90	9 x 8 = 72	7 x 9 = 63
5 x 8 = 40	6 x 6 = 36	8 x 5 = 40
7 x 5 = 35	8 x 9 = 72	8 x 7 = 56
6 x 4 = 24	6 x 4 = 24	7 x 4 = 28
8 x 8 = 64	7 x 3 = 21	4 x 9 = 36
5 x 10 = 50	5 x 9 = 45	6 x 7 = 42
9 x 8 = 72	6 x 8 = 48	4 x 6 = 24
8 x 3 = 24	7 x 7 = 49	7 x 8 = 56
7 x 7 = 49	6 x 9 = 54	6 x 9 = 54
9 x 5 = 45	7 x 8 = 56	10 x 8 = 80
4 x 8 = 32	8 x 4 = 32	6 x 5 = 30
6 x 7 = 42	0 x 9 = 0	8 x 8 = 64
2 x 9 = 18	10 x 10 = 100	7 x 6 = 42
8 x 4 = 32	7 x 6 = 42	6 x 8 = 48
7 x 10 = 70	8 x 7 = 56	9 x 10 = 90
2 x 8 = 16	9 x 6 = 54	8 x 4 = 32
4 x 7 = 28	8 x 6 = 48	7 x 10 = 70
6 x 9 = 54	9 x 9 = 81	5 x 8 = 40
9 x 9 = 81	6 x 7 = 42	8 x 9 = 72

Times tables for division

Knowing the times tables can also help with division problems.
Look at these examples.
3 x 6 = 18 which means that 18 ÷ 3 = 6 and that 18 ÷ 6 = 3
4 x 5 = 20 which means that 20 ÷ 4 = 5 and that 20 ÷ 5 = 4
9 x 3 = 27 which means that 27 ÷ 3 = 9 and that 27 ÷ 9 = 3

Use your knowledge of the times tables to work these division problems.

3 x 8 = 24 which means that 24 ÷ 3 = 8 and that 24 ÷ 8 = 3
4 x 7 = 28 which means that 28 ÷ 4 = 7 and that 28 ÷ 7 = 4
3 x 5 = 15 which means that 15 ÷ 3 = 5 and that 15 ÷ 5 = 3
4 x 3 = 12 which means that 12 ÷ 3 = 4 and that 12 ÷ 4= 3
3 x 10 = 30 which means that 30 ÷ 3 = 10 and that 30 ÷ 10 = 3
4 x 8 = 32 which means that 32 ÷ 4 = 8 and that 32 ÷ 8 = 4
3 x 9 = 27 which means that 27 ÷ 3 = 9 and that 27 ÷ 9 = 3
4 x 10 = 40 which means that 40 ÷ 4 = 10 and that 40 ÷ 10 = 4

These division problems help practice the 3 and 4 times tables.

20 ÷ 4 = 5	15 ÷ 3 = 5	16 ÷ 4 = 4
24 ÷ 4 = 6	27 ÷ 3 = 9	30 ÷ 3 = 10
12 ÷ 3 = 4	18 ÷ 3 = 6	28 ÷ 4 = 7
24 ÷ 3 = 8	32 ÷ 4 = 8	21 ÷ 3 = 7

How many fours in 36? 9	Divide 27 by three. 9
Divide 28 by 4. 7	How many threes in 21? 7
How many fives in 35? 7	Divide 40 by 5. 8
Divide 15 by 3. 5	How many eights in 48? 6

Times tables for division

This page will help you remember times tables by dividing by 2, 3, 4, 5, and 10.
20 ÷ 5 = 4   18 ÷ 3 = 6   60 ÷ 10 = 6

Complete the problems.

40 ÷ 10 = 4	14 ÷ 2 = 7	32 ÷ 4 = 8
25 ÷ 5 = 5	21 ÷ 3 = 7	16 ÷ 4 = 4
24 ÷ 4 = 6	28 ÷ 4 = 7	12 ÷ 2 = 6
45 ÷ 5 = 9	35 ÷ 5 = 7	12 ÷ 3 = 4
10 ÷ 2 = 5	40 ÷ 10 = 4	12 ÷ 4 = 3
20 ÷ 10 = 2	20 ÷ 2 = 10	20 ÷ 2 = 10
6 ÷ 2 = 3	18 ÷ 3 = 6	20 ÷ 4 = 5
24 ÷ 3 = 8	32 ÷ 4 = 8	20 ÷ 5 = 4
30 ÷ 5 = 6	40 ÷ 5 = 8	20 ÷ 10 = 2
30 ÷ 10 = 3	80 ÷ 10 = 8	18 ÷ 2 = 9
40 ÷ 5 = 8	6 ÷ 2 = 3	18 ÷ 3 = 6
21 ÷ 3 = 7	15 ÷ 3 = 5	15 ÷ 3 = 5
14 ÷ 2 = 7	24 ÷ 4 = 6	15 ÷ 5 = 3
27 ÷ 3 = 9	15 ÷ 5 = 3	24 ÷ 3 = 8
90 ÷ 10 = 9	10 ÷ 10 = 1	24 ÷ 4 = 6
15 ÷ 5 = 3	4 ÷ 2 = 2	50 ÷ 5 = 10
15 ÷ 3 = 5	9 ÷ 3 = 3	50 ÷ 10 = 5
20 ÷ 5 = 4	4 ÷ 4 = 1	30 ÷ 3 = 10
20 ÷ 4 = 5	10 ÷ 5 = 2	30 ÷ 5 = 6
16 ÷ 2 = 8	100 ÷ 10 = 10	30 ÷ 10 = 3

Times tables for division

This page will help you remember times tables by dividing by 2, 3, 4, 5, 6, and 10.
30 ÷ 6 = 5   12 ÷ 6 = 2   60 ÷ 10 = 6

Complete the problems.

18 ÷ 6 = 3	27 ÷ 3 = 9	48 ÷ 6 = 8
30 ÷ 10 = 3	18 ÷ 6 = 3	35 ÷ 5 = 7
14 ÷ 2 = 7	20 ÷ 2 = 10	36 ÷ 4 = 9
18 ÷ 3 = 6	24 ÷ 6 = 4	24 ÷ 3 = 8
20 ÷ 4 = 5	24 ÷ 8 = 8	20 ÷ 2 = 10
15 ÷ 5 = 3	24 ÷ 4 = 6	30 ÷ 6 = 5
36 ÷ 6 = 6	30 ÷ 10 = 3	25 ÷ 5 = 5
50 ÷ 10 = 5	18 ÷ 2 = 9	32 ÷ 4 = 8
8 ÷ 2 = 4	18 ÷ 3 = 6	27 ÷ 3 = 9
15 ÷ 3 = 5	36 ÷ 4 = 9	16 ÷ 2 = 8
16 ÷ 4 = 4	36 ÷ 6 = 6	42 ÷ 6 = 7
25 ÷ 5 = 5	40 ÷ 5 = 8	5 ÷ 5 = 1
6 ÷ 6 = 1	100 ÷ 10 = 10	4 ÷ 4 = 1
10 ÷ 10 = 1	16 ÷ 4 = 4	28 ÷ 4 = 7
42 ÷ 6 = 7	42 ÷ 6 = 7	14 ÷ 2 = 7
24 ÷ 4 = 6	48 ÷ 6 = 8	24 ÷ 6 = 4
54 ÷ 6 = 9	54 ÷ 6 = 9	18 ÷ 6 = 3
90 ÷ 10 = 9	60 ÷ 6 = 10	54 ÷ 6 = 9
30 ÷ 6 = 5	60 ÷ 10 = 6	60 ÷ 6 = 10
30 ÷ 5 = 6	30 ÷ 6 = 5	40 ÷ 5 = 8

Times tables for division

This page will help you remember times tables by dividing by 2, 3, 4, 5, 6, and 7.

14 ÷ 7 = 2	28 ÷ 7 = 4	70 ÷ 7 = 10

Complete the problems.

21 ÷ 7 = 3	18 ÷ 6 = 3	49 ÷ 7 = 7
35 ÷ 5 = 7	28 ÷ 7 = 4	35 ÷ 5 = 7
14 ÷ 2 = 7	24 ÷ 6 = 4	35 ÷ 7 = 5
18 ÷ 6 = 3	24 ÷ 4 = 6	24 ÷ 6 = 4
20 ÷ 5 = 4	24 ÷ 2 = 12	21 ÷ 3 = 7
15 ÷ 3 = 5	21 ÷ 7 = 3	70 ÷ 7 = 10
36 ÷ 4 = 9	42 ÷ 7 = 6	42 ÷ 7 = 6
56 ÷ 7 = 8	18 ÷ 3 = 6	32 ÷ 4 = 8
18 ÷ 2 = 9	49 ÷ 7 = 7	27 ÷ 3 = 9
15 ÷ 5 = 3	36 ÷ 4 = 9	16 ÷ 4 = 4
49 ÷ 7 = 7	36 ÷ 6 = 6	42 ÷ 6 = 7
25 ÷ 5 = 5	40 ÷ 5 = 8	45 ÷ 5 = 9
7 ÷ 7 = 1	70 ÷ 7 = 10	40 ÷ 4 = 10
63 ÷ 7 = 9	24 ÷ 3 = 8	24 ÷ 3 = 8
42 ÷ 7 = 6	42 ÷ 6 = 7	14 ÷ 7 = 2
24 ÷ 6 = 4	48 ÷ 6 = 8	24 ÷ 4 = 6
54 ÷ 6 = 9	54 ÷ 6 = 9	18 ÷ 3 = 6
28 ÷ 7 = 4	60 ÷ 6 = 10	56 ÷ 7 = 8
30 ÷ 6 = 5	63 ÷ 7 = 9	63 ÷ 7 = 9
35 ÷ 7 = 5	25 ÷ 5 = 5	48 ÷ 6 = 8

Times tables for division

This page will help you remember times tables by dividing by 2, 3, 4, 5, 6, 7, 8, and 9.

16 ÷ 8 = 2	35 ÷ 7 = 5	27 ÷ 9 = 3

Complete the problems.

42 ÷ 6 = 7	81 ÷ 9 = 9	56 ÷ 7 = 8
32 ÷ 8 = 4	56 ÷ 7 = 8	45 ÷ 5 = 9
14 ÷ 7 = 2	72 ÷ 9 = 8	35 ÷ 7 = 5
18 ÷ 9 = 2	24 ÷ 8 = 3	18 ÷ 9 = 2
63 ÷ 7 = 9	27 ÷ 9 = 3	21 ÷ 3 = 7
72 ÷ 9 = 8	72 ÷ 9 = 8	28 ÷ 7 = 4
72 ÷ 8 = 9	42 ÷ 6 = 7	64 ÷ 8 = 8
56 ÷ 7 = 8	27 ÷ 3 = 9	32 ÷ 8 = 4
18 ÷ 6 = 3	14 ÷ 7 = 2	27 ÷ 9 = 3
81 ÷ 9 = 9	36 ÷ 4 = 9	16 ÷ 8 = 2
63 ÷ 9 = 7	36 ÷ 6 = 6	42 ÷ 6 = 7
45 ÷ 5 = 9	48 ÷ 8 = 6	45 ÷ 9 = 5
54 ÷ 9 = 6	21 ÷ 7 = 3	40 ÷ 4 = 10
70 ÷ 7 = 10	24 ÷ 3 = 8	24 ÷ 8 = 3
42 ÷ 7 = 6	40 ÷ 8 = 5	63 ÷ 7 = 9
30 ÷ 5 = 6	45 ÷ 9 = 5	24 ÷ 6 = 4
54 ÷ 6 = 9	54 ÷ 6 = 9	18 ÷ 6 = 3
56 ÷ 8 = 7	42 ÷ 7 = 6	56 ÷ 7 = 8
30 ÷ 5 = 6	63 ÷ 9 = 7	63 ÷ 9 = 7
35 ÷ 7 = 5	50 ÷ 5 = 10	48 ÷ 8 = 6

Times tables practice grids

This is a times tables grid.

X	3	4	5
7	21	28	35
8	24	32	40

Complete each times tables grid.

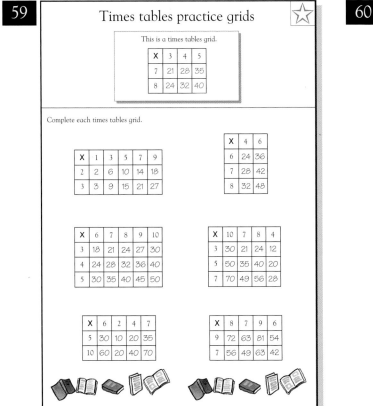

X	1	3	5	7	9
2	2	6	10	14	18
3	3	9	15	21	27

X	4	6
6	24	36
7	28	42
8	32	48

X	6	7	8	9	10
3	18	21	24	27	30
4	24	28	32	36	40
5	30	35	40	45	50

X	10	7	8	4
3	30	21	24	12
5	50	35	40	20
7	70	49	56	28

X	6	2	4	7
5	30	10	20	35
10	60	20	40	70

X	8	7	9	6
9	72	63	81	54
7	56	49	63	42

Times tables practice grids

Here are more times tables grids.

X	2	4	6
5	10	20	30
7	14	28	42

X	8	3	9	2
5	40	15	45	10
6	48	18	54	12
7	56	21	63	14

X	2	3	4	5
8	16	24	32	40
9	18	27	36	45

X	10	9	8	7
6	60	54	48	42
5	50	45	40	35
4	40	36	32	28

X	3	8
2	6	16
3	9	24
4	12	32
5	15	40
6	18	48
7	21	56

X	2	4	6	8
1	2	4	6	8
3	6	12	18	24
5	10	20	30	40
7	14	28	42	56
9	18	36	54	72
0	0	0	0	0

61 — Times tables practice grids

Here are some other times tables grids.

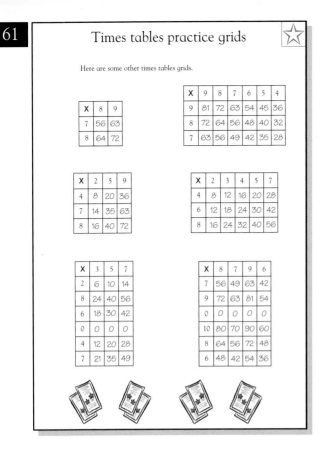

X	8	9
7	56	63
8	64	72

X	9	8	7	6	5	4
9	81	72	63	54	45	36
8	72	64	56	48	40	32
7	63	56	49	42	35	28

X	2	5	9
4	8	20	36
7	14	35	63
8	16	40	72

X	2	3	4	5	7
4	8	12	16	20	28
6	12	18	24	30	42
8	16	24	32	40	56

X	3	5	7
2	6	10	14
8	24	40	56
6	18	30	42
0	0	0	0
4	12	20	28
7	21	35	49

X	8	7	9	6
7	56	49	63	42
9	72	63	81	54
0	0	0	0	0
10	80	70	90	60
8	64	56	72	48
6	48	42	54	36

62 — Speed trials

Try this final test.

27 ÷ 3 = 9	4 x 9 = 36	14 ÷ 2 = 7
7 x 9 = 63	18 ÷ 2 = 9	9 x 9 = 81
64 ÷ 8 = 8	6 x 8 = 48	15 ÷ 3 = 5
90 ÷ 10 = 9	21 ÷ 3 = 7	8 x 8 = 64
6 x 8 = 48	9 x 7 = 63	24 ÷ 4 = 6
45 ÷ 9 = 5	36 ÷ 4 = 9	7 x 8 = 56
3 x 7 = 21	4 x 6 = 24	30 ÷ 5 = 6
9 x 5 = 45	45 ÷ 5 = 9	6 x 6 = 36
48 ÷ 6 = 8	8 x 5 = 40	42 ÷ 6 = 7
7 x 7 = 49	42 ÷ 6 = 7	9 x 5 = 45
3 x 9 = 27	7 x 4 = 28	49 ÷ 7 = 7
56 ÷ 8 = 7	35 ÷ 7 = 5	8 x 6 = 48
36 ÷ 4 = 9	9 x 3 = 27	72 ÷ 8 = 9
24 ÷ 3 = 8	24 ÷ 8 = 3	9 x 7 = 63
36 ÷ 9 = 4	8 x 2 = 16	54 ÷ 9 = 6
6 x 7 = 42	36 ÷ 9 = 4	7 x 6 = 42
4 x 4 = 16	6 x 10 = 60	10 ÷ 10 = 1
32 ÷ 8 = 4	80 ÷ 10 = 8	7 x 7 = 49
49 ÷ 7 = 7	6 x 9 = 54	16 ÷ 8 = 2
25 ÷ 5 = 5	16 ÷ 2 = 8	7 x 9 = 63
56 ÷ 7 = 8	54 ÷ 9 = 6	63 ÷ 7 = 9

63 — Addition, multiplication, and division

Write the missing number in the box.
7 + ? = 7   3 x ? = 3
7 + 0 = 7   3 x 1 = 3

Write the missing number in the box.

4 + 0 = 4	12 x 1 = 12	1 x 9 = 9	6 + 0 = 6
3 + 12 = 15	17 + 8 = 25	11 + 8 = 19	9 + 17 = 26
4 + 5 = 9	12 + 5 = 17	35 ÷ 7 = 5	25 + 15 = 40
15 + 60 = 75	14 + 6 = 20	21 + 32 = 53	49 + 9 = 58
5 x 6 = 30	12 ÷ 4 = 3	50 ÷ 10 = 5	8 x 6 = 48
9 x 6 = 54	100 ÷ 20 = 5	63 x 10 = 630	36 ÷ 9 = 4

Rewrite each equation, and fill in the missing number.

3 x (6 x 4) = (3 x ?) x 4
3 x (6 x 4) = (3 x 6) x 4

(7 x 9) x 3 = 7 x (? x 3)
(7 x 9) x 3 = 7 x (9 x 3)

(2 x 5) x 9 = ? x (5 x 9)
(2 x 5) x 9 = 2 x (5 x 9)

8 x (8 x 7) = (8 x 8) x ?
8 x (8 x 7) = (8 x 8) x 7

5 x (10 + 3) = (5 x 10) + (? x 3)
5 x (10 + 3) = (5 x 10) + (5 x 3)

(8 + 6) x 7 = (8 x 7) + (6 x ?)
(8 + 6) x 7 = (8 x 7) + (6 x 7)

(3 + 7) x 2 = (? x 2) + (7 x 2)
(3 + 7) x 2 = (3 x 2) + (7 x 2)

9 x (5 + 12) = (? x 5) + (? x 12)
9 x (5 + 12) = (9 x 5) + (9 x 12)

Children may have difficulty understanding the distributive property. Perform the operations to show them that 5 x (10 + 3) = (5 x 10) + (5 x 3).

64 — Place value to 10,000,000

How many hundreds are there in 7,000? 70 hundreds (70 x 100 = 7,000)
What is the value of the 9 in 694? 90 (because the 9 is in the tens column)

Write how many tens there are in:

400 — 40 tens	600 — 60 tens	900 — 90 tens
200 — 20 tens	1,300 — 130 tens	4,700 — 470 tens
4,800 — 480 tens	1,240 — 124 tens	1,320 — 132 tens
2,630 — 263 tens	5,920 — 592 tens	4,350 — 435 tens

What is the value of the 7 in these numbers?

76 — 70	720 — 700	137 — 7
7,122 — 7,000	74,301 — 70,000	724 — 700

What is the value of the 3 in these numbers?

324,126 — 300,000	3,927,141 — 3,000,000	214,623 — 3
8,254,320 — 300	3,711,999 — 3,000,000	124,372 — 300

Write how many hundreds there are in:

6,400 — 64 hundreds	8,500 — 85 hundreds
19,900 — 199 hundreds	36,200 — 362 hundreds
524,600 — 5,246 hundreds	712,400 — 7,124 hundreds

What is the value of the 8 in these numbers?

8,214,631 — 8,000,000	2,398,147 — 8,000	463,846 — 800
287,034 — 80,000	8,110,927 — 8,000,000	105,428 — 8

Explain to children that finding how many tens there are in a number is the same as dividing by 10. In the number 400, for example, there are 40 tens, because 400 divided by 10 is 40.

65

Multiplying and dividing by 10

Write the answer in the box.

37 x 10 = **370**   58 ÷ 10 = **5.8**

Write the product in the box.

94 x 10 = **940**   13 x 10 = **130**   37 x 10 = **370**

36 x 10 = **360**   47 x 10 = **470**   54 x 10 = **540**

236 x 10 = **2,360**   419 x 10 = **4,190**   262 x 10 = **2,620**

531 x 10 = **5,310**   674 x 10 = **6,740**   801 x 10 = **8,010**

Write the quotient in the box.

92 ÷ 10 = **9.2**   48 ÷ 10 = **4.8**   37 ÷ 10 = **3.7**

18 ÷ 10 = **1.8**   29 ÷ 10 = **2.9**   54 ÷ 10 = **5.4**

345 ÷ 10 = **34.5**   354 ÷ 10 = **35.4**   723 ÷ 10 = **72.3**

531 ÷ 10 = **53.1**   262 ÷ 10 = **26.2**   419 ÷ 10 = **41.9**

Find the missing factor.

23 x 10 = 230   **75** x 10 = 750   **99** x 10 = 990

48 x 10 = 480   **13** x 10 = 130   **25** x 10 = 250

52 x 10 = 520   **39** x 10 = 390   **27** x 10 = 270

62 x 10 = 620   **86** x 10 = 860   **17** x 10 = 170

Find the dividend.

47 ÷ 10 = 4.7   **68** ÷ 10 = 6.8   **124** ÷ 10 = 12.4

257 ÷ 10 = 25.7   **362** ÷ 10 = 36.2   **314** ÷ 10 = 31.4

408 ÷ 10 = 40.8   **672** ÷ 10 = 67.2   **809** ÷ 10 = 80.9

924 ÷ 10 = 92.4   **327** ÷ 10 = 32.7   **563** ÷ 10 = 56.3

Multiplying a number by 10 is the same as adding a 0 it. Dividing by 10 moves the decimal point one place to the left. Whole numbers (e.g. 58) can be written with a decimal point (58.0). In the last two sections, the inverse operation gives the answer.

66

Ordering sets of measures

Write these measures in order, from least to greatest.

3,100 km   24 km   1,821 km   247 km   4 km   960 km

4 km   24 km   247 km   960 km   1,821 km   3,100 km

Write these measures in order, from least to greatest.

$526	$15,940	$1,504	$826	$37,532
$526	**$826**	**$1,504**	**$15,940**	**$37,532**
720 mi	7,200 mi	27,410 mi	15 mi	247 mi
15 mi	**247 mi**	**720 mi**	**7,200 mi**	**27,410 mi**
70,000 gal	650 gal	26,000 gal	6,500 gal	7,000 gal
650 gal	**6,500 gal**	**7,000 gal**	**26,000 gal**	**70,000 gal**
656 lb	9,565 lb	22,942 lb	752,247 lb	1,327 lb
656 lb	**1,327 lb**	**9,565 lb**	**22,942 lb**	**752,247 lb**
9,520 yrs	320 yrs	4,681 yrs	8,940 yrs	20,316 yrs
320 yrs	**4,681 yrs**	**8,940 yrs**	**9,520 yrs**	**20,316 yrs**
217,846 kg	75,126 kg	8,940 kg	14,632 kg	175 kg
175 kg	**8,940 kg**	**14,632 kg**	**75,126 kg**	**217,846 kg**
9,420 km	764 km	25,811 km	114,243 km	7,240 km
764 km	**7,240 km**	**9,420 km**	**25,811 km**	**114,243 km**
$37,227	$1,365,240	$143,820	$950	$4,212
$950	**$4,212**	**$37,227**	**$143,820**	**$1,365,240**
24,091 ft	59,473 ft	1,237 ft	426 ft	837,201 ft
426 ft	**1,237 ft**	**24,091 ft**	**59,473 ft**	**837,201 ft**
47,632 oz	847 oz	9,625 oz	103,427 oz	2,330 oz
847 oz	**2,330 oz**	**9,625 oz**	**47,632 oz**	**103,427 oz**
7,340 m	249 m	12,746 m	32 m	17,407,321 m
32 m	**249 m**	**7,340 m**	**12,746 m**	**17,407,321 m**

You may need to help children identify the significant digit when sorting a group of numbers. In some cases, when the significant digits are the same, it will be necessary to compare the digits to the right of the significant digit.

67

Appropriate units of measure

Choose the best units to measure the length of each item.

inches   feet   yards

notebook   car   swimming pool
inches   **feet**   **yards**

Choose the best units to measure the length of each item.

inches   feet   yards

bed   bicycle   toothbrush   football field
feet   **feet**   **inches**   **yards**

shoe   driveway   canoe   fence
inches   **feet or yards**   **feet**   **yards**

The height of a door is about 7   **feet** .

The length of a pencil is about 7   **inches** .

The height of a flagpole is about 7   **yards** .

Choose the best units to measure the weight of each item.

ounces   pounds   tons

train   kitten   watermelon   tennis ball
tons   **ounces**   **pounds**   **ounces**

shoe   bag of potatoes   elephant   washing machine
ounces   **pounds**   **tons**   **pounds**

The weight of a hamburger is about 6   **ounces** .

The weight of a bag of apples is about 5   **pounds** .

The weight of a truck is about 4   **tons** .

Children might come up with their own examples of items that measure about 1 inch, 1 foot, and 1 yard, as well as items that weigh about 1 ounce, 1 pound, and 1 ton. They can use these as benchmarks to find the appropriate unit.

Identifying patterns

Continue each pattern.

Intervals of 6:   1   7   13   19   **25**   **31**   **37**

Intervals of 3:   27   24   21   18   **15**   **12**   **9**

Continue each pattern.

0	10	20	**30**	**40**	**50**	**60**
15	20	25	**30**	**35**	**40**	**45**
5	7	9	**11**	**13**	**15**	**17**
2	9	16	**23**	**30**	**37**	**44**
4	7	10	**13**	**16**	19	22
2	10	18	**26**	34	**42**	**50**

Continue each pattern.

44	38	32	**26**	**20**	**14**	**8**
33	29	25	**21**	**17**	**13**	**9**
27	23	19	**15**	**11**	**7**	**3**
56	48	40	**32**	**24**	16	**8**
49	42	35	**28**	**21**	**14**	**7**
28	25	22	**19**	**16**	**13**	10

Continue each pattern.

36	30	24	**18**	12	**6**	**0**
5	14	23	**32**	**41**	**50**	**59**
3	8	13	**18**	**23**	**28**	**33**
47	40	33	**26**	**19**	12	**5**
1	4	7	**10**	**13**	**16**	**19**

Point out that some of the patterns show an increase and some a decrease. Children should see what operation turns the first number into the second, and the second number into the third. They can then continue the pattern.

Recognizing multiples

Circle the multiples of 10.

14　(20)　25　(30)　47　(60)

Circle the multiples of 6.

20　(48)　56　(72)　25　35
1　3　(6)　16　26　(36)

Circle the multiples of 7.

(14)　24　(35)　27　47　(49)
(63)　(42)　52　37　64　71

Circle the multiples of 8.

25　31　(48)　84　(32)　(8)
18　54　(64)　35　(72)　28

Circle the multiples of 9.

17　(81)　(27)　35　92　106
(45)　53　(108)　(90)　33　95
64　(9)　28　(18)　(36)　98

Circle the multiples of 10.

15　35　(20)　46　(90)　(100)
44　37　(30)　29　(50)　45

Circle the multiples of 11.

24　(110)　123　54　(66)　90
45　(33)　87　98　(99)　(121)
43　(44)　65　(55)　21　(22)

Circle the multiples of 12.

136　134　(144)　109　(108)　(132)
(24)　34　58　68　(48)　(60)
35　29　(72)　74　(84)　94

Success on this page basically depends on a knowledge of multiplication tables. Where children experience difficulty, it may be necessary to reinforce multiplication tables.

70

Factors of numbers from 31 to 65

The factors of 40 are　1　2　4　5　8　10　20　40

Circle the factors of 56.

(1)　(2)　3　(4)　5　6　(7)　(8)　(14)　(28)　32　(56)

Find all the factors of each number.

The factors of 31 are	1, 31
The factors of 47 are	1, 47
The factors of 60 are	1, 2, 3, 4, 5, 6, 10, 12, 15, 20, 30, 60
The factors of 50 are	1, 2, 5, 10, 25, 50
The factors of 42 are	1, 2, 3, 6, 7, 14, 21, 42
The factors of 32 are	1, 2, 4, 8, 16, 32
The factors of 48 are	1, 2, 3, 4, 6, 8, 12, 16, 24, 48
The factors of 35 are	1, 5, 7, 35
The factors of 52 are	1, 2, 4, 13, 26, 52

Circle all the factors of each number.

Which numbers are factors of 39?
(1)　2　(3)　4　5　8　9　10　(13)　14　15　20　25　(39)

Which numbers are factors of 45?
(1)　(3)　4　(5)　8　(9)　12　(15)　16　21　24　36　40　44　(45)

Which numbers are factors of 61?
(1)　3　4　5　6　10　15　16　18　20　26　31　40　(61)

Which numbers are factors of 65?
(1)　2　4　(5)　6　8　9　10　12　(13)　14　15　30　60　(65)

Some numbers have only factors of 1 and themselves. They are called prime numbers. Write all the prime numbers between 31 and 65 in the box.

31, 37, 41, 43, 47, 53, 59, 61

Children often miss some of the factors of large numbers. Encourage a systematic method to find factors. Remind children that 1 and the number itself are factors of a number. If necessary, discuss prime numbers with them.

71

Writing equivalent fractions

Make these fractions equal by writing the missing number.

$\frac{20}{100} = \frac{2}{10} = \frac{1}{5}$

$\frac{5}{15} = \frac{1}{3}$

Make these fractions equal by writing a number in the box.

$\frac{10}{100} = \frac{1}{10}$ 　 $\frac{8}{100} = \frac{2}{25}$ 　 $\frac{4}{100} = \frac{1}{25}$

$\frac{2}{20} = \frac{1}{10}$ 　 $\frac{5}{100} = \frac{1}{20}$ 　 $\frac{6}{20} = \frac{3}{10}$

$\frac{3}{5} = \frac{12}{20}$ 　 $\frac{5}{6} = \frac{10}{12}$ 　 $\frac{2}{8} = \frac{6}{24}$

$\frac{2}{3} = \frac{16}{24}$ 　 $\frac{2}{18} = \frac{1}{9}$ 　 $\frac{4}{50} = \frac{2}{25}$

$\frac{11}{12} = \frac{33}{36}$ 　 $\frac{12}{15} = \frac{4}{5}$ 　 $\frac{8}{20} = \frac{2}{5}$

$\frac{2}{12} = \frac{1}{6}$ 　 $\frac{5}{20} = \frac{1}{4}$ 　 $\frac{5}{8} = \frac{10}{16}$

$\frac{7}{8} = \frac{21}{24}$ 　 $\frac{15}{100} = \frac{3}{20}$ 　 $\frac{6}{24} = \frac{1}{4}$

$\frac{5}{25} = \frac{1}{5}$ 　 $\frac{8}{20} = \frac{2}{5}$ 　 $\frac{15}{20} = \frac{3}{4}$

$\frac{5}{30} = \frac{1}{6}$ 　 $\frac{12}{14} = \frac{6}{7}$ 　 $\frac{1}{5} = \frac{4}{20}$

$\frac{9}{18} = \frac{1}{2}$ 　 $\frac{24}{30} = \frac{4}{5}$ 　 $\frac{25}{30} = \frac{5}{6}$

$\frac{1}{8} = \frac{2}{16} = \frac{3}{24} = \frac{4}{32} = \frac{5}{40} = \frac{6}{48}$

$\frac{20}{100} = \frac{5}{25} = \frac{2}{10} = \frac{1}{5} = \frac{10}{50} = \frac{40}{200}$

$\frac{2}{5} = \frac{6}{15} = \frac{8}{20} = \frac{10}{25} = \frac{20}{50} = \frac{40}{100}$

$\frac{1}{6} = \frac{2}{12} = \frac{3}{18} = \frac{4}{24} = \frac{5}{30} = \frac{6}{36}$

$\frac{2}{3} = \frac{16}{24} = \frac{24}{36} = \frac{14}{21} = \frac{6}{9} = \frac{200}{300}$

If children have any problems, point out that fractions retain the same value if you multiply the numerator and denominator by the same number or divide the numerator and denominator by the same number.

Fraction models

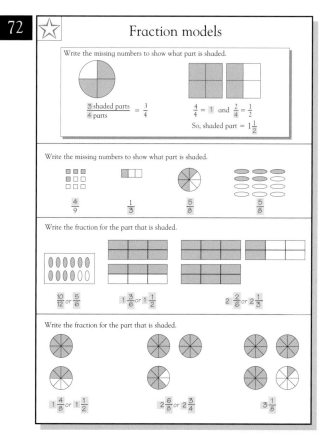

Write the missing numbers to show what part is shaded.

$\frac{3 \text{ shaded parts}}{4 \text{ parts}} = \frac{3}{4}$ 　 $\frac{4}{4} = 1$ and $\frac{2}{4} = \frac{1}{2}$

So, shaded part $= 1\frac{1}{2}$

Write the missing numbers to show what part is shaded.

$\frac{4}{9}$ 　 $\frac{1}{3}$ 　 $\frac{5}{8}$ 　 $\frac{5}{8}$

Write the fraction for the part that is shaded.

$\frac{10}{12}$ or $\frac{5}{6}$ 　 $1\frac{3}{6}$ or $1\frac{1}{2}$ 　 $2\frac{2}{6}$ or $2\frac{1}{3}$

Write the fraction for the part that is shaded.

$1\frac{4}{8}$ or $1\frac{1}{2}$ 　 $2\frac{6}{8}$ or $2\frac{3}{4}$ 　 $3\frac{1}{8}$

Some children may need further explanation of the models of mixed numbers. Point out that when all the parts of a model are shaded, the model shows the number 1.

Converting fractions and decimals ☆

Write these fractions as decimals.

$\frac{7}{10}$ = 0.7

$\frac{3}{100}$ = 0.03

Write these fractions as decimals.

0.2 = $\frac{2}{10}$ = $\frac{1}{5}$

0.47 = $\frac{47}{100}$

Write these fractions as decimals.

$\frac{3}{10}$ = 0.3 $\frac{7}{10}$ = 0.7 $\frac{9}{10}$ = 0.9

$\frac{2}{10}$ = 0.2 $\frac{1}{10}$ = 0.1 $\frac{6}{10}$ = 0.6

$\frac{1}{2}$ = $\frac{5}{10}$ = 0.5 $\frac{8}{10}$ = 0.8 $\frac{4}{10}$ = 0.4

Write these decimals as fractions.

0.1 = $\frac{1}{10}$ 0.2 = $\frac{2}{10}$ = $\frac{1}{5}$ 0.3 = $\frac{3}{10}$

0.4 = $\frac{4}{10}$ = $\frac{2}{5}$ 0.5 = $\frac{5}{10}$ = $\frac{1}{2}$ 0.6 = $\frac{6}{10}$ = $\frac{3}{5}$

0.7 = $\frac{7}{10}$ 0.8 = $\frac{8}{10}$ = $\frac{4}{5}$ 0.9 = $\frac{9}{10}$

Change these fractions to decimals.

$\frac{1}{100}$ = 0.01 $\frac{3}{100}$ = 0.03 $\frac{7}{100}$ = 0.07

$\frac{15}{100}$ = 0.15 $\frac{25}{100}$ = 0.25 $\frac{49}{100}$ = 0.49

$\frac{24}{100}$ = 0.24 $\frac{56}{100}$ = 0.56 $\frac{72}{100}$ = 0.72

Change these decimals to fractions.

0.39 = $\frac{39}{100}$ 0.47 = $\frac{47}{100}$ 0.21 = $\frac{21}{100}$

0.83 = $\frac{83}{100}$ 0.91 = $\frac{91}{100}$ 0.73 = $\frac{73}{100}$

0.51 = $\frac{51}{100}$ 0.43 = $\frac{43}{100}$ 0.17 = $\frac{17}{100}$

A number line showing tenths with their decimal equivalents can help children. If they neglect to include the zeros when converting fractions such as $\frac{7}{100}$ to 0.07, ask them to convert the decimal back to the fraction to realize their error.

74

Using information in tables

Use the table to answer the questions.

Student's favorite sports

Sport	Number of votes
Basketball	4
Soccer	10
Softball	5
Swimming	6

How many students voted for softball? 5

What is the most popular sport? soccer

Use the table to answer the questions.

Pieces made by pottery club

Name	Cups	Bowls	Plates
Carl	5	9	11
Marta	7	2	9
Assam	3	1	12
Colin	8	8	10
Renee	6	9	2

How many plates did Colin make? 10

Who made 7 cups? Marta

Who made the same number of bowls as Renee? Carl

Complete the table, and answer the questions.

Olympic medals 1998

Country	Gold	Silver	Bronze	Total
Austria	3	5	9	17
Canada	6	5	4	15
Germany	12	9	8	29
Norway	10	10	5	25
Russia	9	6	3	18
United States	6	3	4	13

How many more gold medals did Russia win than bronze medals? 6

Which country won the most silver medals? Norway

Which country won three times as many bronze medals as gold medals? Austria

On this page, children have to read, compare or manipulate information in a table. To answer the questions about the third table, children must first complete the final column.

75

Coordinate graphs ☆

Write the coordinates for each point. Remember to write the coordinate for the x-axis first.

A   (2, 4)

B   (3, 2)

C   (5, 3)

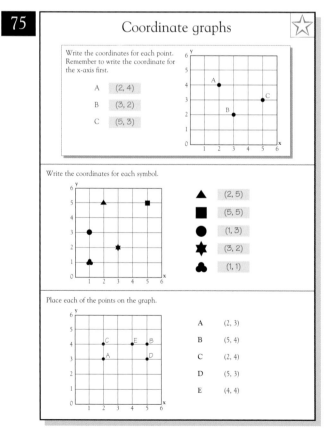

Write the coordinates for each symbol.

▲   (2, 5)

■   (5, 5)

●   (1, 3)

★   (3, 2)

♣   (1, 1)

Place each of the points on the graph.

A   (2, 3)

B   (5, 4)

C   (2, 4)

D   (5, 3)

E   (4, 4)

Most errors on this page result from children using the incorrect order for coordinate pairs. Make sure children know that the x-coordinate is always written before the y-coordinate.

Properties of polygons

Circle the polygon that has two pairs of parallel sides.

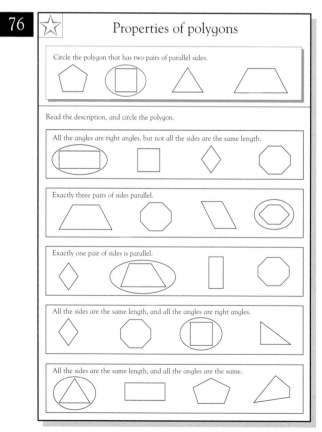

Read the description, and circle the polygon.

All the angles are right angles, but not all the sides are the same length.

Exactly three pairs of sides parallel.

Exactly one pair of sides is parallel.

All the sides are the same length, and all the angles are right angles.

All the sides are the same length, and all the angles are the same.

If children answer questions incorrectly, make sure they understand the concepts of parallel lines, lengths of sides of a polygon, equal angles, and right angles.

Naming polygons

Polygons are named for the number of sides they have.

triangle   quadrilateral   pentagon   hexagon   octagon

Quadrilaterals, which have four sides, can be different shapes.

rectangle   rhombus   square   parallelogram   trapezoid

Circle the quadrilaterals.

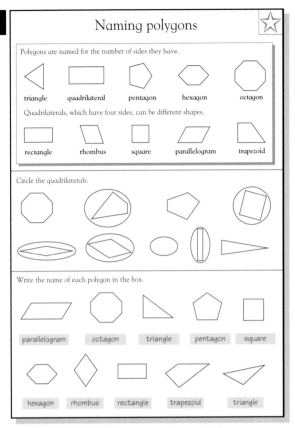

Write the name of each polygon in the box.

parallelogram   octagon   triangle   pentagon   square

hexagon   rhombus   rectangle   trapezoid   triangle

The questions on this page require children to identify and name various polygons. Children may have difficulty differentiating among a square, a parallelogram, a rectangle, and a rhombus. Explain that they are all particular kinds of parallelograms.

78

Adding decimals

Find each sum. Remember to regroup.

$7.49 + $1.36 = $8.85   4.18 + 5.59 = 9.77

Find each sum.

$5.22 + $3.49 = $8.71   4.34 + 2.56 = 6.90 $8.21 + $4.49 = $12.70   3.28 + 9.22 = 12.50

Find each sum.

2.77 m + 4.59 m = 7.36 m   6.58 km + 3.54 km = 10.12 km   7.37 cm + 2.76 cm = 10.13 cm   8.09 m + 4.96 m = 13.05 m

Write each sum in the box.

$3.39 + $5.52 = $8.91 $6.37 + $5.09 = $11.46

$7.46 + $9.53 = $16.99 $8.22 + $1.19 = $9.41

3.77 km + 1.99 km = 5.76 km   5.24 m + 8.37 m = 13.61 m

Solve each problem.

Sandra has saved $3.99. Her mom gives her $1.62. How much does she now have?
$5.61
3.99 + 1.62 = 5.61

Mrs. Jones's car is 4.53 m long. Mr. Jones's car is 5.24 m long. How long must their driveway be in order to fit both cars end to end?
9.77 m
4.53 + 5.24 = 9.77

Children may place the decimal point incorrectly in sums that are presented horizontally (such as those in the third section). Have them rewrite the problems vertically, lining up the decimal points. Remind children to regroup when necessary.

79

Adding decimals

Find each sum. Remember to regroup.

$4.96 + $2.83 = $7.79   7.92 km + 1.68 km = 9.60 km

Find each sum.

8.94 + 5.88 = 14.82 $9.57 + $9.99 = $19.56 $7.96 + $4.78 = $12.74   5.73 + 9.97 = 15.70

6.43 m + 8.57 m = 15.00 m   7.34 cm + 9.99 cm = 17.33 cm   8.62 km + 8.08 km = 16.70 km   3.04 + 5.76 = 8.80

Write each sum in the box.

$5.03 + $6.49 = $11.52   2.74 + 9.61 = 12.35

$8.32 + $9.58 = $17.90   1.29 + 4.83 = 6.12

5.26 km + 9.19 km = 14.45 km   2.04 m + 9.97 m = 12.01 m

Solve each problem.

Anna buys a can of soda for 45¢ and a sandwich for $1.39. How much does she pay?
$1.84
1.39 + 0.45 = 1.84

Mr. Bailey buys two wardrobes. One is 1.29 m wide and the other is 96 cm wide. How much space will they take up if he puts them side by side?
2.25 m
1.29 + 0.96 = 2.25

When the final decimal place of a sum is zero, it can be written, as in the second example, but it can also be omitted—unless the sum is an amount of dollars. To solve the final problem, children must realize that 96 cm is equivalent to 0.96 m.

Subtracting decimals

Find each difference. Remember to regroup.

8.23 − 4.78 = 3.45   2.64 − 1.77 = 0.87

Find each difference.

8.24 − 5.36 = 2.88 $6.27 − $3.48 = $2.79   3.12 − 1.23 = 1.89 $9.47 − $4.79 = $4.68

Find each difference.

5.21 − 2.99 = 2.22   3.64 m − 1.99 m = 1.65 m   9.12 km − 3.99 km = 5.13 km   6.63 cm − 2.94 cm = 3.69 cm

Write each difference in the box.

$2.22 − $1.63 = $0.59   8.14 − 3.25 = 4.89

$9.76 − $3.87 = $5.89   5.71 − 1.92 = 3.79

7.71 − 1.99 = 5.72   3.55 − 1.89 = 1.66

Solve each problem.

Kofi's mother gave him $5.75 to spend at the store. He came back with $1.87. How much did he spend?
$3.88
5.75 − 1.87 = 3.88

The end of Mrs. Brophy's hose was damaged. The hose was 4 m 32 cm long, and she cut off 1 m 49 cm. How much did she have left?
2.83 m, or 2 m 83 cm
4.32 − 1.49 = 2.83

Some children are confused about subtracting decimals. Show them that once they line up the decimal points, they can simply subtract the digits, lining up the decimal point of the answer as well.

Subtracting decimals ⭐

Find each difference. Remember to regroup.

$$\begin{array}{r} {}^{7}\!\!\!\!\!{}^{12}\\ \$8.\overset{2}{\cancel{3}}\overset{11}{\cancel{1}}\\ -\ \$2.94\\ \hline \$5.37 \end{array} \qquad \begin{array}{r} {}^{11}\\ 6.\overset{1}{\cancel{2}}\overset{13}{\cancel{3}}\ m\\ -\ 2.84\ m\\ \hline 3.39\ m \end{array}$$

Find each difference.

$5.31 − $1.89 = **$3.42**	8.24 − 2.87 = **5.37**	7.23 − 3.44 = **3.79**	$6.23 − $1.24 = **$4.99**	$4.11 − $1.12 = **$2.99**

Find each difference.

8.14 m − 2.97 m = **5.17 m**	6.33 km − 2.94 km = **3.39 km**	9.11 cm − 1.32 cm = **7.79 cm**	6.23 − 2.24 = **3.99**	7.48 m − 3.49 m = **3.99 m**

Write each difference in the box.

7.14 − 3.17 = **3.97** $3.39 − $1.47 = **$1.92**

8.51 − 6.59 = **1.92** $6.23 − $5.34 = **$0.89**

8.14 − 3.46 = **4.68**   7.42 m − 4.57 m = **2.85 m**

Solve each problem.

Suzanne goes to the park with $5.13 to spend. She buys a hot dog for $2.49. How much does she have left?

$2.64

$$\begin{array}{r} {}^{10}\\ \overset{4}{\cancel{5}}.\overset{0}{\cancel{1}}\overset{13}{\cancel{3}}\\ -\ 2.49\\ \hline 2.64 \end{array}$$

Gita's garden is 7.43 m long. Josh's garden is 9.21 m long. How much longer is Josh's garden than Gita's?

1.78 m

$$\begin{array}{r} {}^{8}\ {}^{11}\\ \overset{8}{\cancel{9}}.\overset{1}{\cancel{2}}\overset{11}{\cancel{1}}\\ -7.43\\ \hline 1.78 \end{array}$$

This page follows from the previous page. You may need to remind children that they can regroup across a decimal point in the same way as they would if the decimal point were not there.

Multiplying by one-digit numbers

Find each product. Remember to regroup.

$$\begin{array}{r}{}^{1\ 1}\\465\\\times\ \ 3\\\hline 1,395\end{array}\qquad\begin{array}{r}{}^{3}\\391\\\times\ \ 4\\\hline 1,564\end{array}\qquad\begin{array}{r}{}^{3\ 4}\\278\\\times\ \ 5\\\hline 1,390\end{array}$$

Find each product.

563 × 3 = **1,689**	910 × 2 = **1,820**	437 × 3 = **1,311**	812 × 2 = **1,624**
572 × 4 = **2,288**	831 × 3 = **2,493**	406 × 5 = **2,030**	394 × 6 = **2,364**

Find each product.

318 × 3 = **954**	223 × 4 = **892**	542 × 4 = **2,168**	217 × 3 = **651**
127 × 4 = **508**	275 × 5 = **1,375**	798 × 6 = **4,788**	365 × 6 = **2,190**
100 × 5 = **500**	372 × 4 = **1,488**	881 × 4 = **3,524**	953 × 3 = **2,859**

Solve each problem.

A middle school has 255 students. A high school has 6 times as many students. How many children are there at the high school?

1,530 students

$$\begin{array}{r}{}^{3\ 3}\\255\\\times\ \ 6\\\hline 1,530\end{array}$$

A train can carry 365 passengers. How many could it carry on

four trips? **1,460 passengers**

six trips? **2,190 passengers**

$$\begin{array}{r}{}^{2\ 2}\\365\\\times\ \ 4\\\hline 1,460\end{array}\qquad\begin{array}{r}{}^{3\ 3}\\365\\\times\ \ 6\\\hline 2,190\end{array}$$

Make sure children understand the convention of multiplication, i.e. multiply the ones first and work left. Problems on this page may result from gaps in knowledge of the 2, 3, 4, 5, and 6 times tables. Errors will also occur if children neglect to regroup.

Multiplying by one-digit numbers ⭐

Find each product. Remember to regroup.

$$\begin{array}{r}{}^{3\ 3}\\456\\\times\ \ 6\\\hline 2,736\end{array}\qquad\begin{array}{r}{}^{1\ 2}\\823\\\times\ \ 8\\\hline 6,584\end{array}\qquad\begin{array}{r}{}^{4\ 4}\\755\\\times\ \ 9\\\hline 6,795\end{array}$$

Find each product.

394 × 7 = **2,758**	736 × 7 = **5,152**	827 × 8 = **6,616**	943 × 9 = **8,487**
643 × 6 = **3,858**	199 × 6 = **1,194**	821 × 7 = **5,747**	547 × 8 = **4,376**
501 × 7 = **3,507**	377 × 8 = **3,016**	843 × 8 = **6,744**	222 × 9 = **1,998**
471 × 9 = **4,239**	223 × 8 = **1,784**	606 × 6 = **3,636**	513 × 7 = **3,591**
500 × 9 = **4,500**	800 × 9 = **7,200**	900 × 8 = **7,200**	200 × 9 = **1,800**

Solve each problem.

A crate holds 550 apples. How many apples are there in 8 crates?

4,400 apples

$$\begin{array}{r}{}^{4}\\550\\\times\ \ 8\\\hline 4,400\end{array}$$

Keyshawn swims 760 laps each week. How many laps does he swim in 5 weeks?

3,800 people

$$\begin{array}{r}{}^{3}\\760\\\times\ \ 5\\\hline 3,800\end{array}$$

Problems encountered will be similar to the previous page. Gaps in knowledge of the 6, 7, 8, and 9 times table will result in children's errors.

Division with remainders

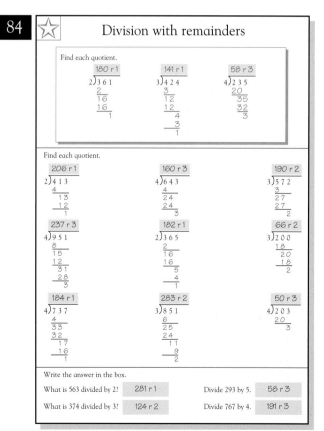

Find each quotient.

$$\begin{array}{r}180\text{ r}1\\2\overline{)361}\\\underline{2}\\16\\\underline{16}\\1\end{array}\qquad\begin{array}{r}141\text{ r}1\\3\overline{)424}\\\underline{3}\\12\\\underline{12}\\4\\\underline{3}\\1\end{array}\qquad\begin{array}{r}58\text{ r}3\\4\overline{)235}\\\underline{20}\\35\\\underline{32}\\3\end{array}$$

Find each quotient.

$$\begin{array}{r}206\text{ r}1\\2\overline{)413}\\\underline{4}\\13\\\underline{12}\\1\end{array}\qquad\begin{array}{r}160\text{ r}3\\4\overline{)643}\\\underline{4}\\24\\\underline{24}\\3\end{array}\qquad\begin{array}{r}190\text{ r}2\\3\overline{)572}\\\underline{3}\\27\\\underline{27}\\2\end{array}$$

$$\begin{array}{r}237\text{ r}3\\4\overline{)951}\\\underline{8}\\15\\\underline{12}\\31\\\underline{28}\\3\end{array}\qquad\begin{array}{r}182\text{ r}1\\2\overline{)365}\\\underline{2}\\16\\\underline{16}\\5\\\underline{4}\\1\end{array}\qquad\begin{array}{r}66\text{ r}2\\3\overline{)200}\\\underline{18}\\20\\\underline{18}\\2\end{array}$$

$$\begin{array}{r}184\text{ r}1\\4\overline{)737}\\\underline{4}\\33\\\underline{32}\\17\\\underline{16}\\1\end{array}\qquad\begin{array}{r}283\text{ r}2\\3\overline{)851}\\\underline{6}\\25\\\underline{24}\\11\\\underline{9}\\2\end{array}\qquad\begin{array}{r}50\text{ r}3\\4\overline{)203}\\\underline{20}\\3\end{array}$$

Write the answer in the box.

What is 563 divided by 2? **281 r 1**   Divide 293 by 5. **58 r 3**

What is 374 divided by 3? **124 r 2**   Divide 767 by 4. **191 r 3**

Children may have difficulty finding quotients with remainders. Have them perform long division until the remaining value to be divided is less than the divisor. That value is the remainder.

Division with remainders

Find each quotient.

$$\begin{array}{r} 62\ r\ 6 \\ 9\overline{)564} \\ 54 \\ \hline 24 \\ 18 \\ \hline 6 \end{array}$$

$$\begin{array}{r} 66\ r\ 1 \\ 7\overline{)463} \\ 42 \\ \hline 43 \\ 42 \\ \hline 1 \end{array}$$

Find each quotient.

$$\begin{array}{r} 57\ r\ 4 \\ 7\overline{)403} \\ 35 \\ \hline 53 \\ 49 \\ \hline 4 \end{array}$$

$$\begin{array}{r} 81\ r\ 7 \\ 8\overline{)655} \\ 64 \\ \hline 15 \\ 8 \\ \hline 7 \end{array}$$

$$\begin{array}{r} 22\ r\ 7 \\ 9\overline{)205} \\ 18 \\ \hline 25 \\ 18 \\ \hline 7 \end{array}$$

$$\begin{array}{r} 63\ r\ 7 \\ 9\overline{)574} \\ 54 \\ \hline 34 \\ 27 \\ \hline 7 \end{array}$$

$$\begin{array}{r} 71\ r\ 5 \\ 6\overline{)431} \\ 42 \\ \hline 11 \\ 6 \\ \hline 5 \end{array}$$

$$\begin{array}{r} 17\ r\ 2 \\ 7\overline{)121} \\ 7 \\ \hline 51 \\ 49 \\ \hline 2 \end{array}$$

$$\begin{array}{r} 24\ r\ 1 \\ 9\overline{)217} \\ 18 \\ \hline 37 \\ 36 \\ \hline 1 \end{array}$$

$$\begin{array}{r} 44\ r\ 8 \\ 9\overline{)404} \\ 36 \\ \hline 44 \\ 36 \\ \hline 8 \end{array}$$

$$\begin{array}{r} 129\ r\ 3 \\ 6\overline{)777} \\ 6 \\ \hline 17 \\ 12 \\ \hline 57 \\ 54 \\ \hline 3 \end{array}$$

Write the answer in the box.

What is 759 divided by 7? 108 r 3

Divide 941 by 9. 104 r 5

What is 463 divided by 8? 57 r 7

Divide 232 by 6. 38 r 4

This page is similar to the previous page, but the divisors are numbers greater than 5. Children will need to know their 6, 7, 8 and 9 times tables.

Real-life problems

Find the answer to each problem.

Jacob spent $4.68 at the store and had $4.77 left. How much did he have to start with?

$9.45

$$\begin{array}{r} {\scriptstyle 1\ 1} \\ 4.77 \\ +\ 4.68 \\ \hline 9.45 \end{array}$$

Tracy receives a weekly allowance of $3.00 a week. How much will she have if she saves all of it for 8 weeks?

$24.00

$$\begin{array}{r} 3.00 \\ \times\ 8 \\ \hline 24.00 \end{array}$$

Find the answer to each problem.

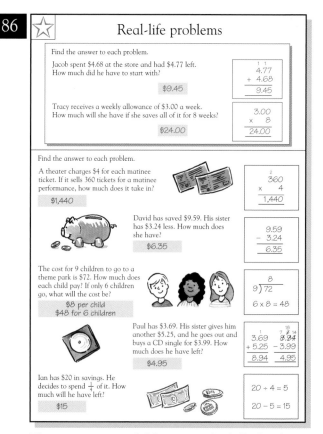

A theater charges $4 for each matinee ticket. If it sells 360 tickets for a matinee performance, how much does it take in?

$1,440

$$\begin{array}{r} {\scriptstyle 2} \\ 360 \\ \times\ 4 \\ \hline 1,440 \end{array}$$

David has saved $9.59. His sister has $3.24 less. How much does she have?

$6.35

$$\begin{array}{r} 9.59 \\ -\ 3.24 \\ \hline 6.35 \end{array}$$

The cost for 9 children to go to a theme park is $72. How much does each child pay? If only 6 children go, what will the cost be?

$8 per child
$48 for 6 children

$$9\overline{)72} \qquad 6 \times 8 = 48$$

Paul has $3.69. His sister gives him another $5.25, and he goes out and buys a CD single for $3.99. How much does he have left?

$4.95

$$\begin{array}{r} {\scriptstyle 1} \\ 3.69 \\ +\ 5.25 \\ \hline 8.94 \end{array} \qquad \begin{array}{r} {\scriptstyle\ \ 18} \\ 8.\cancel{9}4 \\ -\ 3.99 \\ \hline 4.95 \end{array}$$

Ian has $20 in savings. He decides to spend $\frac{1}{4}$ of it. How much will he have left?

$15

$$20 \div 4 = 5 \qquad 20 - 5 = 15$$

This page requires children to apply skills they have learned. If they are unsure about what operation to use, discuss whether they expect the answer to be larger or smaller. This can help them decide whether to add, subtract, multiply or divide.

Real-life problems

Find the answer to each problem.

Nina has an hour to do her homework. She plans to spend $\frac{1}{3}$ of her time on math. How many minutes will she spend doing math?

20 minutes

1 hour is 60 minutes

$$\begin{array}{r} 20 \\ 3\overline{)60} \end{array}$$

In gym class, David makes 2 long jumps of 1.78 m and 2.19 m. How far does he jump altogether?

3.97 m

$$\begin{array}{r} {\scriptstyle 1} \\ 1.78\ m \\ +\ 2.19\ m \\ \hline 3.97\ m \end{array}$$

Find the answer to each problem.

Moishe has a can of lemonade containing 400 ml. He drinks $\frac{1}{4}$ of it. How much is left?

300 ml

$$400 \div 4 = 100$$
$$400 - 100 = 300$$

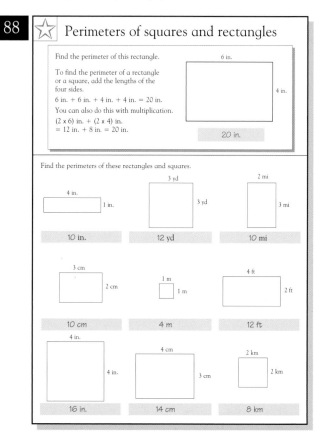

David ran 40 m in 8 seconds. At that speed, how far did he run in 1 second?

5 m

$$40 \div 8 = 5$$

A large jar of coffee contains 1.75 kg. If 1.48 kg is left in the jar, how much has been used?

0.27 kg

$$\begin{array}{r} {\scriptstyle 6\ 15} \\ 1.\cancel{7}\cancel{5} \\ -\ 1.48 \\ \hline 0.27 \end{array}$$

A worker can fill 145 boxes of tea in 15 minutes. How many boxes can he fill in 1 hour?

580 boxes

1 hour = 60 min
$$60 \div 15 = 4$$
$$\begin{array}{r} {\scriptstyle 1\ 2} \\ 145 \\ \times\ 4 \\ \hline 580 \end{array}$$

Jennifer's computer is 41.63 cm wide and her printer is 48.37 cm wide. How much space does she have for books if her desk is 1.5 m wide?

60 cm

1.5 m = 150 cm
$$\begin{array}{r} {\scriptstyle 1\ 1} \\ 41.63 \\ +\ 48.37 \\ \hline 90.00 \end{array} \quad \begin{array}{r} 150 \\ -\ 90 \\ \hline 60 \end{array}$$

This page deals with units other than money. As on the previous page, children have to decide what operation to use. Note that solving the final problem requires two operations.

Perimeters of squares and rectangles

Find the perimeter of this rectangle.

To find the perimeter of a rectangle or a square, add the lengths of the four sides.

6 in. + 6 in. + 4 in. + 4 in. = 20 in.
You can also do this with multiplication.
(2 × 6) in. + (2 × 4) in.
= 12 in. + 8 in. = 20 in.

6 in.
4 in.

20 in.

Find the perimeters of these rectangles and squares.

4 in. / 1 in. → 10 in.

3 yd / 3 yd → 12 yd

2 mi / 3 mi → 10 mi

3 cm / 2 cm → 10 cm

1 m / 1 m → 4 m

4 ft / 2 ft → 12 ft

4 in. / 4 in. → 16 in.

4 cm / 3 cm → 14 cm

2 km / 2 km → 8 km

Make sure that children do not simply add the lengths of two sides of a figure rather than all four sides. You may want to help children realize that the perimeter of a square can be found by multiplying the length of one side by 4.

Problems involving time

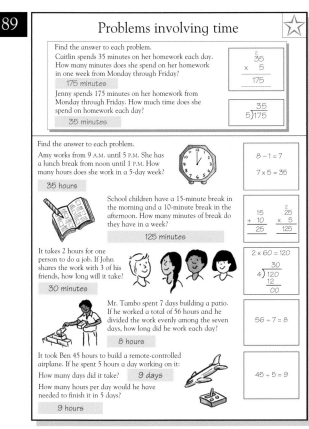

Find the answer to each problem.

Caitlin spends 35 minutes on her homework each day. How many minutes does she spend on her homework in one week from Monday through Friday?

$$\begin{array}{r} \overset{2}{35} \\ \times\ 5 \\ \hline 175 \end{array}$$

175 minutes

Jenny spends 175 minutes on her homework from Monday through Friday. How much time does she spend on homework each day?

$$5\overline{)175}\ \ 35$$

35 minutes

Find the answer to each problem.

Amy works from 9 A.M. until 5 P.M. She has a lunch break from noon until 1 P.M. How many hours does she work in a 5-day week?

$8 - 1 = 7$

$7 \times 5 = 35$

35 hours

School children have a 15-minute break in the morning and a 10-minute break in the afternoon. How many minutes of break do they have in a week?

$$\begin{array}{r} 15 \\ +\ 10 \\ \hline 25 \end{array} \qquad \begin{array}{r} \overset{2}{25} \\ \times\ 5 \\ \hline 125 \end{array}$$

125 minutes

It takes 2 hours for one person to do a job. If John shares the work with 3 of his friends, how long will it take?

$2 \times 60 = 120$

$$\begin{array}{r} 30 \\ 4\overline{)120} \\ 12 \\ \hline 00 \end{array}$$

30 minutes

Mr. Tambo spent 7 days building a patio. If he worked a total of 56 hours and he divided the work evenly among the seven days, how long did he work each day?

$56 \div 7 = 8$

8 hours

It took Ben 45 hours to build a remote-controlled airplane. If he spent 5 hours a day working on it:

How many days did it take? **9 days**

How many hours per day would he have needed to finish it in 5 days?

$45 \div 5 = 9$

9 hours

For the second problem, children should realize that a school week is 5 days. For the third problem, check that children divide by 4 rather than 3.

90

Using bar graphs

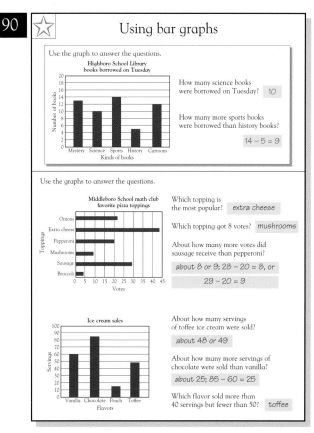

Use the graph to answer the questions.

Highboro School Library books borrowed on Tuesday

How many science books were borrowed on Tuesday? **10**

How many more sports books were borrowed than history books? **14 − 5 = 9**

Use the graphs to answer the questions.

Middleboro School math club favorite pizza toppings

Which topping is the most popular? **extra cheese**

Which topping got 8 votes? **mushrooms**

About how many more votes did sausage receive than pepperoni? **about 8 or 9; 28 − 20 = 8, or 29 − 20 = 9**

Ice cream sales

About how many servings of toffee ice cream were sold? **about 48 or 49**

About how many more servings of chocolate were sold than vanilla? **about 25; 85 − 60 = 25**

Which flavor sold more than 40 servings but fewer than 50? **toffee**

On this page, children have to find specific entries, compare or manipulate information read from a bar graph. Some children may need to be reassured that a horizontal bar graph can be read in much the same way as a vertical bar graph.

91

Congruency

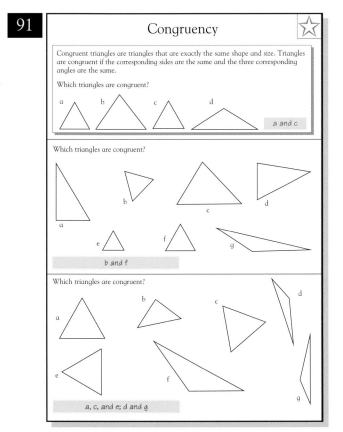

Congruent triangles are triangles that are exactly the same shape and size. Triangles are congruent if the corresponding sides are the same and the three corresponding angles are the same.

Which triangles are congruent?

a   b   c   d

a and c

Which triangles are congruent?

b and f

Which triangles are congruent?

a, c, and e; d and g

You may want to discuss with children the fact that a triangle with congruent corresponding sides also has congruent corresponding angles.

Lines of symmetry

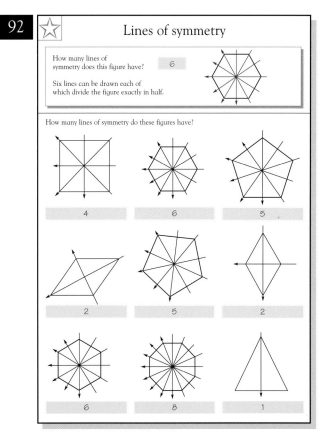

How many lines of symmetry does this figure have? **6**

Six lines can be drawn each of which divide the figure exactly in half.

How many lines of symmetry do these figures have?

4   **6**   **5**

2   **5**   **2**

6   **8**   **1**

Make sure that children understand that the lines of symmetry of the figures on this page could be between opposite vertices, between the mid-points of opposite sides, or between vertices and mid-points of their opposite sides.

Writing equivalent number sentences ⭐

> Write a multiplication sentence that goes with 24 ÷ 6 = 4.
> 6 x 4 = 24 or 4 x 6 = 24
> Write a related subtraction sentence for 5 + 12 = 17.
> 17 − 5 = 12 or 17 − 12 = 5

Write a related subtraction sentence for each sentence.

25 + 12 = 37	37 − 25 = 12 or 37 − 12 = 25
35 + 8 = 43	43 − 35 = 8 or 43 − 8 = 35
13 + 9 = 22	22 − 9 = 13 or 22 − 13 = 9

Write a related addition sentence for each sentence.

35 − 24 = 11	11 + 24 = 35 or 24 + 11 = 35
82 − 23 = 59	23 + 59 = 82 or 59 + 23 = 82
45 − 20 = 25	25 + 20 = 45 or 20 + 25 = 45

Write a related multiplication sentence for each sentence.

36 ÷ 4 = 9	4 x 9 = 36 or 9 x 4 = 36
32 ÷ 2 = 16	16 x 2 = 32 or 2 x 16 = 32
72 ÷ 9 = 8	8 x 9 = 72 or 9 x 8 = 72

Write a related division sentence for each sentence.

8 x 6 = 48	48 ÷ 8 = 6 or 48 ÷ 6 = 8
7 x 12 = 84	84 ÷ 7 = 12 or 84 ÷ 12 = 7
9 x 5 = 45	45 ÷ 9 = 5 or 45 ÷ 5 = 9

If children answer any questions incorrectly, have them check their answers to find out if they have written sentences that do not express facts.

⭐ Multiplying and dividing

> Write the answer in the box.
> 26 x 10 = 260   26 x 100 = 2,600
> 400 ÷ 10 = 40   400 ÷ 100 = 4

Write the product in the box.

33 x 10 = 330	21 x 10 = 210	42 x 10 = 420
94 x 100 = 9,400	36 x 100 = 3,600	81 x 100 = 8,100
416 x 10 = 4,160	204 x 10 = 2,040	513 x 10 = 5,130
767 x 100 = 76,700	821 x 100 = 82,100	245 x 100 = 24,500

Write the quotient in the box.

120 ÷ 10 = 12	260 ÷ 10 = 26	470 ÷ 10 = 47
300 ÷ 100 = 3	800 ÷ 100 = 8	400 ÷ 100 = 4
20 ÷ 10 = 2	30 ÷ 10 = 3	70 ÷ 10 = 7
500 ÷ 100 = 5	100 ÷ 100 = 1	900 ÷ 100 = 9

Write the number that has been multiplied by 100.

59 x 100 = 5,900	714 x 100 = 71,400
721 x 100 = 72,100	234 x 100 = 23,400
11 x 100 = 1,100	470 x 100 = 47,000
84 x 100 = 8,400	441 x 100 = 44,100

Write the number that has been divided by 100.

200 ÷ 100 = 2	800 ÷ 100 = 8
2,100 ÷ 100 = 21	1,800 ÷ 100 = 18
8,600 ÷ 100 = 86	2,100 ÷ 100 = 21
1,000 ÷ 100 = 10	5,900 ÷ 100 = 59

Children should realize that multiplying a whole number by 10 or 100 means writing one or two zeros at the end of it. To divide a multiple of 10 by 10, take the final zero off the number. The two final sections require use of the inverse operation.

Ordering sets of measures ⭐

> Write these amounts in order, from least to greatest.
>
> | 70 cm | 300 mm | 2 km | 6 m | 500 mm |
> |---|---|---|---|---|
> | 300 mm | 500 mm | 70 cm | 6 m | 2 km |

Write these amounts in order, from least to greatest.

500¢	$4.00	$5.50	350¢	640¢
350¢	$4.00	500¢	$5.50	640¢
2 qt	1 gal	12 pt	2 gal	10 qt
12 pt	2 qt	1 gal	10 qt	2 gal
125 min	2 h	3½ h	200 min	¾ h
¾ h	2 h	125 min	200 min	3½ h
2,500 m	2 km	1,000 cm	20 m	1,000 m
1,000 cm	20 m	1,000 m	2 km	2,500 m
$240	3,500¢	$125.00	4,600¢	$50.00
3,500¢	4,600¢	$50.00	$125.00	$240
1 yd	9 ft	24 in.	72 in.	7 ft
24 in.	1 yd	72 in.	7 ft	9 ft
6 qt	8 pt	3 gal	1 qt	4 pt
1 qt	4 pt	8 pt	6 qt	3 gal
2 h	75 min	1½ h	100 min	150 min
75 min	1½ h	100 min	2 h	150 min
44 mm	4 cm	4 m	4 km	40 cm
4 cm	44 mm	40 cm	4 m	4 km
4 yd	36 in.	2 ft	20 in.	2 yd
20 in.	2 ft	36 in.	2 yd	4 yd

Most errors will result from a lack of understanding of the relationship between measures written using different units. Look out for confusion between large numbers of small units and small numbers of large units, such as 350¢ and $4.00.

⭐ Decimal models

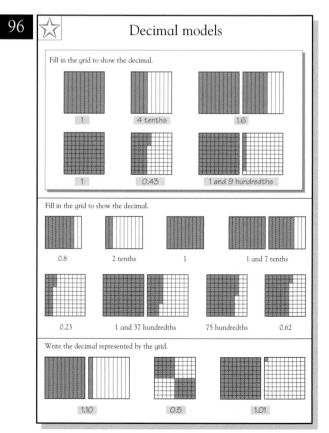

Fill in the grid to show the decimal.

1	4 tenths	1.6
1	0.43	1 and 9 hundredths

Fill in the grid to show the decimal.

0.8	2 tenths	1	1 and 7 tenths
0.23	1 and 37 hundredths	75 hundredths	0.62

Write the decimal represented by the grid.

1.10	0.5	1.01

Children may have difficulty understanding that the zero in a number such as 1.09 is needed. If they write such a number incorrectly, show them that their answer actually represents a different number.

97 Identifying patterns

Continue each pattern.

Steps of 2:	$\frac{1}{2}$	$2\frac{1}{2}$	$4\frac{1}{2}$	$6\frac{1}{2}$	$8\frac{1}{2}$	$10\frac{1}{2}$
Steps of 5:	3.5	8.5	13.5	18.5	23.5	28.5

Continue each pattern.

$5\frac{1}{2}$	$10\frac{1}{2}$	$15\frac{1}{2}$	$20\frac{1}{2}$	$25\frac{1}{2}$	$30\frac{1}{2}$
$1\frac{1}{4}$	$3\frac{1}{4}$	$5\frac{1}{4}$	$7\frac{1}{4}$	$9\frac{1}{4}$	$11\frac{1}{4}$
$8\frac{1}{3}$	$9\frac{1}{3}$	$10\frac{1}{3}$	$11\frac{1}{3}$	$12\frac{1}{3}$	$13\frac{1}{3}$
$55\frac{3}{4}$	$45\frac{3}{4}$	$35\frac{3}{4}$	$25\frac{3}{4}$	$15\frac{3}{4}$	$5\frac{3}{4}$
$42\frac{1}{2}$	$38\frac{1}{2}$	$34\frac{1}{2}$	$30\frac{1}{2}$	$26\frac{1}{2}$	$22\frac{1}{2}$
7.5	6.5	5.5	4.5	3.5	2.5
28.4	25.4	22.4	19.4	16.4	13.4
81.6	73.6	65.6	57.6	49.6	41.6
6.3	10.3	14.3	18.3	22.3	26.3
12.1	13.1	14.1	15.1	16.1	17.1
14.6	21.6	28.6	35.6	42.6	49.6
$11\frac{1}{2}$	$10\frac{1}{2}$	$9\frac{1}{2}$	$8\frac{1}{2}$	$7\frac{1}{2}$	$6\frac{1}{2}$
8.4	11.4	14.4	17.4	20.4	23.4
$7\frac{3}{4}$	$13\frac{3}{4}$	$19\frac{3}{4}$	$25\frac{3}{4}$	$31\frac{3}{4}$	$37\frac{3}{4}$
57.5	48.5	39.5	30.5	21.5	12.5

Although the patterns here are formed by adding or subtracting whole numbers, the items in each are mixed numbers or decimals. The operation that turns the first number into the second, and the second into the third can be used to continue the pattern.

98 Products with odd and even numbers

Find the products of these numbers.

3 and 4 The product of 3 and 4 is 12. 6 and 8 The product of 6 and 8 is 48.

Find the products of these odd and even numbers.

5 and 6	The product of 5 and 6 is 30.	3 and 2	The product of 3 and 2 is 6.
7 and 4	The product of 7 and 4 is 28.	8 and 3	The product of 8 and 3 is 24.
6 and 3	The product of 6 and 3 is 18.	2 and 9	The product of 2 and 9 is 18.
10 and 3	The product of 10 and 3 is 30.	12 and 5	The product of 12 and 5 is 60.

What do you notice about your answers? The product of odd and even numbers is always an even number.

Find the products of these odd numbers.

5 and 7	The product of 5 and 7 is 35.	3 and 9	The product of 3 and 9 is 27.
5 and 11	The product of 5 and 11 is 55.	7 and 3	The product of 7 and 3 is 21.
9 and 5	The product of 9 and 5 is 45.	11 and 7	The product of 11 and 7 is 77.
13 and 3	The product of 13 and 3 is 39.	1 and 5	The product of 1 and 5 is 5.

What do you notice about your answers? The product of two odd numbers is always an odd number.

Find the products of these even numbers.

2 and 4	The product of 2 and 4 is 8.	4 and 6	The product of 4 and 6 is 24.
6 and 2	The product of 6 and 2 is 12.	4 and 8	The product of 4 and 8 is 32.
10 and 2	The product of 10 and 2 is 20.	4 and 10	The product of 4 and 10 is 40.
6 and 10	The product of 6 and 10 is 60.	6 and 8	The product of 6 and 8 is 48.

What do you notice about your answers? The product of two even numbers is always an even number.

Can you write a rule for the products with odd and even numbers?
The product of two numbers will always be even unless both numbers are odd.

Children may need help answering the questions on what they notice about the products. Accept any rule about products that children write as long as it indicates that they have grasped the concept.

99 Squares of numbers

Find the square of 2. 2 x 2 = 4

What is the area of this square? (2 in. by 2 in.) 2 x 2 = 4 Area = 4 in.^{2}

Find the square of these numbers.

3	3 x 3 = 9	1	1 x 1 = 1	6	6 x 6 = 36
7	7 x 7 = 49	8	8 x 8 = 64	5	5 x 5 = 25
9	9 x 9 = 81	4	4 x 4 = 16	10	10 x 10 = 100

Now try these.

13	13 x 13 = 169	20	20 x 20 = 400	40	40 x 40 = 1600
11	11 x 11 = 121	12	12 x 12 = 144	30	30 x 30 = 900

What are the areas of these squares?

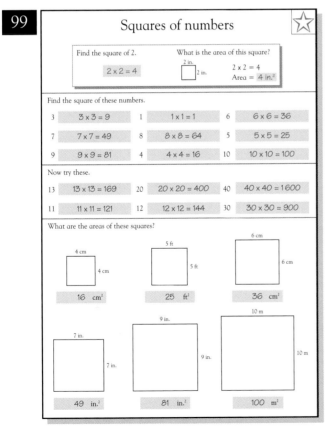

4 cm × 4 cm: 16 cm^2	5 ft × 5 ft: 25 ft^2	6 cm × 6 cm: 36 cm^2
7 in. × 7 in.: 49 in.^{2}	9 in. × 9 in.: 81 in.^{2}	10 m × 10 m: 100 m^2

Make sure that children understand that area is given in square units. You may want to add lines to divide the square in the example into quarters, to show 4 square inches. Check that they are in fact squaring the numbers, and not multiplying by two.

100 Factors of numbers from 66 to 100

The factors of 66 are 1 2 3 6 11 22 33 66

Circle the factors of 94. ① ② 28 32 43 ㊼ 71 86 (94)

Write the factors of each number in the box.

The factors of 70 are 1, 2, 5, 7, 10, 14, 35, 70
The factors of 85 are 1, 5, 17, 85
The factors of 69 are 1, 3, 23, 69
The factors of 83 are 1, 83
The factors of 75 are 1, 3, 5, 15, 25, 75
The factors of 96 are 1, 2, 3, 4, 6, 8, 12, 16, 24, 32, 48, 96
The factors of 63 are 1, 3, 7, 9, 21, 63
The factors of 99 are 1, 3, 9, 11, 33, 99
The factors of 72 are 1, 2, 3, 4, 6, 8, 9, 12, 18, 24, 36, 72

Circle the factors of 68.
① ② 3 ④ 5 6 7 8 9 11 12 ⑰ ㉞ 35 62 (68)

Circle the factors of 95.
① 2 3 4 ⑤ 15 16 17 ⑲ 24 37 85 90 (95) 96

Circle the factors of 88.
① ② 3 ④ 5 6 ⑧ 10 ⑪ 15 ㉒ 25 27 ㊹ 87 (88)

Circle the factors of 73.
① 2 4 5 6 8 9 10 12 13 14 15 30 60 (73)

A prime number only has two factors, 1 and itself.
Write all the prime numbers between 66 and 100 in the box.

67, 71, 73, 79, 83, 89, 97

Children often miss some of the factors of large numbers. Encourage a systematic method of finding factors. Children may forget that 1 and the number itself are factors of a number. If necessary, discuss prime numbers with children.

101 Renaming fractions ☆

Rename these improper fractions as mixed numbers in simplest form.

$$\frac{17}{10} = 1\frac{7}{10} \qquad \frac{25}{6} = 4\frac{1}{6}$$

Rename this improper fraction as a mixed number in simplest form.

$$\frac{16}{10} = 1\frac{\cancel{6}}{\cancel{10}_5}^3 = 1\frac{3}{5}$$

Rename these improper fractions as mixed numbers in simplest form.

$\frac{15}{4} = 3\frac{3}{4}$	$\frac{13}{10} = 1\frac{3}{10}$	$\frac{29}{5} = 5\frac{4}{5}$
$\frac{19}{12} = 1\frac{7}{12}$	$\frac{22}{9} = 2\frac{4}{9}$	$\frac{17}{6} = 2\frac{5}{6}$
$\frac{19}{6} = 3\frac{1}{6}$	$\frac{24}{5} = 4\frac{4}{5}$	$\frac{13}{3} = 4\frac{1}{3}$
$\frac{13}{4} = 3\frac{1}{4}$	$\frac{21}{2} = 10\frac{1}{2}$	$\frac{14}{9} = 1\frac{5}{9}$
$\frac{9}{8} = 1\frac{1}{8}$	$\frac{11}{6} = 1\frac{5}{6}$	$\frac{15}{7} = 2\frac{1}{7}$
$\frac{17}{8} = 2\frac{1}{8}$	$\frac{43}{4} = 10\frac{3}{4}$	$\frac{11}{5} = 2\frac{1}{5}$
$\frac{16}{10} = 1\frac{3}{5}$	$\frac{36}{8} = 4\frac{1}{2}$	$\frac{18}{8} = 2\frac{1}{4}$
$\frac{45}{10} = 4\frac{1}{2}$	$\frac{22}{6} = 3\frac{2}{3}$	$\frac{24}{20} = 1\frac{1}{5}$
$\frac{26}{8} = 3\frac{1}{4}$	$\frac{20}{8} = 2\frac{1}{2}$	$\frac{16}{12} = 1\frac{1}{3}$
$\frac{25}{15} = 1\frac{2}{3}$	$\frac{18}{4} = 4\frac{1}{2}$	$\frac{20}{14} = 1\frac{3}{7}$
$\frac{28}{24} = 1\frac{1}{6}$	$\frac{32}{6} = 5\frac{1}{3}$	$\frac{26}{10} = 2\frac{3}{5}$
$\frac{18}{12} = 1\frac{1}{2}$	$\frac{46}{4} = 11\frac{1}{2}$	$\frac{30}{9} = 3\frac{1}{3}$

To change improper fractions to mixed numbers, children should divide the numerator by the denominator and place the remainder over the denominator. Help them simplify answers by finding common factors for the numerator and denominator.

102 ☆ Ordering sets of decimals

Write these decimals in order, from least to greatest.

0.45	0.21	2.07	1.45	3.62	2.17
0.21	0.45	1.45	2.07	2.17	3.62

Write these decimals in order, from least to greatest.

5.63	2.14	5.6	3.91	1.25	4.63
1.25	2.14	3.91	4.63	5.6	5.63
9.39	0.24	7.63	8.25	7.49	9.40
0.24	7.49	7.63	8.25	9.39	9.40
1.05	2.36	1.09	2.41	7.94	1.50
1.05	1.09	1.50	2.36	2.41	7.94
3.92	5.63	2.29	4.62	5.36	2.15
2.15	2.29	3.92	4.62	5.36	5.63
28.71	21.87	27.18	21.78	28.17	27.81
21.78	21.87	27.18	27.81	28.17	28.71

Write these measures in order, from least to greatest.

$56.25	$32.40	$11.36	$32.04	$55.26	$36.19
$11.36	$32.04	$32.40	$36.19	$55.26	$56.25
94.21 km	87.05 km	76.91 km	94.36 km	65.99 km	110.75 km
65.99 km	76.91 km	87.05 km	94.21 km	94.36 km	110.75 km
$26.41	$47.23	$26.14	$35.23	$49.14	$35.32
$26.14	$26.41	$35.23	$35.32	$47.23	$49.14
19.51 m	16.15 m	15.53 m	12.65 m	24.24 m	16.51 m
12.65 m	15.53 m	16.15 m	16.51 m	19.51 m	24.24 m
7.35 l	8.29 l	5.73 l	8.92 l	10.65 l	4.29 l
4.29 l	5.73 l	7.35 l	8.29 l	8.92 l	10.65 l

Children should take special care when they order sets that include numbers with similar digits that have different place values. Make sure that they understand how place value defines a number: for example, 6.959 is less than 7.1

103 Symmetry ☆

How many lines of symmetry does each figure have?

| 1 | 2 | 5 | 0 |

Is the dashed line a line symmetry? Write yes or no.

| no | yes | no | yes |

Draw the lines of symmetry. Write how many there are.

| 3 | 0 | 4 |

Draw the lines of symmetry. Write how many there are.

| 0 | 1 | 2 |

Draw the lines of symmetry. Write how many there are.

| 6 | 1 | 1 |

Children may have difficulty understanding that a line of symmetry in a pentagon passes through the mid-point of a side and the opposite vertex. Place a pocket mirror upright along a line of symmetry to show how the reflection completes the figure.

104 ☆ Comparing areas

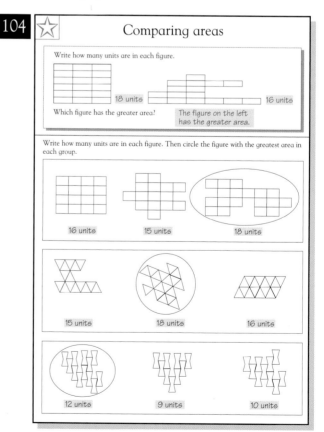

Write how many units are in each figure.

18 units   16 units

Which figure has the greater area?   The figure on the left has the greater area.

Write how many units are in each figure. Then circle the figure with the greatest area in each group.

16 units   15 units   18 units

15 units   18 units   16 units

12 units   9 units   10 units

Children may not realize that they can compare the areas of irregular figures. Make sure that they take care to count the units in each figure, rather than incorrectly assuming that the longest or tallest figure has the greater area.

Probability

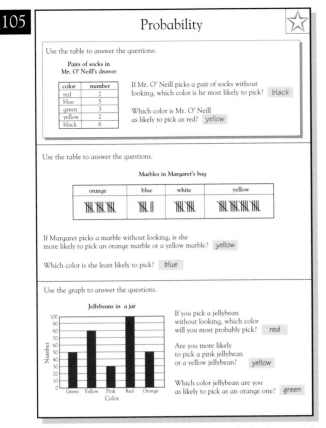

Use the table to answer the questions.

Pairs of socks in Mr. O' Neill's drawer

color	number
red	2
blue	5
green	3
yellow	2
black	6

If Mr. O' Neill picks a pair of socks without looking, which color is he most likely to pick? **black**

Which color is Mr. O' Neill as likely to pick as red? **yellow**

Use the table to answer the questions.

Marbles in Margaret's bag

orange	blue	white	yellow

If Margaret picks a marble without looking, is she more likely to pick an orange marble or a yellow marble? **yellow**

Which color is she least likely to pick? **blue**

Use the graph to answer the questions.

Jellybeans in a jar

If you pick a jellybean without looking, which color will you most probably pick? **red**

Are you more likely to pick a pink jellybean or a yellow jellybean? **yellow**

Which color jellybean are you as likely to pick as an orange one? **green**

Children must read the tally table and the bar graph to compare the numbers of items. Make sure they understand that there is an equal probability of picking either of two items if there is the same number of each.

Column addition

Find these sums.

```
  1 1
 $327          1 2 1
 $644        1,374 km
 $923        2,362 km
+$455        1,690 km
            + 4,216 km
$2,349
            9,642 km
```

Find these sums.

539 yd	206 yd	481 yd	735 yd
965 yd	812 yd	604 yd	234 yd
774 yd	619 yd	274 yd	391 yd
+ 347 yd	+ 832 yd	+ 976 yd	+ 863 yd
2,625 yd	2,469 yd	2,335 yd	2,223 yd
746 lb	817 lb	944 lb	763 lb
201 lb	591 lb	835 lb	861 lb
432 lb	685 lb	391 lb	608 lb
+ 309 lb	+ 245 lb	+ 105 lb	+ 671 lb
1,688 lb	2,338 lb	2,275 lb	2,903 lb
6,329 m	5,245 m	6,431 m	8,690 m
3,251 m	2,845 m	7,453 m	5,243 m
2,642 m	1,937 m	4,650 m	6,137 m
+ 4,823 m	+ 5,610 m	+ 3,782 m	+ 5,843 m
17,045 m	15,637 m	22,316 m	25,913 m
$4,721	$3,654	$8,172	$4,352
$1,711	$5,932	$1,475	$3,920
$8,342	$6,841	$7,760	$8,439
+ $2,365	+ $4,736	+ $8,102	+ $1,348
$17,139	$21,163	$25,509	$18,059
1,573 mi	4,902 mi	3,756 mi	8,010 mi
6,231 mi	7,547 mi	1,150 mi	7,793 mi
2,112 mi	8,463 mi	5,535 mi	1,641 mi
+ 2,141 mi	+ 6,418 mi	+ 3,852 mi	+ 7,684 mi
12,057 mi	27,330 mi	14,293 mi	25,128 mi

This page requires children to perform basic addition. However, with a larger number of addends, there is a greater possibility of neglecting to regroup correctly.

Column addition

Find these sums.

```
  1 1 1          2 2 1
 3,461 km      $3,645
 2,100 km      $4,231
 3,522 km      $8,560
 4,159 km      $7,213
+ 3,614 km    + $9,463
16,856 km     $33,112
```

Find these sums.

3,144 m	2,510 m	3,276 m	1,475 m
2,345 m	1,734 m	1,593 m	2,653 m
8,479 m	5,421 m	6,837 m	2,765 m
1,004 m	3,205 m	1,769 m	3,742 m
+ 6,310 m	+ 2,365 m	+ 3,846 m	+ 5,905 m
21,282 m	15,235 m	17,321 m	16,540 m
$1,480	$4,527	$3,063	$8,741
$6,366	$8,309	$8,460	$6,334
$1,313	$6,235	$2,712	$3,231
$3,389	$4,487	$3,756	$6,063
+ $4,592	+ $4,065	+ $5,650	+ $4,096
$17,140	$27,623	$23,641	$28,465
8,644 km	3,823 km	8,636 km	8,618 km
3,353 km	9,275 km	8,986 km	3,453 km
6,400 km	3,669 km	5,367 km	4,404 km
5,768 km	2,998 km	6,863 km	4,361 km
+ 1,092 km	+ 7,564 km	+ 3,605 km	+ 5,641 km
25,257 km	27,329 km	33,457 km	26,477 km
$3,742	$8,596	$2,739	$8,463
$2,785	$5,430	$6,517	$5,641
$7,326	$8,379	$6,014	$9,440
$1,652	$2,943	$7,115	$8,204
+ $5,753	+ $1,081	+ $2,704	+ $6,326
$21,258	$26,429	$25,089	$38,064

This page is similar to the previous one, but children must find the sum of a larger number of addends.

Adding fractions

Write the sum in simplest form.

$\frac{1}{8} + \frac{3}{8} = \frac{4}{8} = \frac{1}{2}$ $\frac{3}{5} + \frac{3}{5} = \frac{6}{5} = 1\frac{1}{5}$

Write the sum in simplest form.

$\frac{1}{3} + \frac{1}{3} = \frac{2}{3}$ $\frac{2}{9} + \frac{4}{9} = \frac{6}{9} = \frac{2}{3}$

$\frac{1}{4} + \frac{1}{4} = \frac{2}{4} = \frac{1}{2}$ $\frac{5}{7} + \frac{1}{7} = \frac{6}{7}$

$\frac{2}{3} + \frac{2}{3} = \frac{4}{3} = 1\frac{1}{3}$ $\frac{1}{12} + \frac{3}{12} = \frac{4}{12} = \frac{1}{3}$

$\frac{3}{7} + \frac{5}{7} = \frac{8}{7} = 1\frac{1}{7}$ $\frac{5}{11} + \frac{9}{11} = \frac{14}{11} = 1\frac{3}{11}$

$\frac{2}{5} + \frac{4}{5} = \frac{6}{5} = 1\frac{1}{5}$ $\frac{5}{18} + \frac{4}{18} = \frac{9}{18} = \frac{1}{2}$

$\frac{5}{16} + \frac{7}{16} = \frac{12}{16} = \frac{3}{4}$ $\frac{5}{9} + \frac{5}{9} = \frac{10}{9} = 1\frac{1}{9}$

$\frac{3}{8} + \frac{5}{8} = \frac{8}{8} = 1$ $\frac{4}{15} + \frac{7}{15} = \frac{11}{15}$

$\frac{7}{13} + \frac{8}{13} = \frac{15}{13} = 1\frac{2}{13}$ $\frac{2}{5} + \frac{1}{5} = \frac{3}{5}$

$\frac{5}{16} + \frac{7}{16} = \frac{12}{16} = \frac{3}{4}$ $\frac{1}{6} + \frac{5}{6} = \frac{6}{6} = 1$

$\frac{9}{10} + \frac{7}{10} = \frac{16}{10} = \frac{8}{5} = 1\frac{3}{5}$ $\frac{3}{4} + \frac{3}{4} = \frac{6}{4} = \frac{3}{2} = 1\frac{1}{2}$

$\frac{4}{5} + \frac{3}{5} = \frac{7}{5} = 1\frac{2}{5}$ $\frac{1}{8} + \frac{5}{8} = \frac{6}{8} = \frac{3}{4}$

$\frac{7}{12} + \frac{5}{12} = \frac{12}{12} = 1$ $\frac{3}{10} + \frac{9}{10} = \frac{12}{10} = \frac{6}{5} = 1\frac{1}{5}$

$\frac{3}{11} + \frac{5}{11} = \frac{8}{11}$ $\frac{9}{15} + \frac{11}{15} = \frac{20}{15} = \frac{4}{3} = 1\frac{1}{3}$

$\frac{8}{14} + \frac{5}{14} = \frac{13}{14}$ $\frac{1}{20} + \frac{6}{20} = \frac{7}{20}$

Some children may incorrectly add both the numerators and the denominators. Demonstrate that only the numerators should be added when the fractions have the same denominators: $\frac{1}{2} + \frac{1}{2}$ equals $\frac{2}{2}$ or 1, not $\frac{2}{4}$.

Adding fractions ⭐

Write the sum in simplest form.

$\frac{1}{12} + \frac{3}{4} = \frac{1}{12} + \frac{9}{12} = \frac{10}{12} = \frac{5}{6}$ $\frac{3}{5} + \frac{7}{10} = \frac{6}{10} + \frac{7}{10} = \frac{13}{10} = 1\frac{3}{10}$

Write the sum in simplest form.

$\frac{1}{6} + \frac{2}{3} = \frac{1}{6} + \frac{4}{6} = \frac{5}{6}$ $\frac{7}{12} + \frac{7}{36} = \frac{21}{36} + \frac{7}{36} = \frac{28}{36} = \frac{7}{9}$

$\frac{1}{3} + \frac{2}{6} = \frac{2}{6} + \frac{2}{6} = \frac{4}{6} = \frac{2}{3}$ $\frac{6}{10} + \frac{7}{30} = \frac{18}{30} + \frac{7}{30} = \frac{25}{30} = \frac{5}{6}$

$\frac{8}{12} + \frac{5}{24} = \frac{16}{24} + \frac{5}{24} = \frac{21}{24} = \frac{7}{8}$ $\frac{7}{12} + \frac{5}{6} = \frac{7}{12} + \frac{10}{12} = \frac{17}{12} = 1\frac{5}{12}$

$\frac{5}{7} + \frac{7}{14} = \frac{10}{14} + \frac{7}{14} = \frac{17}{14} = 1\frac{3}{14}$ $\frac{9}{25} + \frac{1}{5} = \frac{9}{25} + \frac{5}{25} = \frac{14}{25}$

$\frac{5}{6} + \frac{9}{12} = \frac{10}{12} + \frac{9}{12} = \frac{19}{12} = 1\frac{7}{12}$ $\frac{6}{16} + \frac{1}{4} = \frac{6}{16} + \frac{4}{16} = \frac{10}{16} = \frac{5}{8}$

$\frac{4}{5} + \frac{3}{10} = \frac{8}{10} + \frac{3}{10} = \frac{11}{10} = 1\frac{1}{10}$ $\frac{5}{13} + \frac{5}{30} = \frac{10}{30} + \frac{5}{30} = \frac{15}{30} = \frac{1}{2}$

$\frac{3}{8} + \frac{5}{24} = \frac{9}{24} + \frac{5}{24} = \frac{14}{24} = \frac{7}{12}$ $\frac{7}{8} + \frac{1}{2} = \frac{7}{8} + \frac{4}{8} = \frac{11}{8} = 1\frac{3}{8}$

$\frac{4}{9} + \frac{2}{3} = \frac{4}{9} + \frac{6}{9} = \frac{10}{9} = 1\frac{1}{9}$ $\frac{2}{3} + \frac{7}{15} = \frac{10}{15} + \frac{7}{15} = \frac{17}{15} = 1\frac{2}{15}$

$\frac{7}{8} + \frac{3}{16} = \frac{14}{16} + \frac{3}{16} = \frac{17}{16} = 1\frac{1}{16}$ $\frac{5}{14} + \frac{9}{28} = \frac{10}{28} + \frac{9}{28} = \frac{19}{28}$

$\frac{3}{10} + \frac{7}{20} = \frac{6}{20} + \frac{7}{20} = \frac{13}{20}$ $\frac{3}{33} + \frac{5}{11} = \frac{3}{33} + \frac{15}{33} = \frac{18}{33} = \frac{6}{11}$

On this page, children must rename fractions so that both addends have the same denominator. They should also be aware that they must simplify the sum when necessary.

⭐ Subtracting fractions

Write the answer in simplest form.

$\frac{5}{6} - \frac{4}{6} = \frac{1}{6}$ $\frac{5}{8} - \frac{3}{8} = \frac{2}{8} = \frac{1}{4}$

Write the answer in simplest form.

$\frac{2}{3} - \frac{1}{3} = \frac{1}{3}$ $\frac{7}{9} - \frac{4}{9} = \frac{3}{9} = \frac{1}{3}$

$\frac{1}{4} - \frac{1}{4} = 0$ $\frac{5}{7} - \frac{1}{7} = \frac{4}{7}$

$\frac{7}{12} - \frac{5}{12} = \frac{2}{12} = \frac{1}{6}$ $\frac{5}{11} - \frac{3}{11} = \frac{2}{11}$

$\frac{6}{7} - \frac{5}{7} = \frac{1}{7}$ $\frac{9}{12} - \frac{5}{12} = \frac{4}{12} = \frac{1}{3}$

$\frac{18}{30} - \frac{15}{30} = \frac{3}{30} = \frac{1}{10}$ $\frac{4}{5} - \frac{2}{5} = \frac{2}{5}$

$\frac{3}{6} - \frac{1}{6} = \frac{2}{6} = \frac{1}{3}$ $\frac{7}{8} - \frac{1}{8} = \frac{6}{8} = \frac{3}{4}$

$\frac{11}{16} - \frac{7}{16} = \frac{4}{16} = \frac{1}{4}$ $\frac{5}{9} - \frac{2}{9} = \frac{3}{9} = \frac{1}{3}$

$\frac{7}{13} - \frac{5}{13} = \frac{2}{13}$ $\frac{14}{15} - \frac{4}{15} = \frac{10}{15} = \frac{2}{3}$

$\frac{12}{13} - \frac{8}{13} = \frac{4}{13}$ $\frac{4}{5} - \frac{1}{5} = \frac{3}{5}$

$\frac{9}{10} - \frac{7}{10} = \frac{2}{10} = \frac{1}{5}$ $\frac{5}{6} - \frac{1}{6} = \frac{4}{6} = \frac{2}{3}$

$\frac{8}{17} - \frac{4}{17} = \frac{4}{17}$ $\frac{11}{18} - \frac{8}{18} = \frac{3}{18} = \frac{1}{6}$

$\frac{4}{5} - \frac{3}{5} = \frac{1}{5}$ $\frac{7}{12} - \frac{1}{12} = \frac{6}{12} = \frac{1}{2}$

$\frac{9}{11} - \frac{5}{11} = \frac{4}{11}$ $\frac{8}{14} - \frac{5}{14} = \frac{3}{14}$

$\frac{7}{8} - \frac{5}{8} = \frac{2}{8} = \frac{1}{4}$ $\frac{9}{10} - \frac{3}{10} = \frac{6}{10} = \frac{3}{5}$

$\frac{3}{16} - \frac{2}{16} = \frac{1}{16}$ $\frac{17}{20} - \frac{7}{20} = \frac{10}{20} = \frac{1}{2}$

On this page, children subtract fractions that have the same denominators. If they neglect to simplify their answers, help them find common factors in the numerator and denominator.

Subtracting fractions ⭐

Write the answer in simplest form.

$\frac{3}{4} - \frac{1}{12} = \frac{9}{12} - \frac{1}{12} = \frac{8}{12} = \frac{2}{3}$

$\frac{3}{5} - \frac{4}{10} = \frac{6}{10} - \frac{4}{10} = \frac{2}{10} = \frac{1}{5}$

Write the answer in simplest form.

$\frac{5}{6} - \frac{9}{12} = \frac{10}{12} - \frac{9}{12} = \frac{1}{12}$ $\frac{6}{10} - \frac{7}{30} = \frac{18}{30} - \frac{7}{30} = \frac{11}{30}$

$\frac{6}{14} - \frac{9}{28} = \frac{12}{28} - \frac{9}{28} = \frac{3}{28}$ $\frac{1}{3} - \frac{2}{6} = \frac{2}{6} - \frac{2}{6} = 0$

$\frac{7}{8} - \frac{6}{16} = \frac{14}{16} - \frac{6}{16} = \frac{8}{16} = \frac{1}{2}$ $\frac{5}{15} - \frac{5}{30} = \frac{10}{30} - \frac{5}{30} = \frac{5}{30} = \frac{1}{6}$

$\frac{1}{2} - \frac{5}{12} = \frac{6}{12} - \frac{5}{12} = \frac{1}{12}$ $\frac{8}{9} - \frac{2}{3} = \frac{8}{9} - \frac{6}{9} = \frac{2}{9}$

$\frac{6}{16} - \frac{1}{4} = \frac{6}{16} - \frac{4}{16} = \frac{2}{16} = \frac{1}{8}$ $\frac{6}{7} - \frac{7}{14} = \frac{12}{14} - \frac{7}{14} = \frac{5}{14}$

$\frac{7}{9} - \frac{7}{36} = \frac{28}{36} - \frac{7}{36} = \frac{21}{36} = \frac{7}{12}$ $\frac{2}{5} - \frac{4}{15} = \frac{6}{15} - \frac{4}{15} = \frac{2}{15}$

$\frac{8}{12} - \frac{3}{24} = \frac{16}{24} - \frac{3}{24} = \frac{13}{24}$ $\frac{3}{10} - \frac{3}{20} = \frac{6}{20} - \frac{3}{20} = \frac{3}{20}$

$\frac{7}{8} - \frac{1}{2} = \frac{7}{8} - \frac{4}{8} = \frac{3}{8}$ $\frac{7}{12} - \frac{2}{6} = \frac{7}{12} - \frac{4}{12} = \frac{3}{12} = \frac{1}{4}$

$\frac{5}{7} - \frac{1}{21} = \frac{15}{21} - \frac{1}{21} = \frac{14}{21} = \frac{2}{3}$ $\frac{14}{18} - \frac{5}{9} = \frac{14}{18} - \frac{10}{18} = \frac{4}{18} = \frac{2}{9}$

$\frac{3}{4} - \frac{3}{20} = \frac{15}{20} - \frac{3}{20} = \frac{12}{20} = \frac{3}{5}$ $\frac{1}{2} - \frac{3}{8} = \frac{4}{8} - \frac{3}{8} = \frac{1}{8}$

$\frac{8}{21} - \frac{2}{7} = \frac{8}{21} - \frac{6}{21} = \frac{2}{21}$ $\frac{3}{5} - \frac{6}{15} = \frac{9}{15} - \frac{6}{15} = \frac{3}{15} = \frac{1}{5}$

On this page, children must write both fractions with the same denominator before subtracting. If necessary, point out that fractions have the same value as long as you multiply the numerator and denominator by the same number.

⭐ Multiplying by two-digit numbers

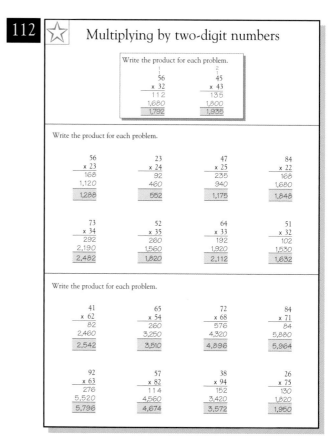

Write the product for each problem.

$\begin{array}{r} \overset{1}{5}6 \\ \times\ 32 \\ \hline 112 \\ 1,680 \\ \hline \mathbf{1,792} \end{array}$ $\begin{array}{r} \overset{2}{4}5 \\ \times\ 43 \\ \hline 135 \\ 1,800 \\ \hline \mathbf{1,935} \end{array}$

Write the product for each problem.

$\begin{array}{r} 56 \\ \times\ 23 \\ \hline 168 \\ 1,120 \\ \hline \mathbf{1,288} \end{array}$ $\begin{array}{r} 23 \\ \times\ 24 \\ \hline 92 \\ 460 \\ \hline \mathbf{552} \end{array}$ $\begin{array}{r} 47 \\ \times\ 25 \\ \hline 235 \\ 940 \\ \hline \mathbf{1,175} \end{array}$ $\begin{array}{r} 84 \\ \times\ 22 \\ \hline 168 \\ 1,680 \\ \hline \mathbf{1,848} \end{array}$

$\begin{array}{r} 73 \\ \times\ 34 \\ \hline 292 \\ 2,190 \\ \hline \mathbf{2,482} \end{array}$ $\begin{array}{r} 52 \\ \times\ 35 \\ \hline 260 \\ 1,560 \\ \hline \mathbf{1,820} \end{array}$ $\begin{array}{r} 64 \\ \times\ 33 \\ \hline 192 \\ 1,920 \\ \hline \mathbf{2,112} \end{array}$ $\begin{array}{r} 51 \\ \times\ 32 \\ \hline 102 \\ 1,530 \\ \hline \mathbf{1,632} \end{array}$

Write the product for each problem.

$\begin{array}{r} 41 \\ \times\ 62 \\ \hline 82 \\ 2,460 \\ \hline \mathbf{2,542} \end{array}$ $\begin{array}{r} 65 \\ \times\ 54 \\ \hline 260 \\ 3,250 \\ \hline \mathbf{3,510} \end{array}$ $\begin{array}{r} 72 \\ \times\ 68 \\ \hline 576 \\ 4,320 \\ \hline \mathbf{4,896} \end{array}$ $\begin{array}{r} 84 \\ \times\ 71 \\ \hline 84 \\ 5,880 \\ \hline \mathbf{5,964} \end{array}$

$\begin{array}{r} 92 \\ \times\ 63 \\ \hline 276 \\ 5,520 \\ \hline \mathbf{5,796} \end{array}$ $\begin{array}{r} 57 \\ \times\ 82 \\ \hline 114 \\ 4,560 \\ \hline \mathbf{4,674} \end{array}$ $\begin{array}{r} 38 \\ \times\ 94 \\ \hline 152 \\ 3,420 \\ \hline \mathbf{3,572} \end{array}$ $\begin{array}{r} 26 \\ \times\ 75 \\ \hline 130 \\ 1,820 \\ \hline \mathbf{1,950} \end{array}$

Children should understand that multiplying a number by 32 is the same as multiplying the number by 2, and by 30, and then adding the two products.

Multiplying by two-digit numbers

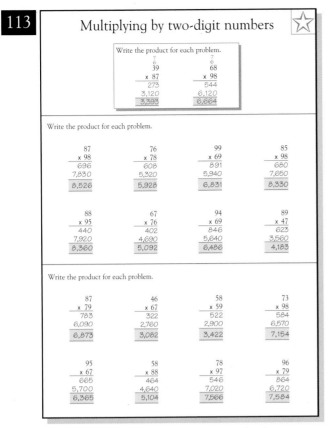

Write the product for each problem.

7	7
6	6
39	68
x 87	x 98
273	544
3,120	6,120
3,393	**6,664**

Write the product for each problem.

87	76	99	85
x 98	x 78	x 69	x 98
696	608	891	680
7,830	5,320	5,940	7,650
8,526	**5,928**	**6,831**	**8,330**

88	67	94	89
x 95	x 76	x 69	x 47
440	402	846	623
7,920	4,690	5,640	3,560
8,360	**5,092**	**6,486**	**4,183**

Write the product for each problem.

87	46	58	73
x 79	x 67	x 59	x 98
783	322	522	584
6,090	2,760	2,900	6,570
6,873	**3,082**	**3,422**	**7,154**

95	58	78	96
x 67	x 88	x 97	x 79
665	464	546	864
5,700	4,640	7,020	6,720
6,365	**5,104**	**7,566**	**7,584**

This page gives further practice of multiplication as on the previous page. Make sure that children do not neglect to regroup when necessary.

Dividing by one-digit numbers

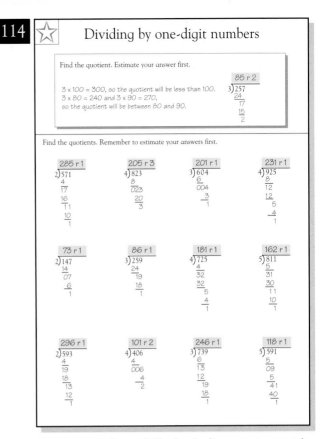

Find the quotient. Estimate your answer first.

3 x 100 = 300, so the quotient will be less than 100.
3 x 80 = 240 and 3 x 90 = 270,
so the quotient will be between 80 and 90.

```
        85 r 2
    3)257
      24
       17
       15
        2
```

Find the quotients. Remember to estimate your answers first.

```
  285 r 1      205 r 3      201 r 1      231 r 1
2)571        4)823        3)604        4)925
  4            8            6            8
  17           023          004          12
  16            20           3           12
   11            3                         5
   10                                      4
    1                                      1
```

```
  73 r 1       86 r 1       181 r 1      162 r 1
2)147        3)259        4)725        5)811
  14           24           4            5
  07           19           32           31
   6           18           32           30
   1            1            5            11
                            4            10
                            1             1
```

```
  296 r 1      101 r 2      246 r 1      118 r 1
2)593        4)406        3)739        5)591
  4            4            6            5
  19           006          13           09
  18            4           12           5
  13            2           19           41
  12                        18           40
   1                         1            1
```

Children may have difficulty finding quotients with remainders. Have them perform long division until the remaining value to be divided is less than the divisor. That value is the remainder.

Dividing by one-digit numbers

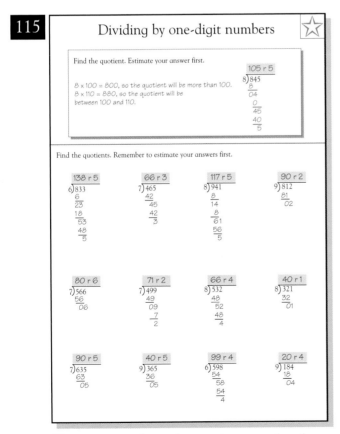

Find the quotient. Estimate your answer first.

8 x 100 = 800, so the quotient will be more than 100.
8 x 110 = 880, so the quotient will be between 100 and 110.

```
        105 r 5
    8)845
      8
      04
       0
       45
       40
        5
```

Find the quotients. Remember to estimate your answers first.

```
  138 r 5      66 r 3       117 r 5      90 r 2
6)833        7)465        8)941        9)812
  6            42           8            81
  23           45           14           02
  18           42            8
  53            3            61
  48                         56
   5                          5
```

```
  80 r 6       71 r 2       66 r 4       40 r 1
7)566        7)499        8)532        8)321
  56           49           48           32
  06           09           52           01
                7           48
                2            4
```

```
  90 r 5       40 r 5       99 r 4       20 r 4
7)635        9)365        6)598        9)184
  63           36           54           18
  05           05           58           04
                            54
                             4
```

This page is similar to the previous page, but the divisors are numbers greater than 5. Children will need to know their 6, 7, 8, and 9 times tables.

Real-life problems

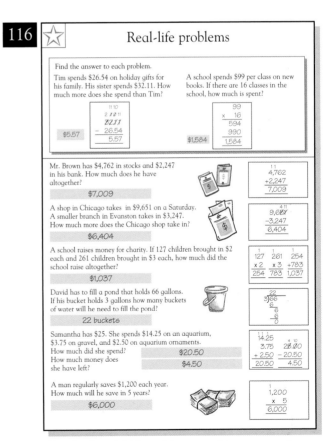

Find the answer to each problem.

Tim spends $26.54 on holiday gifts for his family. His sister spends $32.11. How much more does she spend than Tim?

```
   11 10
  2 7 8 11
   32.11
 - 26.54
    5.57
```
$5.57

A school spends $99 per class on new books. If there are 16 classes in the school, how much is spent?

```
     99
   x 16
    594
    990
  1,584
```
$1,584

Mr. Brown has $4,762 in stocks and $2,247 in his bank. How much does he have altogether?

$7,009

```
    1 1
   4,762
 + 2,247
   7,009
```

A shop in Chicago takes in $9,651 on a Saturday. A smaller branch in Evanston takes in $3,247. How much more does the Chicago shop take in?

$6,404

```
    4 11
   9,651
 - 3,247
   6,404
```

A school raises money for charity. If 127 children brought in $2 each and 261 children brought in $3 each, how much did the school raise altogether?

$1,037

```
   127     261      254
   x 2     x 3    + 783
   254     783    1,037
```

David has to fill a pond that holds 66 gallons. If his bucket holds 3 gallons how many buckets of water will he need to fill the pond?

22 buckets

```
    22
  3)66
    6
    6
    6
    0
```

Samantha has $25. She spends $14.25 on an aquarium, $3.75 on gravel, and $2.50 on aquarium ornaments. How much did she spend?   **$20.50**
How much money does she have left?   **$4.50**

```
   1 1
  14.25        4 10
   3.75      25.00
 + 2.50    - 20.50
  20.50       4.50
```

A man regularly saves $1,200 each year. How much will he save in 5 years?

$6,000

```
   1,200
   x   5
   6,000
```

The third and fifth problems on this page require multiple steps to reach the correct answers. If children have difficulty, help them plan out methods to solve the problems.

Real-life problems

Find the answer to each problem.

Jaime runs round a field 8 times.
If he runs a total of 944 yards,
what is the perimeter of the field?   **118 yd**

$$\begin{array}{r} 118 \\ 8\overline{)944} \\ 8 \\ \hline 14 \\ 8 \\ \hline 64 \\ 64 \\ \hline 0 \end{array}$$

Mr. and Mrs. Green's living room is 5.75 m
long and their dining room is 4.37 m long.
If they knock out the wall between them to
make one room, how long will it be?   **10.12 m**

$$\begin{array}{r} ^{1\ 1} \\ 5.75 \\ +\ 4.37 \\ \hline 10.12 \end{array}$$

A family's car trip took 5 hours. If they travelled 50 miles each
hour, how far did they travel?   **250 mi**

$$\begin{array}{r} 50 \\ \times\ 5 \\ \hline 250 \end{array}$$

Two men weigh $218\frac{1}{2}$ lb and 173 lb.
What is the difference between their weights?   **$45\frac{1}{2}$ lb**

$$\begin{array}{r} 218\frac{1}{2} \\ -\ 173 \\ \hline 45\frac{1}{2} \end{array}$$

An electrician uses 480 yd of electrician wire in 6 apartments. If he
uses the same amount in each, how much does he use per house?   **80 yd**

$$\begin{array}{r} 80 \\ 6\overline{)480} \\ 48 \\ \hline 00 \end{array}$$

A jar of coffee weighs 36 oz.
How much will 7 jars weigh?   **252 oz**

$$\begin{array}{r} 36 \\ \times\ 7 \\ \hline 252 \end{array}$$

A box of pencils is 2 in. wide. How many can be stored
on a shelf 1 yd long?   **18 boxes**

1 yd = 36 in. $2\overline{)36}$

Maria spends 32 hours working on a school project. If she spreads the
work evenly over 8 days, how many hours does she work each day?   **4 h**

$$\begin{array}{r} 4 \\ 8\overline{)32} \\ 32 \\ \hline 0 \end{array}$$

Sean runs 143.26 m in 40 seconds. Malik runs 97.92 m in the
same time. How much farther does Sean run than Malik?   **45.34 m**

$$\begin{array}{r} 143.26 \\ -\ 97.92 \\ \hline 45.34 \end{array}$$

Children will need to know that there are 3 feet,
or 36 inches in a yard to solve the fifth problem
on this page.

Problems involving time

Find the answer to each problem.

A yard sale began at 12 P.M. and
ended at 4:35 P.M. How long did it last?

12:00 → 4:00 = 4 h
4:00 → 4:35 = 35 min
Total = 4 h 35 min   **4 h 35 min**

Fred's watch says 2:27. What time will
it say in 1h 26 min?

2:27 + 1 h = 3:27
3.27 + 26 min = 3:53   **3:53**

Rachel begins painting fences at 12:15 P.M. and finishes at
4:45 P.M. If she paints 3 fences, how long does each one take?   **1.5 h**

12:15 → 4:15 = 4 h
4:15 → 4:45 = 0.5 h
$\begin{array}{r} 4.0 \\ +\ 0.5 \\ \hline 4.5 \end{array}$ $3\overline{)4.5}$

Joy works from 9 A.M. until 5 P.M. every day.
If she takes an hour's lunch break, how many hours
does she work altogether from Monday through Friday?   **35 h**

9 A.M. → 5 P.M. = 8 h
8 h − 1 h = 7 h
$\begin{array}{r} 7 \\ \times\ 5 \\ \hline 35 \end{array}$

A train leaves at 2:29 P.M. and arrives at 10:47 P.M.
How long does the trip take?   **8 h 18 min**

2:29 → 10:29 = 8 h
10:29 → 10:47 = 18 min

A castle has a 24-hour guard on the gate. Three soldiers share
the work equally. If the first soldier starts his duty at 2:30 P.M.,
what times will the other two soldiers start their duties?

Soldier 2   **10:30 P.M.**

Soldier 3   **6:30 A.M.**

$\begin{array}{r} 8 \\ 3\overline{)24} \\ \hline 0 \end{array}$ 8 h each

2:30 P.M. + 8 h = 10:30 P.M.
10:30 P.M. + 8h = 6:30 A.M.

Kobe wants to videotape a program that starts
at 3:30 P.M. and finishes at 5 P.M. If the program
is on every day for the next five days, how many
hours will he videotape?   **7.5 h**

3:30 → 4:30 = 1 h
4:30 → 5:00 = 0.5 h
1 h + 0.5 h = 1.5 h
$\begin{array}{r} 1.5 \\ \times\ 5 \\ \hline 7.5 \end{array}$

You may need to help children understand time
periods so that they can manage the questions
more easily. For example, borrowing an hour in
a subtraction problem is the same as borrowing
60 minutes.

Looking at graphs

Derek recorded the temperature in
his garden during one day.
At what time was the temperature
at its highest?   **noon**

By how much did the
temperature fall between
6 P.M. and midnight?   **15°F**

Kate keeps a record of her last 10 spelling test scores.

What was Kate's score
in week 3?   **14**

In which 2 consecutive weeks did Kate's
score stay the same?   **weeks 3 and 4**

What was Kate's best score?   **16**

How much did her score improve
between weeks 4 and 5?   **by 2 points**

The local tourist board produced a graph to show the maximum temperatures in
Charleston between April and August.

What was the maximum
temperature in April?   **50°F**

Overall, what is happening to the
temperature between April and August?   **It is rising.**

How much did the temperature rise
between May and July?   **70°F − 60°F = 10°F**

Which two months had the same
maximum temperature?   **May and June**

On this page, children are required to find two or
more pieces of information on a graph. They then
have to compare or find the difference in value.
In the first question, make sure that children
understand the meaning of consecutive.

Place value for whole numbers

Write the value of 7 in 573 in standard form and word form.
70   **seventy**

What happens to the value of 247 if you change the 2 to a 3?
The value of the number increases by 100.

Write the value of the 6 in these numbers in standard form and word form.

26	162	36,904	12,612
6	**60**	**6,000**	**600**
six	sixty	six thousand	six hundred

Circle the numbers that have a 7 with a value of seventy.

457,682   (67,974)   870,234   372,987

(177,079)   (767,777)   (79,875)   16,757

Write what happens to the value of each number.

Change the 6 in 3,586 to 3.   **The value of the number decreases by 3.**

Change the 9 in 1,921 to 8.   **The value of the number decreases by 100.**

Change the 7 in 7,246 to 9.   **The value of the number increases by 2,000.**

Change the 1 in 817 to 9.   **The value of the number increases by 80.**

Change the 5 in 50,247 to 1.   **The value of the number decreases by 40,000.**

Change the 2 in 90,205 to 9.   **The value of the number increases by 700.**

Children may need help completing the final section
of the page. If so, help them work through the first
question of the section. Have children write the
new number for each question before trying to
find the answer.

Place value for decimals

Write the value of 5 in 7.53 in standard form and word form.

0.5   5 tenths

What happens to the value of 2.48 if you change the 8 to a 1?

The value of the number decreases by 0.07.

Write the value of the 9 in these numbers in standard form and written form.

2.9	0.19	975.04	9.12
0.9	0.09	900	9
9 tenths	9 hundredths	9 hundred	nine

0.89	591.65	19.85	3.96
0.09	90	9	0.9
9 hundredths	ninety	nine	9 tenths

Write what happens to the value of each number.

Change the 8 in 35.86 to 7.   The value of the number decreases by 0.1.

Change the 2 in 1.02 to 6.   The value of the number increases by 0.04.

Change the 3 in 3,460 to 9.   The value of the number increases by 6,000.

Change the 1 in 8.17 to 6.   The value of the number increases by 0.5.

Change the 5 in 8.35 to 1.   The value of the number decreases by 0.04.

Circle the numbers that have an 8 with a value of 8 tenths.

457.68   (1.8)   8.09   (35.85)   388.1

Circle the numbers that have a 5 with a value of 5 hundredths.

550.7   (5.25)   (99.95)   16.53   (68.95)

Circle the numbers that have a 3 with a value of 3 tenths.

(3,603.3)   0.93   32.45   (5.33)   23.53

This page is similar to the previous one, but involves decimals rather than whole numbers. For the second section of questions, it may help children to write the new numbers and then find the difference between them and the original numbers.

Reading tally charts

Use the chart to answer the questions.

Club members' pets

Pet	Number
dog	卌 卌 ‖‖
cat	卌 卌 卌 ‖
fish	卌 ‖‖

What is the most popular pet for club members? cats

How many more club members have cats than have fish?

16 − 8 = 8,   8 members

Use the chart to answer the questions.

Birds seen at feeder

sparrow	junco	blue jay	chickadee
卌 卌 卌 ‖‖‖	卌 ‖‖‖	卌 卌 ‖	卌 卌 卌 卌

What kinds of birds were seen at the feeder more than 12 times?   sparrows and chickadees

What is the total number of sparrows and chickadees seen at the feeder?   19 + 20 = 39

How many more blue jays than juncos were seen?   11 − 8 = 3

Use the chart to answer the questions.

Snacks chosen by students

carrots	chips	cookies	pretzels
‖‖‖	卌 卌 ‖‖‖	卌 卌 卌 ‖‖	卌 卌 卌 卌 ‖‖

What snack did fewer than 10 students choose?   carrots

What is the most popular snack for students?   pretzels

Was the total number of students who chose chips and cookies greater than or less than the total number who chose carrots and pretzels?

13 + 17 = 30;   4 + 22 = 26;   greater than

If children have difficulty reading tally charts, show them that they can count by 5s for groups of tallies that are crossed out.

Volumes of cubes

This cube is 1 cm long, 1 cm high, and 1 cm wide. We say it has a volume of 1 cubic centimeter (1 cm³).

If we put 4 of these cubes together the new shape has a volume of 4 cm³.

These shapes are made of 1 cm³ cubes. What are their volumes?

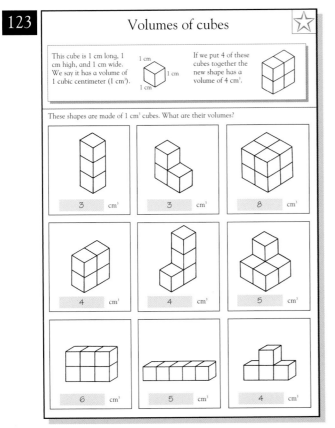

3 cm³   3 cm³   8 cm³

4 cm³   4 cm³   5 cm³

6 cm³   5 cm³   4 cm³

To find the volume of some of the shapes on this page, children must visualize in order to determine how many blocks cannot be seen in the illustrations. In the third and sixth shapes there is one block that is not shown.

Acute and obtuse angles

A right angle forms a square corner.

An obtuse angle is greater than a right angle.

An acute angle is less than a right angle.

Look at these angles.

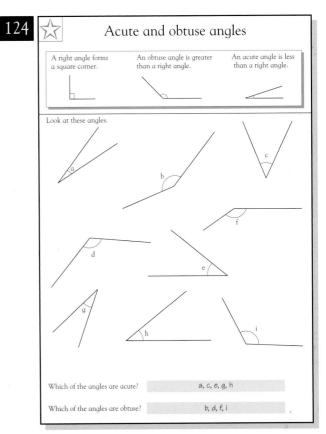

Which of the angles are acute?   a, c, e, g, h

Which of the angles are obtuse?   b, d, f, i

Children should have no difficulty identifying each angle if they compare it to a right angle.

Acute and obtuse angles

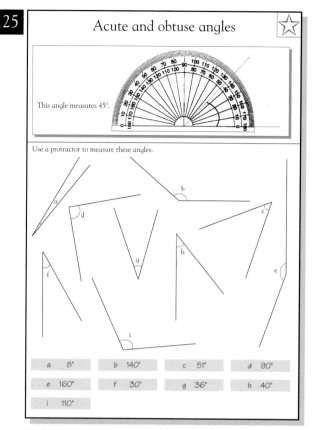

This angle measures 45°.

Use a protractor to measure these angles.

a	8°	b	140°	c	51°	d	90°
e	160°	f	30°	g	36°	h	40°
i	110°						

If children make errors on this page, the most likely
reasons are that they have placed the protractor
inaccurately above the vertex of the angle or that
they have read the protractor from the wrong
direction.

Addition fact families

Circle the number sentence that is in the same fact family.

| 12 − 5 = 7
5 + 7 = 12 | 12 − 4 = 8 | (7 + 5 = 12) | 12 + 12 = 24 |
| 10 − 8 = 2
8 + 2 = 10 | 8 − 6 = 2 | (2 + 8 = 10) | 8 − 2 = 6 |

Circle the number sentence that is in the same fact family.

7 + 8 = 15 8 + 7 = 15	7 + 5 = 12	(15 − 8 = 7)	8 − 7 = 1
17 − 6 = 11 11 + 6 = 17	(17 − 11 = 6)	17 + 6 = 23	5 + 6 = 11
14 − 5 = 9 14 − 9 = 5	9 − 3 = 6	14 + 9 = 23	(5 + 9 = 14)
9 + 7 = 16 7 + 9 = 16	(16 − 9 = 7)	16 + 7 = 23	9 − 7 = 2
19 − 9 = 10 19 − 10 = 9	9 + 3 = 12	(9 + 10 = 19)	18 − 8 = 10
4 + 7 = 11 11 − 4 = 7	11 + 4 = 15	(7 + 4 = 11)	7 + 7 = 14

Write the fact family for each group of numbers.

5, 6, 11	6, 10, 4	5, 13, 8
5 + 6 = 11	6 + 4 = 10	5 + 8 = 13
6 + 5 = 11	4 + 6 = 10	8 + 5 = 13
11 − 6 = 5	10 − 6 = 4	13 − 8 = 5
11 − 5 = 6	10 − 4 = 6	13 − 5 = 8

Children should understand that subtraction
"undoes" addition. You may want to use counters
to show the addition fact families.

Odds and evens

Write the answer in the box.

| 3 + 3 = | 6 | 4 + 6 = | 10 | 7 + 3 = | 10 | 2 + 6 = | 8 |

Add the even numbers to the even numbers.

4 + 8 =	12	12 + 6 =	18	10 + 6 =	16	8 + 14 =	22
20 + 14 =	34	14 + 12 =	26	16 + 10 =	26	30 + 20 =	50
14 + 16 =	30	18 + 6 =	24	22 + 8 =	30	20 + 40 =	60

What do you notice about each answer?   All the answers are even numbers.

Add the odd numbers to the odd numbers.

7 + 9 =	16	5 + 7 =	12	11 + 5 =	16	9 + 5 =	14
7 + 7 =	14	9 + 3 =	12	15 + 5 =	20	13 + 7 =	20
11 + 3 =	14	17 + 9 =	26	15 + 9 =	24	13 + 15 =	28

What do you notice about each answer?   All the answers are even numbers.

Add the odd numbers to the even numbers.

3 + 8 =	11	9 + 12 =	21	5 + 18 =	23	7 + 14 =	21
11 + 4 =	15	13 + 10 =	23	15 + 6 =	21	21 + 4 =	25
7 + 20 =	27	13 + 30 =	43	11 + 16 =	27	17 + 6 =	23

What do you notice about each answer?   All the answers are odd numbers.

Add the even numbers to the odd numbers.

6 + 7 =	13	8 + 5 =	13	10 + 9 =	19	2 + 17 =	19
10 + 29 =	39	14 + 3 =	17	8 + 13 =	21	12 + 5 =	17
14 + 7 =	21	8 + 51 =	59	16 + 9 =	25	30 + 17 =	47

What do you notice about each answer?   All the answers are odd numbers.

Children should notice that adding two even
numbers results in an even number and adding two
odd numbers results in an odd number. Adding an
odd and an even number gives an odd number. The
order in which numbers are added is not important.

Word problems

Write the answer in the box.
I multiply a number by 6 and the answer is 24.
What number did I begin with?   4

Write the answer in the box.

A number multiplied by 7 equals 35. What is the number?	5
I divide a number by 10 and the answer is 3. What number did I divide?	30
I multiply a number by 4 and the answer is 20. What is the number I multiplied?	5
After dividing a piece of wood into four equal sections, each section is 4 in. long. How long was the piece of wood I started with?	16 in.
A number multiplied by 6 gives the answer 24. What is the number?	4
Some money is divided into five equal amounts. Each amount is 10 cents. How much money was there before it was divided?	50¢
I multiply a number by 9 and the result is 45. What number was multiplied?	5
A number divided by 6 is 3. What number was divided?	18
Three children share 18 peanuts equally among themselves. How many peanuts does each child receive?	6
A number divided by 4 is 8. What is the number?	32
I multiply a number by 6 and the answer is 30. What is the number?	5
Four sets of a number equal 16. What is the number?	4
A number divided by 5 is 5. What is the number?	25
A child divides a number by 8 and gets 2. What number was divided?	16
Three groups of a number equal 27. What is the number?	9
I multiply a number by 10 and the result is 100. What is the number?	10

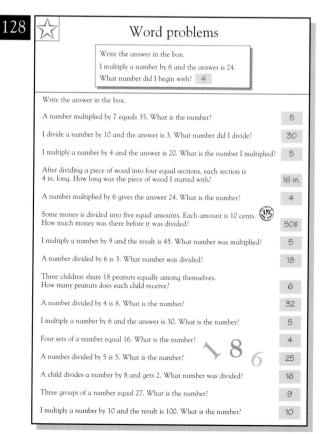

Some children find these sorts of problems difficult
even if they are good with times tables and division.
Many of the problems require children to perform
the inverse operation. Have children check their
answers to make sure they are correct.

129 — Word problems

Write the answer in the box.
A child is given four dimes. How much money does she have altogether? 40¢

Write the answer in the box.

A box contains 6 eggs. How many boxes would I need to buy to have 18 eggs? 3

When Peter multiplies his apartment number by 3, the result is 75. What is his apartment number? 25

A boy is given three bags of candy. There are 20 pieces in each bag. How many pieces of candy does the boy have in total? 60

One photograph costs $1.80. How much will two photographs cost? $3.60

Four lifeboats carry a total of 100 people. How many people are in each boat? 25

A dog buries 20 bones on Monday, 30 bones on Tuesday, and 40 bones on Wednesday. How many bones has the dog buried altogether? 90

A shepherd had 200 sheep but 70 were lost in a snowstorm. How many sheep does the shepherd have left? 130

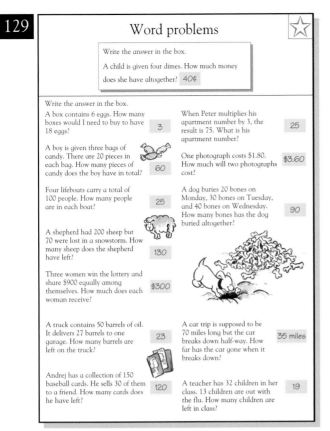

Three women win the lottery and share $900 equally among themselves. How much does each woman receive? $300

A truck contains 50 barrels of oil. It delivers 27 barrels to one garage. How many barrels are left on the truck? 23

A car trip is supposed to be 70 miles long but the car breaks down half-way. How far has the car gone when it breaks down? 35 miles

Andrej has a collection of 150 baseball cards. He sells 30 of them to a friend. How many cards does he have left? 120

A teacher has 32 children in her class. 13 children are out with the flu. How many children are left in class? 19

Children will need to think carefully about how they will solve each problem. If they have difficulty, talk each problem through with them.

130 — Multiples

Circle the multiples of 3.

4   7   ⑨   14   20   ㉔

Circle the multiples of 3.

4	7	10	⑮	㉑	㉚	35	50
2	4	⑥	8	10	⑫	14	16
1	③	5	7	⑨	11	13	⑮
2	5	8	11	14	17	20	23
5	10	⑮	20	25	㉚	35	40
0	③	⑥	⑨	⑫	⑮	⑱	㉑
10	20	㉚	40	50	㉠	70	80
5	8	11	14	17	20	23	26
2	7	13	17	㉑	25	㉝	㉠

Circle the multiples of 4.

2	7	11	15	19	23	㉘	31
2	④	6	⑧	10	⑫	14	⑯
1	3	5	7	9	11	13	15
3	6	9	⑫	15	18	21	㉔
④	⑫	14	18	22	㉔	㉘	34
5	10	15	㉠	25	30	35	㊵
3	5	⑫	17	㉔	26	㉜	㉠
1	5	9	13	18	㉠	㉠	⑩⓪
10	㉠	30	㊵	50	㉠	70	㊶

Children may not know the rule for finding a multiple of 3: if the digits of a number add up to a multiple of 3, then the number itself is a multiple of 3. For example, 2 + 7 = 9, which is a multiple of 3, so 27 is a multiple of 3 (and so is 72).

131 — Factors

Write the factors of each number.

6 1, 2, 3, 6   8 1, 2, 4, 8

Write the factors of each number.

4	1, 2, 4	10	1, 2, 5, 10	14	1, 2, 7, 14
9	1, 3, 9	3	1, 3	12	1, 2, 3, 4, 6, 12
7	1, 7	15	1, 3, 5, 15	17	1, 17
5	1, 5	20	1, 2, 4, 5, 10, 20	19	1, 19
2	1, 2	24	1, 2, 3, 4, 6, 8, 12, 24	11	1, 11
13	1, 13	30	1, 2, 3, 5, 6, 10, 15, 30	16	1, 2, 4, 8, 16

Write the factors of each number.

1	1	4	1, 2, 4	16	1, 2, 4, 8, 16
25	1, 5, 25	36	1,2,3,4,6,9,12,18,36	49	1, 7, 49
64	1,2,4,8,16,32,64	81	1, 3, 9, 27, 81	100	1,2,4,5,10,20,25,50,100

Do you notice anything about the number of factors each of the numbers has?
Each number has an odd number of factors.
Do you know the name for these special numbers? These are squares.

Write the factors of each number.

2	1, 2	3	1, 3	5	1, 5
7	1, 7	11	1, 11	13	1, 13
17	1, 17	19	1, 19	23	1, 23
29	1, 29	31	1, 31	37	1, 37

Do you notice anything about the number of factors each of the numbers has?
The factors of each number are 1 and the number itself.
Do you know the name for these special numbers? These are prime numbers.

Children may neglect to include 1 and the number itself as factors of a number. For larger numbers, they may not include all the factors in their answers. Point out that 1 is not a prime number.

132 — Fractions

Write the answer in the box.

$1\frac{1}{2} + \frac{1}{4} = 1\frac{3}{4}$ $2\frac{1}{2} + 3\frac{1}{2} = 6$ $1\frac{1}{4} + 2\frac{1}{2} = 3\frac{3}{4}$

Write the answer in the box.

$2\frac{1}{4} + 1\frac{1}{4} = 3\frac{1}{2}$ $1\frac{1}{2} + 1\frac{1}{2} = 3$ $1\frac{1}{4} + \frac{1}{4} = 1\frac{1}{2}$

$3\frac{1}{2} + 1 = 4\frac{1}{2}$ $3\frac{1}{2} + 1\frac{1}{4} = 4\frac{3}{4}$ $2\frac{1}{4} + 4 = 6\frac{1}{4}$

$4\frac{1}{2} + 1\frac{1}{4} = 5\frac{3}{4}$ $2\frac{1}{2} + 1\frac{1}{2} = 4$ $5 + 1\frac{1}{2} = 6\frac{1}{2}$

$3\frac{1}{4} + 1\frac{1}{2} = 4\frac{3}{4}$ $2 + 3\frac{1}{2} = 5\frac{1}{2}$ $7 + \frac{1}{2} = 7\frac{1}{2}$

$3 + \frac{1}{4} = 3\frac{1}{4}$ $4\frac{1}{4} + \frac{1}{4} = 4\frac{1}{2}$ $5 + 4\frac{1}{2} = 9\frac{1}{2}$

Write the answer in the box.

$1\frac{1}{3} + 2\frac{1}{3} = 3\frac{2}{3}$ $3\frac{1}{3} + 4\frac{2}{3} = 8$ $1\frac{2}{3} + 5 = 6\frac{2}{3}$

$3\frac{2}{3} + 2 = 5\frac{2}{3}$ $4\frac{1}{3} + 1\frac{2}{3} = 6$ $2\frac{2}{3} + 1\frac{2}{3} = 4\frac{1}{3}$

$1\frac{2}{3} + 1\frac{2}{3} = 3\frac{1}{3}$ $4\frac{1}{3} + 2\frac{1}{3} = 6\frac{2}{3}$ $3 + 2\frac{1}{3} = 5\frac{1}{3}$

$6 + 2\frac{2}{3} = 8\frac{2}{3}$ $1\frac{1}{3} + 3\frac{1}{3} = 4\frac{2}{3}$ $3\frac{1}{3} + 1\frac{1}{3} = 4\frac{2}{3}$

$5\frac{2}{3} + 2\frac{2}{3} = 8\frac{1}{3}$ $7 + \frac{1}{3} = 7\frac{1}{3}$ $2\frac{2}{3} + 5\frac{2}{3} = 8\frac{1}{3}$

Write the answer in the box.

$2\frac{1}{5} + 2\frac{2}{5} = 4\frac{3}{5}$ $3\frac{1}{5} + 2\frac{3}{5} = 5\frac{4}{5}$ $1\frac{4}{5} + 6 = 7\frac{4}{5}$

$3\frac{1}{5} + 3\frac{2}{5} = 6\frac{3}{5}$ $4 + 2\frac{2}{5} = 6\frac{2}{5}$ $5\frac{3}{5} + 1\frac{1}{5} = 6\frac{4}{5}$

$\frac{3}{5} + \frac{3}{5} = 1\frac{1}{5}$ $3\frac{2}{5} + \frac{4}{5} = 4\frac{1}{5}$ $3\frac{2}{5} + \frac{2}{5} = 3\frac{4}{5}$

It is technically correct if children add $\frac{1}{4}$ and $\frac{1}{4}$ to get $\frac{2}{4}$, but they should be encouraged to simplify this to $\frac{1}{2}$. Some children may not simplify improper fractions that are part of a mixed number (such as $3\frac{6}{5}$). Show them how to do this.

Fractions and decimals ⭐

Write each fraction as a decimal.

$1\frac{1}{10}$ = 1.1 $1\frac{2}{10}$ = 1.2 $1\frac{7}{10}$ = 1.7

Write each decimal as a fraction.

2.5 = $2\frac{1}{2}$ 1.9 = $1\frac{9}{10}$ 3.2 = $3\frac{2}{10}$

Write each fraction as a decimal.

$2\frac{1}{2}$ 2.5 $3\frac{1}{10}$ 3.1 $4\frac{3}{10}$ 4.3 $1\frac{1}{2}$ 1.5

$5\frac{1}{10}$ 5.1 $2\frac{3}{10}$ 2.3 $8\frac{1}{10}$ 8.1 $5\frac{1}{2}$ 5.5

$7\frac{8}{10}$ 7.8 $2\frac{4}{10}$ 2.4 $6\frac{1}{2}$ 6.5 $8\frac{1}{2}$ 8.5

$7\frac{6}{10}$ 7.6 $9\frac{1}{2}$ 9.5 $6\frac{7}{10}$ 6.7 $10\frac{1}{2}$ 10.5

Write each decimal as a fraction.

3.2 $3\frac{2}{10}$ 4.5 $4\frac{1}{2}$ 1.7 $1\frac{7}{10}$ 1.2 $1\frac{1}{2}$

6.5 $6\frac{1}{2}$ 2.7 $2\frac{7}{10}$ 5.2 $5\frac{2}{10}$ 5.5 $5\frac{1}{2}$

7.2 $7\frac{2}{10}$ 8.5 $8\frac{1}{2}$ 9.7 $9\frac{7}{10}$ 10.2 $10\frac{2}{10}$

11.5 $11\frac{1}{2}$ 12.7 $12\frac{7}{10}$ 13.2 $13\frac{2}{10}$ 14.5 $14\frac{1}{2}$

15.7 $15\frac{7}{10}$ 16.2 $16\frac{2}{10}$ 17.5 $17\frac{1}{2}$ 18.7 $18\frac{7}{10}$

Write each fraction as a decimal.

$\frac{1}{2}$ = 0.5 $\frac{2}{10}$ = 0.2 $\frac{3}{10}$ = 0.3

Write each decimal as a fraction.

0.5 = $\frac{1}{2}$ 0.2 = $\frac{2}{10}$ 0.7 = $\frac{7}{10}$

If children have difficulty, you may want to use a number line showing fractions and decimals.

Real-life problems

Write the answer in the box.

A number multiplied by 8 is 56. What is the number?   7

I divide a number by 9 and the result is 6. What is the number?   54

Write the answer in the box.

A number multiplied by 6 is 42. What is the number?   7

I divide a number by 4 and the result is 7. What is the number?   28

I divide a number by 8 and the result is 6. What number did I begin with?   48

A number multiplied by itself gives the answer 25. What is the number?   5

I divide a number by 7 and the result is 7. What number did I begin with?   49

A number multiplied by itself gives the answer 49. What is the number?   7

When I multiply a number by 7 I end up with 56. What number did I begin with?   8

Seven times a number is 63. What is the number?   9

What do I have to multiply 8 by to get the result 72?   9

Nine times a number is 81. What is the number?   9

When 6 is multiplied by a number the result is 42. What number was 6 multiplied by?   7

A number divided by 8 gives the answer 10. What was the starting number?   80

I multiply a number by 9 and end up with 45. What number did I multiply?   5

I multiply a number by 9 and the result is 81. What number did I begin with?   9

Some children find these sorts of problems difficult even if they are good with times tables and division. Many of the problems require children to perform the inverse operation. Have them check their answers to make sure they are correct.

Symmetry ⭐

The dotted line is a mirror line. Complete each shape.

Complete each shape.

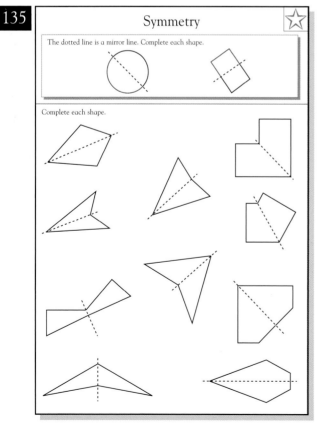

If children have difficulties with these shapes, let them use a mirror. Even if they are confident, let them check the shapes they have drawn with a mirror when they finish.

Fractions and decimals

Write each fraction as a decimal.

$\frac{1}{2}$ = 0.5 $\frac{1}{10}$ = 0.1

Write each decimal as a fraction.

0.25 = $\frac{1}{4}$ 0.4 = $\frac{4}{10}$

Write each fraction as a decimal.

$\frac{1}{10}$ 0.1 $\frac{1}{2}$ 0.5 $\frac{3}{10}$ 0.3 $\frac{5}{10}$ 0.5

$\frac{2}{10}$ 0.2 $\frac{9}{10}$ 0.9 $\frac{6}{10}$ 0.6 $\frac{1}{10}$ 0.1

$\frac{2}{10}$ 0.2 $\frac{3}{10}$ 0.3 $\frac{4}{10}$ 0.4 $\frac{5}{10}$ 0.5

$\frac{6}{10}$ 0.6 $\frac{7}{10}$ 0.7 $\frac{8}{10}$ 0.8 $\frac{9}{10}$ 0.9

Write each decimal as a fraction.

0.8 $\frac{8}{10}$ 0.5 $\frac{5}{10}$ 0.3 $\frac{3}{10}$ 0.4 $\frac{2}{5}$

0.25 $\frac{1}{4}$ 0.7 $\frac{7}{10}$ 0.2 $\frac{1}{5}$ 0.75 $\frac{3}{4}$

0.2 $\frac{2}{10}$ 0.6 $\frac{6}{10}$ 0.5 $\frac{1}{2}$ 0.8 $\frac{4}{5}$

0.1 $\frac{1}{10}$ 0.4 $\frac{4}{10}$ 0.6 $\frac{3}{5}$ 0.9 $\frac{9}{10}$

Write the answer in the box.

Which two of the fractions above are the same as 0.5? $\frac{5}{10}$, $\frac{1}{2}$

Which two of the fractions above are the same as 0.8? $\frac{8}{10}$, $\frac{4}{5}$

Which two of the fractions above are the same as 0.6? $\frac{6}{10}$, $\frac{3}{5}$

Which two of the fractions above are the same as 0.2? $\frac{2}{10}$, $\frac{1}{5}$

Which two of the fractions above are the same as 0.4? $\frac{4}{10}$, $\frac{2}{5}$

Children should realize that $\frac{1}{10}$ is equivalent to 0.1. If necessary, help them understand that $\frac{2}{10}$ is equivalent to 0.2, and so on. Children also need to know the decimal equivalents of $\frac{1}{4}$ and $\frac{3}{4}$.

Fractions of shapes

Shade $\frac{3}{5}$ of each shape.

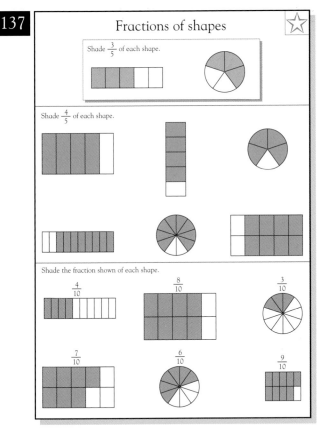

Shade $\frac{4}{5}$ of each shape.

Shade the fraction shown of each shape.

$\frac{4}{10}$ $\frac{8}{10}$ $\frac{3}{10}$

$\frac{7}{10}$ $\frac{6}{10}$ $\frac{9}{10}$

Children may shade in any combination of the sections as long as the shaded area represents the correct fraction.

Fractions

Color $\frac{3}{4}$ of each shape.

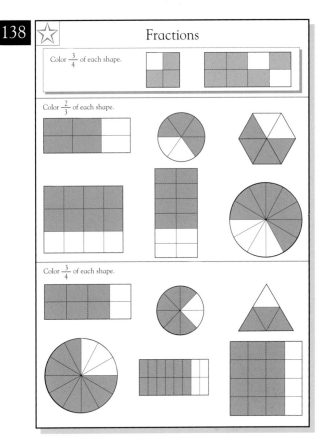

Color $\frac{2}{3}$ of each shape.

Color $\frac{3}{4}$ of each shape.

Children may shade in any combination of the sections as long as the shaded area represents the correct fraction.

Reading timetables

	Frostburg	Elmhusrt	Badger Farm	Winchester
Redline Bus	8:00	8:05	8:15	8:25
Blueline tram	8:05	No stop	8:12	8:20
City taxi	8:30	8:35	8:45	8:55
Greenline Trolley	8:07	No stop	No stop	8:15

The timetable shows the times it takes to travel using different transport companies between Frostburg and Winchester.

Write the answer in the box.

How long does Redline take between Frostburg and Winchester? — **25 minutes**

When does the tram arrive at Badger Farm? — **8:12**

Where does the trolley not stop? — **Elmhurst and Badger farm**

Where is City taxi at 8.35? — **Elmhurst**

Does the tram stop at Elmhurst? — **No**

How long does the bus take to travel between Badger Farm and Winchester? — **10 minutes**

Which is the fastest trip between Frostburg and Winchester? — **Greenline trolley**

Which service arrives at five minutes to nine? — **City taxi**

How long does City taxi take between Frostburg and Badger Farm? — **15 minutes**

Where is the tram at twelve minutes past eight? — **Badger farm**

Children should find this exercise fairly straightforward. If they have difficulty, help them read across the rows and down the columns to find the information they need.

Averages

Write the average of this row in the box.

4   2   2   2   6   3   2

The average is   **3** .

Write the average of each row in the box.

2	3	7	4	2	7	2	5	4
7	4	5	4	8	5	3	4	5
5	3	5	3	5	2	4	5	4
7	5	9	7	2	4	8	6	6
4	3	4	3	4	3	4	7	4
1	4	2	7	3	8	2	5	4
3	2	1	2	2	3	2	1	2
8	3	6	3	8	2	8	2	5

Write the average of each row in the box.

4	8	6	3	9	6	6	6
5	9	2	6	9	1	3	5
6	3	8	6	1	5	6	5
3	8	6	7	5	9	4	6
1	8	3	4	2	6	4	4
9	5	8	7	4	7	9	7
1	3	2	3	1	2	2	2
6	3	7	4	5	8	2	5

If necessary, remind children that the average of a set of quantities is the sum of the quantities divided by the total number of quantities.

Multiplying larger numbers by ones

Write the product for each problem.

```
   13            131
  529           1273
x   4         x    5
 2,116         6,365
```

Write the product for each problem.

```
  724          831          126          455
x   2        x   3        x   3        x   4
1,448        2,493          378        1,820

  161          282          349          253
x   4        x   5        x   6        x   6
  644        1,410        1,745        1,518

  328          465          105          562
x   6        x   4        x   4        x   4
1,968        2,790          420        2,248
```

Write the product for each problem.

```
 4,261        1,582        3,612        4,284
x    3       x    3       x    4       x    4
12,783        4,746       14,448       17,136

 5,907        1,263        1,303        1,467
x    5       x    5       x    6       x    6
29,535        6,315        7,818        8,802

 6,521        8,436        1,599        3,761
x    6       x    6       x    6       x    6
39,126       50,616        9,594       22,566

 5,837        6,394        8,124        3,914
x    4       x    5       x    6       x    6
23,348       31,970       48,744       23,484
```

Children should understand the convention of multiplication problems, i.e. to multiply the ones first and work left, carrying when necessary. Problems on this page will highlight gaps in knowledge of 2, 3, 4, 5, and 6 times tables.

Multiplying larger numbers by ones

Write the product for each problem.

```
    14           174
  417           2,185
x   7         x    9
2,919         19,665
```

Write the product for each problem.

```
  419          604          715          327
x   7        x   7        x   8        x   7
2,933        4,228        5,720        2,289

  425          171          682          246
x   8        x   9        x   8        x   8
3,400        1,539        5,456        1,968

  436          999          319          581
x   9        x   9        x   9        x   9
3,488        8,991        2,871        5,229
```

Write the product for each problem.

```
 4,331        2,816        1,439        2,617
x    7       x    7       x    8       x    8
30,317       19,712       11,512       20,936

 3,104        4,022        3,212        2,591
x    8       x    8       x    9       x    9
24,832       32,176       28,908       23,319

 1,710        3,002        2,468        1,514
x    9       x    8       x    7       x    8
15,390       24,016       17,276       12,112

 4,624        2,993        3,894        4,361
x    7       x    8       x    8       x    9
32,368       23,944       31,152       39,249
```

Any problems encountered on this page will be similar to those of the previous page. Gaps in the child's knowledge of 7, 8, and 9 times tables will be highlighted here.

Real-life multiplication problems

There are 157 apples in a box. How many will there be in three boxes?

```
  12
 157
x  3
 471
```

471 apples

A stamp album can hold 550 stamps. How many stamps will 5 albums hold?

2,750 stamps

```
 550
x  5
2,750
```

A train can take 425 passengers. How many can it take in four trips?

1,700 passengers

```
 425
x  4
1,700
```

Mr Jenkins puts $256 a month into the bank. How much will he have put in after six months?

$1,536

```
 256
x  6
1,536
```

A theater can seat 5,524 people. If a play runs for 7 days, what is the maximum number of people who will be able to see it?

38,668 people

```
 5,524
x    7
38,668
```

A car costs $9,956. How much will it cost a company to buy nine cars for its people?

$89,604

```
 9,956
x    9
89,604
```

Installing a new window for a house costs $435. How much will it cost to install 8 windows of the same size?

$3,480

```
 435
x  8
3,480
```

An airplane flies at a steady speed of 550 mph. How far will it travel in 7 hours?

3,850 mph

```
 550
x  7
3,850
```

This page provides an opportunity for children to apply their skills of multiplication to real life problems. As with previous multiplication work, gaps in their knowledge of multiplication facts will be highlighted here.

Area of rectangles and squares

Find the area of this rectangle

To find the area of a rectangle or square, we multiply length (l) by width (w).

Area = 800 in.²

```
    1
   32
x  25
  160
+ 640
  800 in.²
```

Find the area of these rectangles and squares. You may need to do your work on a separate sheet.

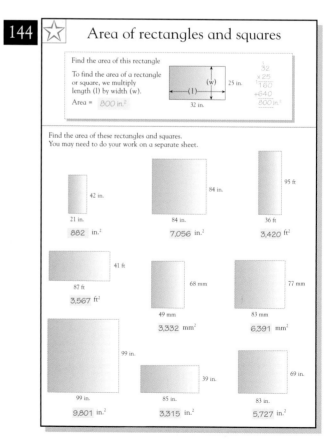

21 in. × 42 in.
882 in.²

84 in. × 84 in.
7,056 in.²

36 ft × 95 ft
3,420 ft²

87 ft × 41 ft
3,567 ft²

49 mm × 68 mm
3,332 mm²

83 mm × 77 mm
6,391 mm²

99 in. × 99 in.
9,801 in.²

85 in. × 39 in.
3,315 in.²

83 in. × 69 in.
5,727 in.²

Children may confuse area and perimeter, and add the sides together instead of multiplying the two sides to arrive at the area. If any answers are wrong, check the long multiplication, and if necessary, revise the method.

145 — Perimeter of shapes

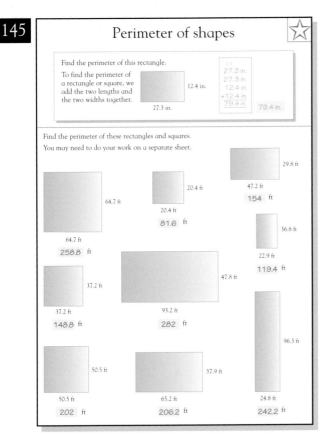

Find the perimeter of this rectangle.

To find the perimeter of a rectangle or square, we add the two lengths and the two widths together.

27.3 in.
27.3 in.
12.4 in.
+12.4 in.
79.4 in.   79.4 in.

Find the perimeter of these rectangles and squares.
You may need to do your work on a separate sheet.

29.8 ft / 47.2 ft — **154** ft

20.4 ft / 20.4 ft — **81.6** ft

64.7 ft / 64.7 ft — **258.8** ft

36.8 ft / 22.9 ft — **119.4** ft

37.2 ft / 37.2 ft — **148.8** ft

47.8 ft / 93.2 ft — **282** ft

96.3 ft / 24.8 ft — **242.2** ft

50.5 ft / 50.5 ft — **202** ft

37.9 ft / 65.2 ft — **206.2** ft

On this page and the next, the most likely problem will be confusion with the area work done on the previous page. Remind children to add the four sides together.

146 — Adding fractions

Work out the answer to the problem.

$$\frac{1}{5} + \frac{3}{5} = \frac{4}{5} \qquad \frac{4}{9} + \frac{2}{9} = \frac{6}{9} = \frac{2}{3}$$

Remember to reduce to simplest form if you need to.

Work out the answer to each sum. Reduce to simplest form if you need to.

$\frac{2}{7} + \frac{3}{7} = \frac{5}{7}$ $\frac{2}{9} + \frac{5}{9} = \frac{7}{9}$ $\frac{1}{3} + \frac{1}{3} = \frac{2}{3}$

$\frac{3}{10} + \frac{4}{10} = \frac{7}{10}$ $\frac{1}{8} + \frac{2}{8} = \frac{3}{8}$ $\frac{2}{9} + \frac{3}{9} = \frac{5}{9}$

$\frac{2}{5} + \frac{1}{5} = \frac{3}{5}$ $\frac{1}{7} + \frac{5}{7} = \frac{6}{7}$ $\frac{4}{9} + \frac{1}{9} = \frac{5}{9}$

$\frac{3}{20} + \frac{4}{20} = \frac{7}{20}$ $\frac{3}{100} + \frac{8}{100} = \frac{11}{100}$ $\frac{7}{10} + \frac{2}{10} = \frac{9}{10}$

$\frac{1}{6} + \frac{2}{6} = \frac{3}{6} = \frac{1}{2}$ $\frac{31}{100} + \frac{19}{100} = \frac{50}{100} = \frac{1}{2}$ $\frac{11}{20} + \frac{4}{20} = \frac{15}{20} = \frac{3}{4}$

$\frac{3}{10} + \frac{3}{10} = \frac{6}{10} = \frac{3}{5}$ $\frac{1}{12} + \frac{5}{12} = \frac{6}{12} = \frac{1}{2}$ $\frac{2}{6} + \frac{2}{6} = \frac{4}{6} = \frac{2}{3}$

$\frac{3}{8} + \frac{3}{8} = \frac{6}{8} = \frac{3}{4}$ $\frac{3}{8} + \frac{1}{8} = \frac{4}{8} = \frac{1}{2}$ $\frac{5}{12} + \frac{3}{12} = \frac{8}{12} = \frac{2}{3}$

$\frac{1}{4} + \frac{1}{4} = \frac{2}{4} = \frac{1}{2}$ $\frac{3}{20} + \frac{2}{20} = \frac{5}{20} = \frac{1}{4}$ $\frac{2}{6} + \frac{2}{6} = \frac{4}{6} = \frac{2}{3}$

$\frac{2}{7} + \frac{4}{7} = \frac{6}{7}$ $\frac{2}{9} + \frac{2}{9} = \frac{4}{9}$ $\frac{13}{20} + \frac{5}{20} = \frac{18}{20} = \frac{9}{10}$

$\frac{81}{100} + \frac{9}{100} = \frac{90}{100} = \frac{9}{10}$ $\frac{7}{20} + \frac{6}{20} = \frac{13}{20}$ $\frac{3}{8} + \frac{2}{8} = \frac{5}{8}$

$\frac{6}{10} + \frac{2}{10} = \frac{8}{10} = \frac{4}{5}$ $\frac{29}{100} + \frac{46}{100} = \frac{75}{100} = \frac{3}{4}$ $\frac{73}{100} + \frac{17}{100} = \frac{90}{100} = \frac{9}{10}$

Difficulty in reducing the sum to its simplest form points to a weakness in finding common factors of the numerator and denominator. Children can reduce the answer in stages, first looking at whether 2 is a common factor, then 3, and so on.

147 — Adding fractions

Write the answer to each problem.

$$\frac{3}{8} + \frac{5}{8} = \frac{8}{8} = 1 \qquad \frac{3}{4} + \frac{3}{4} = \frac{6}{4} = \frac{3}{2} = 1\frac{1}{2}$$

Write the answer to each problem.

$\frac{7}{10} + \frac{6}{10} = \frac{13}{10} = 1\frac{3}{10}$ $\frac{6}{7} + \frac{5}{7} = \frac{11}{7} = 1\frac{4}{7}$ $\frac{2}{3} + \frac{2}{3} = \frac{4}{3} = 1\frac{1}{3}$

$\frac{5}{10} + \frac{6}{10} = \frac{11}{10} = 1\frac{1}{10}$ $\frac{8}{13} + \frac{5}{13} = \frac{13}{13} = 1$ $\frac{7}{8} + \frac{4}{8} = \frac{11}{8} = 1\frac{3}{8}$

$\frac{7}{8} + \frac{5}{8} = \frac{12}{8} = \frac{3}{2} = 1\frac{1}{2}$ $\frac{2}{5} + \frac{3}{5} = \frac{5}{5} = 1$ $\frac{5}{8} + \frac{5}{8} = \frac{10}{8} = \frac{5}{4} = 1\frac{1}{4}$

$\frac{10}{20} + \frac{15}{20} = \frac{25}{20} = \frac{5}{4} = 1\frac{1}{4}$ $\frac{2}{3} + \frac{1}{3} = \frac{3}{3} = 1$ $\frac{5}{6} + \frac{5}{6} = \frac{10}{6} = \frac{5}{3} = 1\frac{2}{3}$

$\frac{5}{6} + \frac{3}{6} = \frac{8}{6} = \frac{4}{3} = 1\frac{1}{3}$ $\frac{6}{12} + \frac{7}{12} = \frac{13}{12} = 1\frac{1}{12}$ $\frac{8}{10} + \frac{6}{10} = \frac{14}{10} = \frac{7}{5} = 1\frac{2}{5}$

$\frac{12}{20} + \frac{10}{20} = \frac{22}{20} = \frac{11}{10} = 1\frac{1}{10}$ $\frac{3}{10} + \frac{7}{10} = \frac{10}{10} = 1$ $\frac{75}{100} + \frac{75}{100} = \frac{150}{100} = \frac{3}{2} = 1\frac{1}{2}$

$\frac{10}{20} + \frac{16}{20} = \frac{26}{20} = \frac{13}{10} = 1\frac{3}{10}$ $\frac{4}{5} + \frac{4}{5} = \frac{8}{5} = 1\frac{3}{5}$ $\frac{11}{21} + \frac{17}{21} = \frac{28}{21} = \frac{4}{3} = 1\frac{1}{3}$

If children leave the answer as a fraction or do not reduce it, they are completing only one of the two steps to finding the simplest form. Have them first write the answer as a mixed number, and then reduce the fraction part.

148 — Subtracting fractions

Write the answer to each problem.

$$\frac{4}{5} - \frac{2}{5} = \frac{2}{5} \qquad \frac{8}{9} - \frac{5}{9} = \frac{3}{9} = \frac{1}{3}$$

Reduce to simplest form if you need to.

Write the answer to each problem. Reduce to simplest form if you need to.

$\frac{3}{5} - \frac{1}{5} = \frac{2}{5}$ $\frac{6}{7} - \frac{3}{7} = \frac{3}{7}$ $\frac{9}{10} - \frac{6}{10} = \frac{3}{10}$

$\frac{7}{10} - \frac{4}{10} = \frac{3}{10}$ $\frac{5}{9} - \frac{4}{9} = \frac{1}{9}$ $\frac{2}{3} - \frac{1}{3} = \frac{1}{3}$

$\frac{7}{8} - \frac{3}{8} = \frac{4}{8} = \frac{1}{2}$ $\frac{14}{20} - \frac{10}{20} = \frac{4}{20} = \frac{1}{5}$ $\frac{5}{6} - \frac{1}{6} = \frac{4}{6} = \frac{2}{3}$

$\frac{11}{12} - \frac{5}{12} = \frac{6}{12} = \frac{1}{2}$ $\frac{17}{20} - \frac{12}{20} = \frac{5}{20} = \frac{1}{4}$ $\frac{9}{12} - \frac{3}{12} = \frac{6}{12} = \frac{1}{2}$

$\frac{8}{10} - \frac{6}{10} = \frac{2}{10} = \frac{1}{5}$ $\frac{12}{12} - \frac{2}{12} = \frac{10}{12} = \frac{5}{6}$ $\frac{9}{10} - \frac{3}{10} = \frac{6}{10} = \frac{3}{5}$

$\frac{8}{9} - \frac{2}{9} = \frac{6}{9} = \frac{2}{3}$ $\frac{7}{8} - \frac{1}{8} = \frac{6}{8} = \frac{3}{4}$ $\frac{9}{12} - \frac{3}{12} = \frac{6}{12} = \frac{1}{2}$

$\frac{3}{4} - \frac{2}{4} = \frac{1}{4}$ $\frac{6}{8} - \frac{3}{8} = \frac{3}{8}$ $\frac{18}{20} - \frac{8}{20} = \frac{10}{20} = \frac{1}{2}$

$\frac{4}{6} - \frac{2}{6} = \frac{2}{6} = \frac{1}{3}$ $\frac{5}{12} - \frac{4}{12} = \frac{1}{12}$ $\frac{3}{8} - \frac{2}{8} = \frac{1}{8}$

$\frac{5}{7} - \frac{1}{7} = \frac{4}{7}$ $\frac{5}{16} - \frac{1}{16} = \frac{4}{16} = \frac{1}{4}$ $\frac{90}{100} - \frac{80}{100} = \frac{10}{100} = \frac{1}{10}$

See the notes for the previous page.

Showing decimals

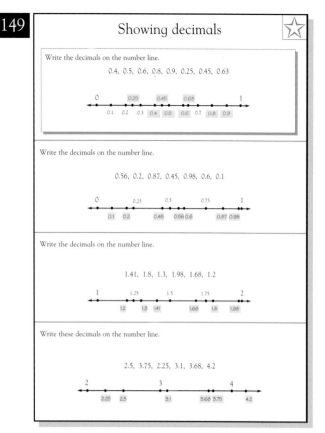

Write the decimals on the number line.

0.4, 0.5, 0.6, 0.8, 0.9, 0.25, 0.45, 0.63

Write the decimals on the number line.

0.56, 0.2, 0.87, 0.45, 0.98, 0.6, 0.1

Write the decimals on the number line.

1.41, 1.8, 1.3, 1.98, 1.68, 1.2

Write these decimals on the number line.

2.5, 3.75, 2.25, 3.1, 3.68, 4.2

If children are confused as to where to place the hundredths, have them first fill in all of the tenths on the number line. Then ask them to find those tenths between which the hundredths fall.

Conversions: length

Units of length	
12 inches	1 foot
3 feet	1 yard
5,280 feet	1 mile
1,760 yards	1 mile

This conversion table shows how to convert inches, feet, yards, and miles.

Brian's rope is 60 inches long. How many feet long is it?

60 ÷ 12 = 5   5 feet long

Neilika's rope is 3 yards long. How many inches long is it?

3 x 3 = 9   9 feet long
9 x 12 = 108   108 inches long

Convert each measurement to feet.

36 inches	12 inches	48 inches	72 inches
36 ÷ 12 = 3	12 ÷ 12 = 1	48 ÷ 12 = 4	72 ÷ 12 = 6
3 feet	1 foot	4 feet	6 feet

Convert each measurement to yards.

6 feet	12 feet	27 feet	36 feet
6 ÷ 3 = 2	12 ÷ 3 = 4	27 ÷ 3 = 9	36 ÷ 3 = 12
2 yards	4 yards	9 yards	12 yards

Convert each measurement to inches.

4 feet	12 feet	8 feet	5 feet
4 x 12 = 48	12 x 12 = 144	8 x 12 = 96	5 x 12 = 60
48 inches	144 inches	96 inches	60 inches

Convert each measurement to feet.

6 yards	2 yards	7 yards	5 yards
6 x 3 = 18	2 x 3 = 6	7 x 3 = 21	5 x 3 = 15
18 feet	6 feet	21 feet	15 feet

Convert each measurement.

4 yards	5 yards	4 miles	1 mile
4 x 3 x 12 = 144	5 x 3 x 12 = 180	4 x 5,280 = 21,120	1 x 5,280 x 12 = 63,360
144 inches	180 inches	21,120 feet	63,360 inches

15,840 feet	31,680 feet	1,760 yards	3,520 yards
15,840 ÷ 5,280 = 3	31,680 ÷ 5,280 = 6	1760 ÷ 1760 = 1	3520 ÷ 1760 = 2
3 miles	6 miles	1 mile	2 miles

If children are confused whether to multiply or divide, ask them if the new unit is a longer or shorter unit. If the unit is longer, there will be fewer of them, so division would be the appropriate operation.

Conversions: capacity

Units of capacity	
8 fluid ounces	1 cup
2 cups	1 pint
2 pints	1 quart
4 quarts	1 gallon

This conversion table shows how to convert ounces, cups pints, quarts, and gallons.

Katya's thermos holds 8 pints. How many cups does it hold?

8 x 2 = 16   16 cups

Hannah's thermos holds 6 cups. How many pints does it hold?

6 ÷ 2 = 3   3 pints

Convert each measurement to cups.

32 fluid ounces	16 fluid ounces	96 fluid ounces	80 fluid ounces
32 ÷ 8 = 4	16 ÷ 8 = 2	96 ÷ 8 = 12	80 ÷ 8 = 10
4 cups	2 cups	12 cups	10 cups

Convert each measurement to pints.

6 cups	12 cups	36 cups	50 cups
6 ÷ 2 = 3	12 ÷ 2 = 6	36 ÷ 2 = 18	50 ÷ 2 = 25
3 pints	6 pints	18 pints	25 pints

4 quarts	12 quarts	30 quarts	6 quarts
4 x 2 = 8	12 x 2 = 24	30 x 2 = 60	6 x 2 = 12
8 pints	24 pints	60 pints	12 pints

Convert each measurement to gallons.

16 quarts	32 quarts	100 quarts	20 quarts
16 ÷ 4 = 4	32 ÷ 4 = 8	100 ÷ 4 = 25	20 ÷ 4 = 5
4 gallons	8 gallons	25 gallons	5 gallons

Convert each measurement.

3 gallons	5 quarts	36 cups	72 pints
3 x 4 x 2 = 24	5 x 2 x 2 = 20	36 ÷ 2 ÷ 2 = 9	72 ÷ 2 ÷ 4 = 9
24 pints	20 cups	9 quarts	9 gallons

1 quart	240 fluid ounces	7 quarts	11 gallons
1 x 2 x 2 x 8 = 32	240 ÷ 8 ÷ 2 = 15	7 x 4 = 28	11 x 4 x 2 = 88
32 fluid ounces	15 pints	28 cups	88 pints

See the comments for the previous page.

Rounding money

Round to the nearest dollar.

$3.95 rounds to $4

$2.25 rounds to $2

Round to the nearest ten dollars.

$15.50 rounds to $20

$14.40 rounds to $10

Round to the nearest dollar.

$2.60 rounds to $3 $8.49 rounds to $8 $3.39 rounds to $3

$9.55 rounds to $10 $1.75 rounds to $2 $4.30 rounds to $4

$7.15 rounds to $7 $6.95 rounds to $7 $2.53 rounds to $3

Round to the nearest ten dollars.

$37.34 rounds to $40 $21.75 rounds to $20 $85.03 rounds to $90

$71.99 rounds to $70 $66.89 rounds to $70 $52.99 rounds to $50

$55.31 rounds to $60 $12.79 rounds to $10 $15.00 rounds to $20

Round to the nearest hundred dollars.

$307.12 rounds to $300 $175.50 rounds to $200 $115.99 rounds to $100

$860.55 rounds to $900 $417.13 rounds to $400 $650.15 rounds to $700

$739.10 rounds to $700 $249.66 rounds to $200 $367.50 rounds to $400

If children have difficulty, have them decide which are the two nearest hundred dollars, and which is closest to the number.

153 — Estimating sums of money

Round to the leading digit. Estimate the sum.

$3.26 → $3 + $4.82 → + $5 is about **$8**	$68.53 → $70 + $34.60 → + $30 is about **$100**

Round to the leading digit. Estimate the sum.

$52.61 → $50
+ $27.95 → + $30
is about **$80**

$19.20 → $20
+ $22.13 → + $20
is about **$40**

$70.75 → $70
+ $12.49 → + $10
is about **$80**

$701.34 → $700
+ $100.80 → + $100
is about **$800**

$339.50 → $300
+ $422.13 → + $400
is about **$700**

$160.07 → $200
+ $230.89 → + $200
is about **$400**

$25.61 → $30
+ $72.51 → + $70
is about **$100**

$61.39 → $60
+ $19.50 → + $20
is about **$80**

$18.32 → $20
+ $13.90 → + $10
is about **$30**

$587.35 → $600
+ 251.89 → + $300
is about **$900**

$109.98 → $100
+ $210.09 → + $200
is about **$300**

$470.02 → $500
+ $203.17 → + $200
is about **$700**

Round to the leading digit. Estimate the sum.

$75.95 + $17.95 → **$100**

$41.67 + $20.35 → **$60**

$49.19 + $38.70 → **$90**

$784.65 + $101.05 → **$900**

$516.50 + $290.69 → **$800**

$58.78 + $33.25 → **$90**

$82.90 + $11.79 → **$90**

$90.09 + $14.50 → **$100**

In section 2, children need to estimate by rounding mentally. If they have trouble, have them write the rounded numbers above the originals, and then add them.

154 — Estimating differences of money

Round the numbers to the leading digit. Estimate the differences.

$8.75 → $9 – $5.10 → – $5 is about **$4**	$61.47 → $60 + $35.64 → + $40 is about **$20**

Round the numbers to the leading digit. Estimate the differences.

$17.90 → $20
– $12.30 → – $10
is about **$10**

$6.40 → $6
– $3.75 → – $4
is about **$2**

$87.45 → $90
– $54.99 → – $50
is about **$40**

$34.90 → $30
– $12.60 → – $10
is about **$20**

$8.68 → $9
– $4.39 → – $4
is about **$5**

$363.24 → $400
– $127.66 → – $100
is about **$300**

$78.75 → $80
+ $24.99 → – $20
is about **$60**

$64.21 → $60
– $28.56 → – $30
is about **$30**

$723.34 → $700
– $487.12 → – $500
is about **$200**

Round the numbers to the leading digit. Estimate the differences.

$8.12 – $1.35
→ $8 – $1 = **$7**

$49.63 – $27.85
→ $50 – $30 = **$20**

$7.50 – $3.15
→ $8 – $3 = **$5**

$85.15 – $42.99
→ $90 – $40 = **$50**

$5.85 – $4.75
→ $6 – $5 = **$1**

$634.60 – $267.25
→ $600 – $300 = **$300**

$37.35 – $16.99
→ $40 – $20 = **$20**

$842.17 – $169.54
→ $800 – $200 = **$600**

$56.95 – $20.58
→ $60 – $20 = **$40**

$628.37 – $252.11
→ $600 – $300 = **$300**

See the comments for the previous page.

155 — Estimating sums and differences

Round the numbers to the leading digit. Estimate the sum or difference.

3,576 → 4,000 + 1,307 → +1,000 is about **5,000**	198,248 → 200,000 – 116,431 → – 100,000 is about **100,000**

Round the numbers to the leading digit. Estimate the sum or difference.

685 → 700
+ 489 → + 500
is about **1,200**

21,481 → 20,000
– 12,500 → – 10,000
is about **10,000**

7,834 → 8,000
+ 3,106 → + 3,000
is about **11,000**

682,778 → 700,000
+ 130,001 → + 100,000
is about **800,000**

58,499 → 60,000
– 22,135 → – 20,000
is about **40,000**

902,276 → 900,000
– 615,999 → – 600,000
is about **300,000**

46,801 → 50,000
+ 34,700 → + 30,000
is about **80,000**

9,734 → 10,000
– 8,306 → – 8,000
is about **2,000**

65,606 → 70,000
+ 85,943 → + 90,000
is about **160,000**

5,218 → 5,000
– 3,673 → – 4,000
is about **1,000**

745 → 700
+ 451 → + 500
is about **1,200**

337,297 → 300,000
– 168,931 → – 200,000
is about **100,000**

Write < or > for each problem.

329 + 495 **>** 800

11,569 – 6,146 **<** 6,000

563 – 317 **<** 300

8,193 – 6,668 **>** 1,000

41,924 – 12,445 **<** 50,000

634,577 + 192,556 **>** 800,000

18,885 + 12,691 **>** 30,000

713,096 – 321,667 **<** 400,000

In section 2, children need to think about their estimates more carefully if the estimate is very close to the number on the right side of the equation. Have them look at the digits in the next place to adjust their estimates up or down.

156 — Conversion tables

Draw a table to convert dollars to cents.

$	cents
1	100
2	200
3	300

Complete the conversion chart below.

Weeks	Days
1	7
2	14
3	21
4	28
5	35
6	42
7	49
8	56
9	63
10	70

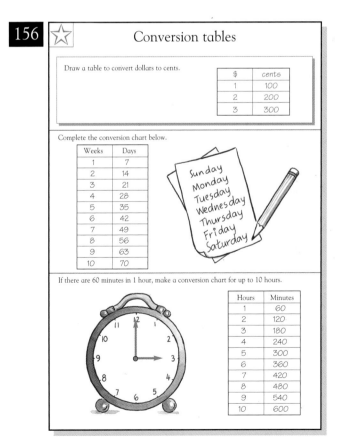

Sunday
Monday
Tuesday
Wednesday
Thursday
Friday
Saturday

If there are 60 minutes in 1 hour, make a conversion chart for up to 10 hours.

Hours	Minutes
1	60
2	120
3	180
4	240
5	300
6	360
7	420
8	480
9	540
10	600

Children will grasp that they are dealing in multiples of 7 and later, 60. Any problems will be due to weaknesses in times tables or from missing numbers as they work down the chart. Encourage care and concentration.